MW00657366

Transparent Minds

Dorrit Cohn

Transparent Minds

Narrative Modes for
Presenting Consciousness
in Fiction

Princeton University Press
Princeton, New Jersey

Copyright © 1978 by Princeton University Press

Published by Princeton University Press,
Princeton, New Jersey
In the United Kingdom: Princeton University Press,
Chichester, West Sussex

All Rights Reserved

Library of Congress Cataloging in Publication Data will be
found on the last printed page of this book

Publication of this book has been aided by a grant
from The Andrew W. Mellon Foundation

This book has been composed in VIP Bembo

Princeton University Press books are printed on acid-free
paper and meet the guidelines for permanence and
durability of the Committee on Production Guidelines for
Book Longevity of the Council on Library Resources

Printed in the United States of America

ISBN 0-691-06369-9
ISBN 0-691-10156-6 (pbk.)

First Princeton Paperback printing, with corrections, 1983

9   8   7   6

Preface

The questions that gave rise to this book arose empirically, at the point where my interest in narrative form
came to meet my predilection for novels with thoughtful
characters and scenes of self-communion. The need to account for analogies and variations sent me to narrative theory
just long enough to contemplate what Todorov calls "the vir-
tualities of literary discourse." Equipped with these basic
abstractions I could then travel around in narrative literature,
selecting works and passages in works that would best display
the entire spectrum of possibilities, while in turn allowing
these works themselves to reveal unforeseen hues. The result
is a critical text woven of a multitude of paradigmatic quotations and close analyses, all held within a firm typological
frame.

My textual repertoire rarely departs from the corpus of narrative literature most familiar to students of fictional form. A
century of psychological realism—roughly 1850 to 1950—
provides the majority of illustrations, with some additions
from as far back as Sterne and as far forward as Sarraute.
When I move sideways to less familiar ground—usually to the
German domain, which I know best—it is always to point up
anomalies that illuminate the norm.

Even though my approach follows typological rather than
chronological lines, I have not altogether disregarded the historical dimension. The direction in which I sweep across the
principal techniques generally corresponds to evolutionary
changes of fictional form: from vocal to hushed authorial
voices, from dissonant to consonant relations between narrators and protagonists, from maximal to minimal removes
between the language of the text and the language of consciousness. On a larger scale, the fact that I begin with narrators who exclude inside views and end with interior-
monologue texts that exclude narrators also suggests that my
typological lines are not entirely disengaged from the historical axis.

But my study lays no claim to encompassing the entire realm of fictional form, either synchronically or diachronically. It explores a special and specific subject, to which a general poetics of fiction—including the most comprehensive and rigorous one to date, Gérard Genette's *Discours du récit*—can usually devote only a short section. Yet it is a privileged subject: not only because so much modern fiction plays within the consciousness of its characters, but also because fictional consciousness is the special preserve of narrative fiction. For this reason the devices through which it is presented are closely allied—and frequently confused—with the modes for presenting the fictional world as a whole: narrative situation or point of view.

This brings me to a final prefatory point. The problem of narrative perspective, more than any other narratological problem, has polarized literary scholarship in the last decades between the two Pascalian spirits: the proliferating *finesse* of criticism and the reductive *géometrie* of linguistics. In terms of expository idioms: to one side the urbane, metaphoric, highly readable style and thought of the critic who refuses to engage in what he regards as hairsplitting definitions and distinctions; to the other the unreadable abbreviations and formulae of the linguist who refuses to communicate with readers unwilling or unable to decipher his code. At the risk of falling between stools, I have tried for a compromise: to use (and, when necessary, to coin) a consistent, rigorous, but not recondite terminology for my subject, which I continue to use in unabbreviated form and in whole sentences, no matter how awkward or monotonous the resulting prose.

Since the most important criteria I employ for typological distinctions are basic grammatical forms (especially tense and person), I have found that significant features in quotations could be preserved in translation, provided only that I scrupulously sacrificed elegance to accuracy. For this reason the majority of translations from French and German are my own; in some cases I was able to adapt, and, in a very few cases, to adopt, existing translations. But readers who know these languages will want to check my analyses against the original, reproduced at the bottom of the page. I would have preferred to use only works that I could read in the original myself. But the Russians were, of course, indispensable, as was one great Scandinavian (Hamsun); experts in these languages were kind enough to check and amend for me some passages from published translations. All editions from which I quote, as well as those on which I base my translations, are listed at the back of the book.

Some of my ideas were rehearsed in article form, and I wish to thank the editors of *Comparative Literature, PMLA, Germanisch-romanische Monatsschrift* and *Festschrift für Käte Hamburger* for permission to expand this material and to integrate it into my larger scheme. This scheme itself was worked out during a year generously supported by the John Simon Guggenheim Memorial Foundation, as well as by Indiana University and Harvard University. Several friends and colleagues read my manuscript in whole or in part at various stages of composition and offered valuable critical advice: Ruby Cohn, Ann Fehn, Paul Hernadi, Jan Hokenson, Breon Mitchell. I am deeply grateful to each of them. I would also like to express my thanks to a number of persons who, in varied but essential ways, helped me to overcome moments of discouragement in the course of my work on this book: Iso Camartin, Ruby Cohn (again), Dr. James Dalsimer, Judith Kates, Frank Ryder, Maria Tatar, and my sons Steve and Rick.

Further thanks go to Annemarie Bestor and Sara Milder for their punctual help with the preparation of the manuscript; and, finally, to Jerry Sherwood of Princeton University Press, for all the expert skill and care she gave this book, from first to last.

Cambridge, Massachusetts
December 1977.

Contents

Transparent Minds

but the within, all that inner space one never sees, the brain and heart and other caverns where thought and feeling dance their sabbath . . .
            Samuel Beckett, Molloy

Introduction

The Greek god Momus, critic of his fellow gods and of created reality, is said to have blamed Vulcan because in the human form, which he had made of clay, he had not placed a window in the breast, by which whatever was felt or thought there might easily be brought to light. It is to this myth that Tristram Shandy refers when he sets out to draw his uncle Toby's character. Had Momus had his way, he tells us, "nothing more would have been wanting, in order to have taken a man's character, but to have taken a chair and gone softly, as you would to a dioptrical bee-hive, and looked in,—viewed the soul stark naked; . . . then taken your pen and ink and set down nothing but what you had seen, and could have sworn to." "But," Tristram adds in realistic resignation, "this is an advantage not to be had by the biographer in this planet; . . . our minds shine not through the body, but we are wrapt up here in a dark covering of uncrystallized flesh and blood; so that, if we would come to the specific characters of them, we must go some other way to work."[1] This is when Tristram decides to "draw my uncle Toby's character from his Hobby-Horse"—choosing an emphatically behavioristic "other way," as befits a biographer (and autobiographer) in this planet.

A similar optical wish-dream shows up at the other end of the gamut of fictional genres, in a German Romantic fairy tale. In E.T.A. Hoffmann's *Master Flea*, the microscopic magician of the title gives to his human friend Peregrinus Tyss a tiny magic lens that, when inserted in the pupil of his eye, enables him to peer through the skulls of all fellow human beings he encounters, and to discern their hidden thoughts. Peregrinus soon curses this "indestructible glass" for giving him an intelligence that rightfully belongs only to "the eternal being who sees through to man's innermost self because he rules it."[2]

Both these fantasies, in their invocation of unreal transparencies, can stand as metaphors for the singular power possessed by the novelist: creator of beings whose inner lives he can reveal at will. Hoffmann's image, by placing the glass in the eye of the beholder rather than in the body of his object, is the more suggestive of "omniscient" narrators. Tristram facing his opaque uncle, by contrast, can stand for all incarnated narrators who inhabit the fictional reality they narrate. Proust's Marcel, himself a member of this second class, can have only the first class of narrators in mind when he tells us that "the ingenuity of the first novelist . . . consisted in the suppression pure and simple of real people." He too resorts to optical imagery to explain how this is done and what advantages ensue: "A real person, profoundly as we may sympathize with him, is in a great measure perceptible only through our senses, that is to say, he remains opaque, offers a dead weight which our sensibilities have no strength to lift. . . . The novelist's happy discovery was to think of substituting for those opaque sections, impenetrable by the human spirit, their equivalent in immaterial sections, things, that is, which the spirit can assimilate to itself."[3]

That the distinction\Proust draws between the people we know in real life and those we know in novels is a matter of common, if not commonly conscious, knowledge is illustrated by a statement on the back cover of *In Cold Blood*: "TRUMAN CAPOTE plumbed the minds and souls of real-life characters." The publishers evidently thought this sentence sufficiently sensational to place it amidst other, more lurid blurbs. And they were right. The technique Capote uses to present the "real-life" murderers Perry and Dick is sensationally contradictory. I quote a random example:

> Waiting for Perry outside the post-office, Dick was in excellent spirits; he had reached a decision that he was certain would eradicate his current difficulties and start him on a new road, with a new rainbow in view. The decision involved impersonating an Air Force officer. . . . By writing worthless checks right around the clock, he

    expected to haul in three, maybe four thousand dollars within a twenty-four hour period. That was half the plot; the second half was: Goodbye, Perry. Dick was sick of him. . . .[4]

This passage bears the unmistakable stamp of fiction. Dick's train of thoughts is known and conveyed by a voice that can only belong to a clairvoyant, disincarnated narrator. And by adopting this voice the reporter Truman Capote has taken on the pose of a novelist, has fictionalized his relationship to the real Dick Hickock and transformed this gruesomely real person into a realistic fictional character.

    As E. M. Forster noted, the same process takes place when a novelist creates a fictional character who bears the name of a historical personage. Forster even insists that a novelist has no business writing a Queen-Victoria-novel unless he plans "to reveal the hidden life at its source: to tell us more about Queen Victoria than could be known, and thus to produce a character who is not the Queen Victoria of history."[5] Quite aside from the hidden *matter* such a novel may revealingly invent, it is its irreverent *manner* that gives piquancy to fictionalized biography, and adds shock value to a narrative episode that presents a famous mind by purely fictional techniques: for example, the monologizing Goethe waking from sleep in Thomas Mann's *Lotte in Weimar*.

    If the real world becomes fiction only by revealing the hidden side of the human beings who inhabit it, the reverse is equally true: the most real, the "roundest" characters of fiction are those we know most intimately, precisely in ways we could never know people in real life. "I confess," writes Mann in an essay on a rival art, "that in everything regarding knowledge of men as individual beings, I regard drama as an art of the silhouette, and only narrated man as round, whole, real, and fully shaped."[6] But this means that the special life-likeness of narrative fiction—as compared to dramatic and cinematic fictions—depends on what writers and readers know least in life: how another mind thinks, another body feels. In depicting the inner life, the novelist is truly a fabricator. Even as he draws on psychological theory and on introspection, he creates what Ortega called "imaginary psychology . . . the psychology of possible human minds"—a field of knowledge the Spanish critic also believed to be "the material proper to the novel."[7]

The more surprising, then, that the novelists most concerned with the exact representation of life are also those who place at the live centers of their works this invented entity whose verisimilitude it is impossible to verify. Stendhal describes the novel as "un miroir qu'on promène le long d'un chemin" in the very novel where he observes a character's thought processes more closely than writers had done before him. And despite the elaborate realistic apparatus that attests to the "reality" of his fictional facts, he never bothers to tell us—nor are we at all moved to ask—in what mirror, along what pathway, he saw the reflection of Julien Sorel's psyche.

The mutual dependence of realistic intent and imaginary psychology is even more graphically illustrated in the work of Henry James. His most famous conceit for the novel—the house of fiction with a million windows—is no less realistic in its spatio-optical clarity than Stendhal's portable mirror, in line with the verisimilar conception of the genre he expressed more directly elsewhere: "The only reason for the existence of a novel is that it does attempt to represent life"; "the air of reality (solidity of specification) seems to me to be the supreme virtue of a novel."[8] But in the preface to *The Portrait of a Lady*, as he stands at his own window in the house of fiction, "a figure with a pair of eyes, or at least with a field-glass,"[9] these sober instruments of vision soon turn as magical as the lens Master Flea gave to Peregrinus Tyss. For he is now watching another house of fiction on a reduced scale, "a square and spacious house . . . put up around my young woman," and *this* house is so constructed that its center is "in the young woman's own consciousness," and even in "her relation to herself."[10] But beyond this, the ultimate sight and central site of this entire nest of houses and mixed metaphors is the solitary and totally inward scene of "my young woman's extraordinary meditative vigil," the famous chapter 42, which James called "obviously the best thing in the book, but . . . only a supreme illustration of the general plan."[11] It is also a supreme illustration of the paradox that narrative fiction attains its greatest "air of reality" in the representation of a lone figure thinking thoughts she will never communicate to anyone.

This paradox lies at the very heart of narrative realism, and has important theoretical and historical implications. Most writers on the novel have taken the transparency of fictional minds for granted; a few—like Proust, Forster, Mann, and Ortega—have mentioned it in passing. But the first literary theorist who has fully explored its meaning is Käte Hamburger in *The Logic of Literature*.[12] For Hamburger the representation of characters' inner lives is the touchstone that simultaneously sets fiction apart from reality and builds the semblance (*Schein*) of another, non-real reality. She argues this thesis and explores its causes and results in two successive stages: 1) starting out from Aristotelian mimesis (understood as representation, not as imitation) she arrives at a theoretical differentiation between the language of fiction and the statement-language of reality; and 2) starting out from textual observations, she demonstrates that certain language patterns are unique to fiction, and dependent on the presence of fictional minds within the text. These language patterns are primarily the conveyors or signals of mental activity: verbs of consciousness, interior and narrated monologues, temporal and spatial adverbs referring to the characters' here and now. Hamburger concludes: "Epic fiction is the sole epistemological instance where the I-originarity (or subjectivity) of a third-person *qua* third person can be portrayed."[13] In approximate translation: narrative fiction is the only literary genre, as well as the only kind of narrative, in which the unspoken thoughts, feelings, perceptions of a person other than the speaker can be portrayed. Hamburger's statement pinpoints the representation (mimesis) of consciousness as the subject

that distinguishes narrative fiction from non-fictional narrative to one side, from non–narrative fiction to the other (i.e.,
from drama and film, the other genres populated by invented
persons).[14]

Hamburger's *Logic*, as this summary barely suggests, gives
a stringently argued theoretical grounding to the interde-
pendence of narrative realism and the mimesis of consciousness. In light of her analysis, the "inward turn" of which
Erich Kahler and other historians of the novel have spoken,[15]
would signify a gradual unfolding of the genre's most distinctive potential, to its full Bloom in the stream-of-consciousness novel and beyond. Modern writers of Joyce's generation
themselves thought of the history of the novel in this fashion.
Thomas Mann postulated a "principle of internalization" that
initially sublimated the outer adventures of the epic hero into
the inner adventures of the *Bildungsheld*, then continued moving inward to greater passivity and complexity.[16] Virginia
Woolf believed that "Modern Fiction" would be returning to
its "circular tendency," with novels where "there would be
no plot, no comedy, no tragedy, no love interest or catastrophe in the accepted style," but only "this varying, this un-
circumscribed spirit . . . with as little admixture of the alien
and external as possible."[17] More surprisingly, one can find
similar statements in the earliest novel theorists, especially in
Germany. Friedrich von Blanckenburg, in his *Essay on the
Novel* of 1774 wrote (with his neo-classical tone nearly hiding
the Hamburgerian insight): "A writer, lest he wish to dis-
honor himself, can not hold to the pretense that he is unacquainted with the inner world of his characters. He is their
creator: they have received from him all their character traits,
their entire being, they live in a world that he himself has
fashioned."[18] Blanckenburg was so bent, in fact, on a novel's
telling solely "the inner history of a man" that he wanted to
exclude even the protagonist's death from fiction, on the
grounds that it was an externally determined event. (On this
last point he relented after reading Goethe's *Werther*.) Some
decades later, Schopenhauer anticipated the moderns even

more clearly: "The more *inner* and the less *outer* life a novel presents, the higher and nobler will be its purpose. . . . Art consists in achieving the maximum of inner motion with the minimum of outer motion; for it is the inner life which is the true object of our interest."[19]

This same call, sounding from such different times and places (and many more voices could be cited), suggests the importance of the mimesis of consciousness for the history of the novel. One could probably argue for a theory of cyclical (or spiral) return of the genre to its inward matrix whenever its characters get hyper-active, its world too cluttered, its orientation too veristic. Woolf and her generation, reacting against the Edwardians, would then figure as just one such return in a series starting with Cervantes' reaction against the chivalric epic (as Thomas Mann suggests), and ending provisionally with the reaction of New Novelists like Nathalie Sarraute against the "behaviorism" of the Hemingway school. This sketch of a spiral suggests that the "inward-turning" of the stream-of-consciousness novel is not nearly so singular a phenomenon, nor so radical a break with tradition as has been assumed, both by critics who applaud it (Edel, Daiches) and by critics who deplore it (Lukács, Auerbach, Wolfgang Kayser).[20] To quote Ortega again, who has perhaps suggested the most accurate image for the relationship between the stream-of-consciousness novel and the Realist tradition: the Proust-Joyce generation, he says, has "overcome realism by merely putting too fine a point on it and discovering, lens in hand, the micro-structure of life."[21] This lens, another optical instrument to add to our collection, estranges as it magnifies. But what it estranges when it is trained on a fictional mind is something that had never been visible outside the pages of fiction in an earlier age either. Despite its scientific power, Ortega's lens is no less (and no more) magic than Stendhal's mirror or James' field-glass.

This view of the historical continuity underlies my typological approach to the presentation of consciousness in fiction. Despite the theoretical and historical importance of the subject, previous studies of its formal implications have been disappointingly rapid and incomplete. They fall into two basic categories:

1. Studies (mostly published in the United States) that focus on the stream-of-consciousness novel, and especially on *Ulysses*, generally treating the subject as though consciousness had appeared in fiction only on Bloomsday. This limited orientation oversimplifies the formal problem by reducing all techniques to a single and vague "stream-of-consciousness technique," and at the same time overcomplicates it by association with broad psychological and aesthetic issues.[22] Leon Edel's influential historical study, *The Modern Psychological Novel*, for example, yields no clarity at all concerning formal devices.[23] Robert Humphrey's brief chapter on basic techniques in *Stream of Consciousness in the Modern Novel* is the most differentiated discussion that has come out of this approach, but it suffers from characteristic limitations and confusions.[24]

2. Studies (mostly published abroad) that apply to the techniques for presenting consciousness the model of the techniques for quoting spoken discourse. They have generally applied simple correspondences between direct discourse and interior monologue, between indirect discourse and narrative analysis, and between the intermediary "free indirect" forms of both spoken and silent discourse (*style indirect libre* in French, *erlebte Rede* in German). This approach, which has a long and venerable history in French and German stylistics, has been updated by stylistic linguists in the last decade and applied in the context of modern fictional modes. An article by Derek Bickerton is of special interest in this regard, since it forges a bridge between literary and linguistic approaches to the subject: he translates the techniques Humphrey identified empirically in the stream-of-consciousness novel into the basic grammatical categories of quotation.[25] The same basic method is applied by the French literary structuralists, notably by Gérard Genette in his influential "Discours du récit."

Under the heading "récit de paroles," Genette pairs spoken and silent discourse according to degrees of "narrative distance," arriving at a threefold division between the poles of pure narration (diegesis) and pure imitation (mimesis).[26]

This linguistically based approach has the great advantage of supplying precise grammatical and lexical criteria, rather than relying on vague psychological and stylistic ones. But it oversimplifies the literary problems by carrying too far the correspondence between spoken discourse and silent thought. Speech is, by definition, always verbal. Whether thought is always verbal is to this day a matter of definition and dispute among psychologists. Most people, including most novelists, certainly conceive of consciousness as including "other mind stuff" (as William James called it), in addition to language. This "stuff" cannot be quoted—directly or indirectly; it can only be narrated. One of the drawbacks of this linguistic approach is therefore that it tends to leave out of account the entire nonverbal realm of consciousness, as well as the entire problematic relationship between thought and speech.

Though my own discussion of the modes for rendering consciousness will be more literary than linguistic in its attention to stylistic, contextual, and psychological aspects, I take simple linguistic criteria for my starting-point in naming and defining three basic techniques.

1. *Psycho-narration*. The most indirect technique has no fixed name; the terms "omniscient description" and "internal analysis" have been applied, but neither is satisfactory.[27] "Omniscient description" is too general: anything, not only the psyche, can be described "omnisciently." "Internal analysis" is misleading: "internal" implies a process occurring *in*, rather than *applied to*, a mind (cf. internal bleeding); "analysis" does not allow for the plainly reportorial, or the highly imagistic ways a narrator may adopt in narrating consciousness.

My neologism "psycho-narration" identifies both the subject-matter and the activity it denotes (on the analogy to psychology, psychoanalysis). At the same time it is frankly distinctive, in order to focus attention on the most neglected of the basic techniques. Stream-of-consciousness critics have acknowledged its existence only grudgingly, since all fictional psyches since *Ulysses* supposedly come at the reader directly, without the aid of a narrator; Robert Humphrey even declares that it is "something of a shock" to find writers like Dorothy Richardson "using conventional description by an omniscient author—without any attempt on the part of the author to disguise the fact."[28] And linguistic-structuralist critics, by reducing the technique to an unvoiced indirect discourse, disregard the ironic or lyric, reductive or expansive, sub- or superverbal functions that psycho-narration can perform, precisely because it is *not* primarily a method for presenting mental language.[29]

2. *Quoted monologue.* The tendency to polarize techniques historically has even more lastingly confused the technique that, from a purely grammatical point of view, is simplest to define. According to the post-Joycean canon interior monologue was supposed not to have existed before *Ulysses* (with the notable exception of Dujardin's novel *Les Lauriers sont coupés*). But what was to be done with direct thought-quotations in novels like *Le Rouge et le noir* or *Crime and Punishment*? Most critics accepted the thesis developed by Dujardin in his book *Le monologue intérieur*, where he draws a sharply divisive line between quotations of the mind found in stream-of-consciousness novels and those found in more traditional novels. Insisting that the term "interior monologue" should be reserved for the modern "flowing" variety of thought-quotations, they have suggested such terms as "traditional monologue" or "silent soliloquy" for thought-quotations found in pre-Joycean novels.[30] The tendency has been to distinguish between them on both psychological and stylistic grounds: the interior monologue is described as associative, illogical, spontaneous; the soliloquy as rhetorical, rational, deliberate.[31] Staccato rhythms, ellipses, profuse imagery are attributed to the interior monologue; more ordinary discursive language patterns to the soliloquy.

Even though this division has a certain historical validity, it is impossible to decide on the basis of such nuances whether a text is, or is not, an interior monologue: many quotations of fictional minds (in both pre- and post-Joycean novels) contain both logical *and* associative patterns, so that their degree of "fluidity" may vary from moment to moment (and from interpreter to interpreter). The interior monologue–soliloquy distinction, moreover, makes one lose track of the twin denominators common to all thought-quotations, regardless of their content and style: the reference to the thinking self in the first person, and to the narrated moment (which is also the moment of locution) in the present tense. This overarching grammatical structure clearly differentiates the most direct technique from the other techniques for rendering consciousness in a third-person context.[32]

As for the term "interior monologue": since the interiority (silence) of self-address is generally assumed in modern narrative, "interior" is a near-redundant modifier, and should, on strictly logical grounds, be replaced by "quoted." But the term "interior monologue" is so solidly entrenched (and has such a long and colorful history in the modern tradition) that more would be lost than gained in discarding it completely. I will therefore use the combined term "quoted interior monologue," reserving the option to drop the second adjective at will, and the first whenever the context permits.

3. *Narrated monologue*. The final basic technique in the third-person context is the least well-known in English criticism. Even such sophisticated genre critics as Scholes and Kellogg discern only "two principal devices for presenting the inner life": narrative analysis and interior monologue.[33] This dual division leaves a wide empty middle for the technique that probably renders the largest number of figural thoughts in the fiction of the last hundred years, but bears no standard English name. The French and German terms (*style indirect libre* and *erlebte Rede*) are sometimes used, as well as "free indirect speech," "indirect interior monologue," "reported speech," etc. I have previously tagged this technique "nar-

rated monologue,"[34] a name that suggests its position astride narration and quotation. Linguistically it is the most complex of the three techniques: like psycho-narration it maintains the third-person reference and the tense of narration, but like the quoted monologue it reproduces verbatim the character's own mental language.

In sum, three types of presentation of consciousness can be identified in the context of third-person narration, to each of which I devote a chapter in the first part of my study. In capsule formulation: 1. psycho-narration: the narrator's discourse about a character's consciousness; 2. quoted monologue: a character's mental discourse; 3. narrated monologue: a character's mental discourse in the guise of the narrator's discourse.

Strangely, the study of techniques for rendering consciousness has focused almost exclusively on third-person narrative texts (with the notable exception of texts cast entirely in interior monologue form). The fact that autobiographical narrators also have inner lives (their own past inner lives) to communicate has passed almost unnoticed. But *retro*spection into a consciousness, though less "magical," is no less important a component of first-person novels than *in*spection of a consciousness is in third-person novels. The same basic types of presentation appear, the same basic terms can apply, modified by prefixes to signal the modified relationship of the narrator to the subject of his narration: psycho-narration becomes self-narration (on the analogy with self-analysis), and monologues can now be either self-quoted, or self-narrated.

If it were merely a matter of surveying an analogous territory in which "he thought" is replaced by "I thought" the bipartite division of my study into third- and first-person narrative forms would lead to nothing but redundancies.[35] But the parallelism between them stops as soon as one goes beyond the definition of the basic techniques. There is, for one thing, a profound change in narrative climate as one moves between the two territories—a change that has been underrated in recent structuralist approaches.[36] It stems from the al-

tered relationship between the narrator and his protagonist
when that protagonist is his own past self. The narration of
inner events is far more strongly affected by this change of
person than the narration of outer events; past thought must
now be presented as *remembered* by the self, as well as expressed by the self (i.e., subject to what David Goldknopf
calls the "confessional increment").[37] All this substantially alters the function of the three basic techniques in autobiographical narration.

But there is another and far more important reason for the
division by person: where the most direct method for the presentation of consciousness is concerned, a radical dissym-
metry appears between third- and first-person forms. In
third-person context the direct expression of a character's
thought (in first-person form) will always be a quotation, a
quoted monologue. But this direct expression of thought can
be presented outside a narrative context as well, and can shape
an independent first-person form of its own: the type of text
also normally referred to as "interior monologue" (*Les Lauriers
sont coupés*, "Penelope"). At this point it becomes clear that
the term "interior monologue" has been designating two
very different phenomena, without anyone's ever stopping to
note the ambiguity: 1) a narrative technique for presenting a
character's consciousness by direct quotation of his thoughts
in a surrounding narrative context; and 2) a narrative *genre*
constituted in its entirety by the silent self-communion of a
fictional mind.[38] Though the technique and the genre share
some psychological implications and stylistic features, their
narrative presentations are entirely different: the first is
mediated (quoted explicitly or implicitly) by a narrating voice
that refers to the monologist by third-person pronoun in the
surrounding text; the second, unmediated, and apparently
self-generated, constitutes an autonomous first-person form,
which it would be best to regard as a variant—or better, a
limit-case—of first-person narration.

This terminological ambiguity too originated with Dujardin, who had a special reason to conflate the two meanings:

his claim that *Les Lauriers sont coupés* was the sole ancestor of *Ulysses* would have been weakened if he had drawn attention to the basic structural difference between the two works: the absence of a narrative context in his own novel, and its presence in Joyce's. But it is obvious on the face of it that *Ulysses* is not an interior-monologue novel in the same sense as *Les Lauriers* is. Joyce's awareness of this difference is apparent in his own description of Dujardin's novel, as reported by Valéry Larbaud: "In that book the reader finds himself established, from the first lines, in the thoughts of the principal personage, and the uninterrupted unrolling of that thought, replacing the usual form of narrative, conveys to us what this personage is doing and what is happening to him."[39] He could scarcely have meant this description to apply to *Ulysses*, since (with the notable exception of the final "Penelope" section) interior monologue is everywhere embedded in a third-person narrative medium. The "first lines" of most of its sections (including of course the first lines of the entire work), far from establishing the reader "in the thoughts of the principal personage," are clearly told in "the usual form of narrative."[40] Wherever the monologue technique appears in *Ulysses*, it alternates with narration, and these narratorial incursions, no matter how brief, permeate the self-locution with a discontinuous element, even as they relieve it of certain notorious difficulties of the autonomous form (e.g., the description of the monologist's own gestures and surroundings). No matter how untraditional their Joycean modulations, such sections as "Proteus" or "Hades" are therefore *structurally* analogous to the quoted monologues in the novels of Stendhal or Dostoevsky rather than to the autonomous form of Dujardin's novel.

It is probably no coincidence that Joyce's comment on *Les Lauriers* dates precisely from the time when he was writing "Penelope,"[41] the only section of *Ulysses* that does have a structure analogous to that of Dujardin's novel. The comment itself still stands today as the most accurate capsule description we have of the interior monologue as a separate fictional form: a first-person genre that, for the sake of clarity, I will call "*autonomous* interior monologue," a term that accurately reflects its same-different relationship to the quoted interior monologue.[42] For this autonomous form also, we can again safely drop the second adjective in most instances. An alternate term I will sometimes use is "interior monologue text" (or "novel").

Despite its notoriety, the autonomous interior monologue in its pure form is a very rare species, even if we count in (as we must) the separate sections from larger texts that take this form ("Penelope," or Mann's Goethe monologue). Yet it is a genre that is entwined with other first-person genres in far more intricate ways than has generally been understood. Both typologically and historically there are multiple intermediate stages between autobiographical and monologic texts, and the two categories can be separated only by closely examining these transitional variations. In this region, the study of techniques for rendering consciousness therefore necessarily spills over into the larger problem of narrative genres (and *the* narrative genre), with the autonomous monologue acting as an essential touchstone for defining what the "usual form of narrative" is—by what it isn't.

This review of my terminology has also served as a preview and preliminary charting of the terrain that will unfold in the successive chapters.

Part I

*Consciousness in
Third-Person Context*

1 / Psycho-Narration

When Becky Sharp believes that she has successfully
ensnared Joseph Sedley, and expects him to ask for her
hand the following day, her narrator escorts her to bed and
informs us: "How Miss Sharp lay awake, thinking, will he
come or not to-morrow? need not be told here." The next
sentence, without so much as a paragraph break, reads: "To-
morrow came, and, as sure as fate, Mr. Joseph Sedley made
his appearance before luncheon."[1] The narrator of *Vanity Fair*
is not much interested in his heroine's night thoughts, eager
as he is to pass on to some action—or at least to some talk.
Becky's meditation can be summarily dismissed because it
would add little to the understanding of a fictional character
or a fictional world that has already been amply explored in
preceding episodes of social interaction.

This avoidance of psycho-narration is characteristic for a
novel in which a hyperactive narrator deals with a multitude
of characters and situations by rapid shifts in time and space.
This pattern dominates the third-person novel well into the
nineteenth century. While prolonged inside views were
largely restricted to first-person forms, third-person novels
dwelt on manifest behavior, with the characters' inner selves
revealed only indirectly through spoken language and telling
gesture. The profusion of directly quoted conversations in the
typical nineteenth-century novel, and the rare opportunity for
self-communion, indicate this tendency toward dramatic
form. In most works by Dickens, Turgenev, Fontane, and

other masters of the novel of manners, character portrayal is far more "contextual" than "intrinsic," and thereby moves in directions lying outside the central compass of this study.[2]

As Ian Watt has shown in detail, a similar narrative rhythm is coupled with similar avoidance of inside views in *Tom Jones*,[3] where the narrator is even more explicit about his refusal to look inside:

> A gentle sigh stole from Sophia at these words, which perhaps contributed to form a dream of no very pleasant kind; but as she never revealed this dream to any one, so the reader cannot expect to see it related here.

> As to the present situation of her [Sophia's] mind, I shall adhere to a rule of Horace, by not attempting to describe it, from despair of success.[4]

Although the Fielding narrator is regularly evasive about the emotions of the passive female of the species, he is somewhat less reluctant to present the mind of the more worldly and active male, who retains a sober—and more easily narrated—mind even in the worst of circumstances. After banishment from Sophia, Tom relieves his emotions in "a flood of tears," which "possibly prevented his misfortunes from either turning his head or bursting his heart," and thus greatly simplify the narrator's task. His faculties unimpaired, Tom then easily turns to the practical problems of where to go and how to earn a living, and thus returns the text to a social context; this is the realm of the narrator's greatest competence, and it gives him occasion for a pithy gnomic pronouncement: "every man who is greatly destitute of money, is on that account entirely excluded from all means of acquiring it."[5]

The last quotation points up another tendency that Fielding and Thackeray share and that deflects their novels from inside views: the presence of a vocal authorial narrator, unable to refrain from embedding his character's private thoughts in his own generalizations about human nature. Not only is he far more interested in his own commentary on events than in the meditations these events may release within his characters, he

is also committed by his narrative stance to explicit, often di-
dactic, evaluation. A typical passage of psycho-narration in a
narrator-oriented novel starts with a brief sentence or two in
the past, followed by several longer and more elaborate sentences in the present. The extent to which such authorial
rhetoric can stunt the inner life is illustrated in another passage
from *Vanity Fair*. Here the narrator accompanies Becky ("this
dauntless worldling") into the room where Amelia is sorrow-
ing after her husband has gone to war:

> Until this dauntless worldling came in and broke the
> spell, and lifted the latch, we too have foreborne to
> enter into that sad chamber. How long had that poor girl
> been on her knees! what hours of speechless prayer and
> bitter prostration had she passed there! the war-chron-
> iclers who write brilliant stories of fight and triumph
> scarcely tell us of these. These are too mean parts of the
> pageant: and you don't hear widows' cries and mothers'
> sobs in the midst of the shouts and jubilation in the great
> Chorus of Victory. And yet when was the time, that
> such have not cried out: heart-broken, humble protes-
> tants, unheard in the uproar of the triumph.[6]

The evasion of an inside view could not be more complete.
The narrator, obviously more interested in his dauntless
worldling than in Amelia's silent sorrow, enters this realm
almost inadvertently—and escapes as swiftly as he can. By
generalizing the individual sorrow of "that poor girl" into
"widows' cries and mothers' sobs," he makes Amelia just as
inaudible among the other "heart-broken, humble protes-
tants"as the latter are among "the great Chorus of Victory."
   In pronouncedly authorial narration, then, the inner life of
an individual character becomes a sounding-board for general
truths about human nature. This typifying tendency determines analogous approaches to the inner life by novelists who
are in other respects as different as Fielding, Thackeray, and
Balzac. Balzac's design, as announced in the preface to the
Comédie humaine, was explicitly paradigmatic: "the description of social species," by the creation of an array of types

representative of the society of his time. No matter how
greatly he may have departed from this design in other respects, his inside views are true to type: it is hard to find in the
Comédie humaine an instance of psycho-narration that is not
followed and dwarfed by authorial glosses, as in the following from *Le Père Goriot*:

> The next day Rastignac dressed himself very elegantly,
> and at about three o'clock in the afternoon went to call
> on Mme de Restaud, indulging on the way in those diz-
> zily foolish dreams which fill the lives of young men
> with so much excitement: they then take no account of
> obstacles nor of dangers, they see success in everything,
> poeticize their existence simply by the play of their imag-
> ination, and render themselves unhappy or sad by the
> collapse of projects that had as yet no existence save in
> their heated fancy; if they were not ignorant and timid,
> the social world would not be possible. Eugène walked
> with extreme caution in order not to get muddy. . . .[7]

No sooner does the narrator mention an inner happening
("indulging . . . in . . . dreams") than he imposes a value
judgment ("dizzily foolish"), which is immediately followed
by a change of tense from narrative past to gnomic present,
and a change of subject from the specific Rastignac to the
species "young men." The text then proceeds with a detailed
and extended psychological analysis, only to end in an even
broader generalization: "if they were not ignorant or timid,
the social world would not be possible." When the text at
length returns to Rastignac, we have learned much about his
peer group, but little about his own thoughts.

* Le lendemain Rastignac s'habilla fort élégamment, et alla, vers trois
heures de l'après-midi, chez madame de Restaud en se livrant pendant la
route à ces espérances étourdiment folles qui rendent la vie des jeunes gens si
belle d'émotions: ils ne calculent alors ni les obstacles ni les dangers, ils voient
en tout le succès, poétisent leur existence par le seul jeu de leur imagination,
et se font malheureux ou tristes par le renversement de projets qui ne vivaient
encore que dans leurs désirs effrénés; s'ils n'étaient pas ignorants et timides, le
monde social serait impossible. Eugène marchait avec mille précautions pour
ne se point crotter . . .

In these texts, even as the narrator draws the reader's attention away from the individual fictional character, he fixes it
on his own articulate self: a discursive intelligence who communicates with the reader about his character—behind his
character's back. This communication can even become a
dialogue, with a narrator engaging an implied reader in a discussion regarding his fictional hero. Wieland's Bildungsro-
man *Agathon* (1766), contains a chapter entitled "Moral State
of our Hero," in which the narrator quotes "a few moving
voices" belonging to his female readers. They protest against
the hero's unheroic thoughts when he reaches a momentary
nadir in the building of his personality. The spirited exchange
that ensues, though it ostensibly deals with the mental behavior of Agathon, tells us less about the "state of our hero" than
it tells about the moral criteria of his narrator and of the typical reader for whom he wrote.

Our discussion up to this point suggests a relation of in-
verse proportion between authorial and figural minds: the
more conspicuous and idiosyncratic the narrator, the less apt
he is to reveal the depth of his characters' psyches or, for that
matter, to create psyches that have depth to reveal.[8] It almost
seems as though the authorial narrator jealously guards his
prerogative as the sole thinking agent within his novel, sens-
ing that his equipoise would be endangered by approaching
another mind too closely and staying with it too long; for this
other mind, contrary to his own disincarnated mental existence, belongs to an incarnated and therefore distinctly limited
being.

The historical development of the novel clearly bears out
the old-fashioned narrator's self-preservative instinct: with
the growing interest in the problems of individual psychology, the audible narrator disappears from the fictional world.
Not because, as Wayne Booth misleadingly asserts, "any sustained inside view . . . temporarily turns the character whose
mind is shown into a narrator,"[9] but because a fully developed figural consciousness siphons away the emotional and
intellectual energy formerly lodged in the expansive narrator.

Even when he passes from center stage, the narrator continues to narrate, becoming the neutral but indispensable
accessory to figure-oriented narration. It is therefore no coincidence that those writers who first insisted on the removal of
vociferous narrators from fiction—notably Flaubert and
Henry James—were also the creators of fictional minds with
previously unparalleled depth and complexity.

Dissonance and Consonance

Although the image of the seesawing relationship between
authorial and figural minds has a certain historical validity, it
becomes invalid once the more extreme forms of authorial
narration have been abandoned. In psychological novels,
where a fictional consciousness holds center stage, there is
considerable variation in the manner of narrating this consciousness. These variations range between two principal
types: one is dominated by a prominent narrator who, even as
he focuses intently on an individual psyche, remains emphatically distanced from the consciousness he narrates; the other is
mediated by a narrator who remains effaced and who readily
fuses with the consciousness he narrates.[10] Two well-known
modern narrative texts will exemplify these two types of
psycho-narration: Thomas Mann's *Death in Venice* and
Joyce's *Portrait of the Artist*.

Thomas Mann is one of the several twentieth-century
novelists—Lawrence, Musil, Gide, and Broch are others—
who reintroduce an audible narrator into third-person fiction,
and put him at the service of individual psychology. *Death in
Venice* concentrates fully on the inner adventures of its
writer-protagonist, with Aschenbach's mind rendered largely
by means of psycho-narration, and only occasional moments
of quoted or narrated monologue. The narrator of the story
holds the unwavering stance of a wise and rational psychologist, whose special field is the psychology of creative artists.
The consistency of his views can be verified in a dozen authorial glosses scattered throughout the text. As Aschenbach's

psychological state changes, as he gravitates from reason to eros and from life to death, the distance between narrator and protagonist increases: in the early sections, when Aschenbach is still in full control of his rational faculties, his self-image very nearly coincides with his narrator's image of him, whereas in the later sections there is a marked ironic gap. The quoted passage occurs somewhat past the midpoint of the story, when Aschenbach is already quite "far gone." Having followed the boy Tadzio with the intention of striking up a casual conversation, Aschenbach finds himself too strongly moved to speak.

Too late, he thought at this moment. Too late! But was it too late? This step he had failed to take, it might quite possibly have led to goodness, levity, gaiety, to salutary sobriety. But the fact doubtless was, that the aging man did not want the sobering, that the intoxication was too dear to him. Who can decipher the nature and pattern of artistic creativity? Who can comprehend the fusion of disciplined and dissolute instincts wherein it is so deeply rooted? For not to be capable of wanting salutary sobering is dissoluteness. Aschenbach was no longer disposed to self-criticism; the tastes, the spiritual dispositions of his later years, self-esteem, maturity, and tardy single-mindedness disinclined him from analyzing his motives, and from deciding whether it was his conscience, or immorality and weakness that had prevented him from carrying out his intention.[11]

---

* Zu spät! dachte er in diesem Augenblick. Zu spät! Jedoch war es zu spät? Dieser Schritt, den zu tun er versäumte, er hätte sehr möglicherweise zum Guten, Leichten und Frohen, zu heilsamer Ernüchterung geführt. Allein es war wohl an dem, dass der Alternde die Ernüchterung nicht wollte, dass der Rausch ihm zu teuer war. Wer enträtselt Wesen und Gepräge des Künstlertums! Wer begreift die tiefe Instinktverschmelzung von Zucht und Zügellosigkeit, worin es beruht! Denn heilsame Ernüchterung nicht wollen zu können, ist Zügellosigkeit. Aschenbach war zur Selbstkritik nicht mehr aufgelegt; der Geschmack, die geistige Verfassung seiner Jahre, Selbstachtung, Reife und späte Einfachheit machten ihn nicht geneigt, Beweggründe zu zergliedern und zu entscheiden, ob er aus Gewissen, ob aus Liederlichkeit und Schwäche sein Vorhaben nicht ausgeführt habe.

The narrator distances himself from Aschenbach immediately, by questioning the directly quoted exclamation "too late," and by then interpreting the failed action as a symptom of abnormal behavior—a form of behavior contrary to the norms held by the narrator. These norms are summed up in the notion of sobriety, which is called salutary when it follows "goodness, levity, gaiety." But his subject has by now rejected these congeries: Aschenbach's supreme value is intoxication. This places him in an eccentric position, makes him into an enigma, the subject of the narrator's dismay: "Who can decipher? . . . Who can comprehend?"; but it is a cool dismay that falls into pointed sententiousness. Couched in the gnomic present—the tense used for timeless generalizations—the authorial rhetoric addresses itself to the mysteries and verities of the human condition, and this authorial wisdom is explicitly denied to Aschenbach when the last sentence returns to him: "Aschenbach was no longer disposed to self-criticism." In that last sentence, the refusal of self-criticism itself becomes the subject of the narrator's criticism.

   A number of features in this passage are typical of psycho-narration with maximal dissonance. The most conspicuous is the presence of the ex cathedra statements, unmistakably set apart from the narration proper by their gnomic present tense. Beyond this, a highly abstract analytical vocabulary is used to describe the inner world, or to elucidate the obscurer sides of the psyche. Without necessarily implying omniscience—Mann's narrator rather takes on a pose of speculative puzzlement—this conceptual language shows that a dominant narrator presents the inner life in a manner as far removed from the psychic experience itself as a psychiatrist's diagnostic notes might be from his patient's free associations. Nowhere does the narrator make the slightest attempt to espouse the syntax or the images of Aschenbach's own consciousness. The initial "too late" pointedly calls attention to the disparity between the narrator's elaborations and his subject's silent thoughts. The same is true for the distancing appellation "the aging man," hardly an epithet that Aschenbach would apply to himself in this moment of would-be rejuvenation. This perceptible hiatus between the narrator's and the character's idioms is one of the clearest signs of authorial orientation in the description of inner events.

These stylistic features all point in one direction: the narrator's superior knowledge of the character's inner life and his superior ability to present it and assess it. To some degree this superiority is implied in all psycho-narration, even where there is greater cohesion between the narrating and the figural consciousness. But the stronger the authorial cast, the more emphatic the cognitive privilege of the narrator. And this cognitive privilege enables him to manifest dimensions of a fictional character that the latter is unwilling or unable to betray. Two such dimensions are of particular importance, the one leading to the exploration of psychic depth, the other to the assessment of ethical worth. The cognitive and linguistic disparity between a narrator and his character is of particular relevance to the narration of those levels of consciousness that cannot be clearly shaped into verbal patterns by the fictional mind itself. I examine this problem in some detail later in this chapter, in discussing the capacity of psycho-narration to penetrate the subliminal zones of the mind.

As for the second, the ethical dimension, it leads to the possibility of explicit judgment of the fictional figure by his narrator. For this reason markedly dissonant psycho-narration is generally favored by critics (like Wayne Booth) who demand moral guidance for the readers of novels, and condemned by those who (like Jean-Paul Sartre[12]) want to grant readers the freedom to form their own judgments. Both tend to forget that a narrator's moral evaluations are not necessarily reliable, especially in modern novels that use intrusive narrators for ironic effect. Authorial glosses can therefore compound the ambiguities of a fictional text, raising more problems than they solve. In *Death in Venice*, at any rate, the identity of narrator and author cannot be taken for granted. Erich Heller even maintains that the narrator represents a parody of the pompous neo-classical artist à la Aschenbach, whose moralistic judgments are meant to be read against the grain.[13] Similar uncertainties arise with the narrator of Gide's *Counterfeiters* when he stops in mid-novel to assess his characters "at his leisure." Though he applies modern value-standards (sincerity, vitality, etc.), his obvious mimicry of his eighteenth-century ancestors casts a parodistic light on his opinionated assessments.

Joyce's *Portrait* shares a number of features with Mann's *Death in Venice*. Both protagonists are artists—one on the rise, the other on the wane—whose intense mental lives range from high rationality to surreal vision. Both works are focused on these central figures, invariably adopting their angle of vision in the presentation of the world surrounding them. Yet the narration of the protagonists' consciousness differs in the two works: in sharpest contrast to Mann's narrator, Joyce's cannot be grasped as a separate entity within the text. His most striking characteristic is, in fact, that he is ungraspably chameleonic. He persistently adapts his style to the age and mood of his hero, coloring it with baby-talk in the beginning section, with the bathos of the budding artist-in-revolt at the end, and in between with a spectrum of psychological states and developmental stages.[14] Though no single passage can demonstrate the narrator's adaptability, the following passage features the most important characteristics of the consonant type of psycho-narration:

> He shook the sound out of his ears by an angry toss of his head and hurried on, stumbling through the mouldering offal, his heart already bitten by an ache of loathing and bitterness. His father's whistle, his mother's mutterings, the screech of an unseen maniac were to him now so many voices offending and threatening to humble the pride of his youth. He drove the echoes even out of his heart with an execration: but, as he walked down the avenue and felt the grey morning light falling about him through the dripping trees and smelt the strange wild smell of the wet leaves and bark, his soul was loosed of her miseries.

The rain-laden trees of the avenue evoked in him, as
always, memories of the girls and women in the plays of
Gerhardt Hauptmann; and the memory of their pale sorrows and the fragrance falling from the wet branches
mingled in a mood of quiet joy.[15]

In contrast to the passage from *Death in Venice*, there is a striking absence here of the more obvious signs of disparity between the narrating and the figural consciousness: no gnomic
present statements, no speculative or explanatory commentary, no distancing appellations. On closer inspection we find
that the narrator avoids prominent analytic or conceptual
terms, as well as reportorial indirection; note the absence of
subordination of the "he thought (felt, knew) that" variety.
The narrator is still there, he is still reporting, with phrases
denoting inner happenings: "He shook the sound out of his
ears," "his heart already bitten by an ache," "he drove the
echoes even out of his heart," and so forth, to the "memory," "sorrows," and "joy" of the final sentence. Yet these
phrases show the discretion of the narrating voice, how it
yields to the figural thoughts and feelings even as it reports
them: not by abstract statement, but by metaphor, not in a
neutral tone, but in one tinged with bathos.

Another pattern that induces cohesion is the manner in
which thoughts and feelings are intertwined with sensations.
The passage follows a typical moment of Irish domesticity,
with the father's commandeering whistle, the mother's nag-
ging, and a mad nun's screeching in a neighboring asylum.
Stephen's negative obsessions, as he leaves the house, are in-
duced by these sounds, and then appeased by sensations of
outdoor sights and odors, while his reactions are enhanced by
literary memories. Why he associates rain-laden trees with
Hauptmann's women is never made clear, but the over-all
associative complex suggests his revolt from family, country,
and religion, and his movement toward aesthetic experience
and cosmopolitan culture.

Because of the absence of authorial rhetoric, the narrator's
knowledge of Stephen's psyche seems to coincide with
Stephen's self-knowledge. There is nothing to indicate cogni-

tive privilege on the narrator's part, with the possible exception of the phrase "the pride of his youth," which fleetingly injects a semblance of authorial abstraction. This consonant type of psycho-narration displays disparity of values even less than disparity of knowledge. The absence from *A Portrait* of any sort of evaluative judgments has led to the unresolved discussion of its author's attitude toward Stephen; but Joyce's avoidance of a marked authorial presence is surely sufficient proof that the portrait of a problematic artist as a problematic young man demands from the reader the same tolerance for ambiguities that went into its making.[16]

Psycho-narration in *A Portrait* often becomes more noticeably tinged with Stephen's idiom than in the passage just analyzed. An almost complete intermingling of authorial and figural voices occurs, for example, in the lengthy sequence describing the matinal composition of the villanelle. In these pages the nearly suffocating lushness of Stephen's neo-romantic mood floods the narrative account. Modulating the erotic dream (never fully related) to its poetic expression (eventually quoted in full), the intervening creative meditation is reported by a narrative voice that emulates the imagistic pattern in Stephen's mind.[17] Its inception leads up to the first stanza of the villanelle:

> Towards dawn he awoke. O what sweet music! His soul was all dewy wet. Over his limbs in sleep pale cool waves of light had passed. He lay still, as if his soul lay amid cool waters, conscious of faint sweet music. His mind was waking slowly to a tremulous morning knowledge, a morning inspiration. A spirit filled him, pure as the purest water, sweet as dew, moving as music. But how faintly it was inbreathed, how passionlessly, as if the seraphim themselves were breathing upon him! His soul was waking slowly, fearing to awake wholly.[18]

The predominant technique of this passage is still psycho-narration, determined by the profusion of verbs and nouns of consciousness. But its vocabulary and rhythm is so vividly colored by Stephen's poetic idiom in-the-making that one may speak of "stylistic contagion." This term was first suggested by Leo Spitzer, in a rather different context: when he discovered that a narrator's style is sometimes peppered with elements of figural dialect or vulgarity.[19] Applied to the techniques for rendering consciousness, the phrase "stylistic contagion" can serve to designate places where psycho-narration verges on the narrated monologue, marking a kind of midpoint between the two techniques where a reporting syntax is maintained, but where the idiom is strongly affected (or infected) with the mental idiom of the mind it renders.

Passages of psycho-narration involving stylistic contagion rarely continue for long stretches without lapsing into sentences of pure narrated monologue, most often in the form of those exclamations and interrogations so characteristic of the latter technique. In the cited passage, the two exclamatory sentences illustrate this tendency, which increases as the text approaches the strophic quotation. That quotation itself must be understood as an instance of *quoted* monologue,[20] and the fact that the villanelle contains many of the key words and images from the narration that precedes it gives additional proof of the symbiosis between narrating and figural voices that takes place throughout this text.

The proximity of this consonant type of psycho-narration to the more direct monologic techniques for rendering figural thought accounts in part for its abundant occurrence in the stream-of-consciousness novel, where its presence has been so reluctantly acknowledged by theorists of the genre.[21] The remainder of this chapter focuses on some special effects that can be attained via this technique, and some special functions it performs in modern as well as in traditional fictional contexts.

Summary and Expansion

In quoted and narrated monologues the rendering of consciousness is temporally restricted to the sequential instants of

silent locution, the time of narration roughly coinciding with
the narrated time. But psycho-narration has almost unlimited
temporal flexibility. It can as readily summarize an inner development over a long period of time as it can render the flow
of successive thoughts and feelings, or expand and elaborate a
mental instant.

Mental descriptions in a large time-frame are found in most
Realist novels, and Jane Austen works them with particular
skill:

> Emma continued to entertain no doubt of her being in
> love. Her ideas only varied as to the how much. At first
> she thought it was a good deal; and afterwards but little.
> She had great pleasure in hearing Frank Churchill talked
> of; and, for his sake, greater pleasure than ever in seeing
> Mr. and Mrs. Weston; she was very often thinking of
> him, and quite impatient for a letter, that she might
> know how he was, how were his spirits, how was his
> aunt, and what was the chance of his coming to Randalls
> again this spring. But, on the other hand, she could not
> admit herself to be unhappy, nor, after the first morning,
> to be less disposed for employment than usual; she was
> still busy and cheerful; and, pleasing as he was, she could
> yet imagine him to have faults; and further, though
> thinking of him so much, and, as she sat drawing or
> working, forming a thousand amusing schemes for the
> progress and close of their attachment, fancying interest-
> ing dialogues, and inventing elegant letters; the conclu-
> sion of every imaginary declaration on his side was that
> she *refused him*. Their affection was always to subside into
> friendship. Everything tender and charming was to mark
> their parting; but still they were to part. When she be-
> came sensible of this, it struck her that she could not be
> very much in love. . . . [Austen's emphasis][22]

A kind of panoramic view of Emma's inner self is achieved
here, to render the progression of her inner debate on the
"how much" of her love. Though there are no precise time
indicators, the third sentence sets the limit points of the inner

events: "At first she thought it was a good deal; and afterwards but little [in love]." The "afterwards" thus anticipates the ultimate moment of realization "that she could not be very much in love." This anticipation is a clear indication of the narrator's temporal omniscience; he views the events from a distant perspective, looking over the entire time span he recounts. Only that telescopic perspective makes it possible for him to order and digest the events in the process of displaying them.

The summation itself is achieved by a number of lexical and syntactic means, among which we can distinguish at least three different rhythms of time condensation: iterative, durative, and mutative.[23] Iterative summary organizes events on a pattern of recurrence: Emma is *"very often* thinking of him," she forms *"a thousand* amusing schemes," she concludes *"every* imaginary declaration" with a refusal, and so forth. Durative summary organizes events on a pattern of persistence: throughout the period recounted, Emma *"continued* to entertain no doubt of her being in love" because she experiences positive emotions toward Frank Churchill in different situations mentioned in the passage; "but, on the other hand," throughout the same period her inner calm remains unaffected: she is no "less disposed for employment *than usual*," *"still* busy and cheerful." Toward the end of the passage the durative rhythm is further underlined by the several present participles: "thinking of him so much . . . as she sat drawing or working, forming . . . fancying . . . and inventing. . . ." Both iterative and durative summaries compress time by focusing on the invariant aspects of the narrated span. By contrast, a mutative summary recounts a change that takes place gradually over an extended period of time. Only the second and third sentences of the quotation summarize in this fashion. But since these sentences anticipate the final mental happening—"it struck her that she could not be very much in love"—they contain the essential summary statement, which the durative and iterative modes support, expand, and substantiate.

The difference between the iterative-durative and the mutative type of summary is more clearly apparent in French than it is in English, where the imperfect is as a rule used for the former, the *passé simple* for the latter. Compare, for example, the following two passages from *Madame Bovary* (which must be quoted in the original):

> Mais elle *était* pleine de convoitises, de rage, de haine. Cette robe aux plis droits cachait un coeur bouleversé, et ces lèvres si pudiques n'en *racontaient* pas la tourmente. Elle *était* amoureuse de Léon, et elle *recherchait* la solitude, afin de pouvoir plus à l'aise se délecter de son image. La vue de sa personne *troublait* la volupté de cette médita-tion. Emma *palpitait* au bruit de ses pas: puis, en sa pré-sence, l'émotion *tombait*, et il ne lui *restait* ensuite qu'un immense étonnement qui se *finissait* en tristesse. [my emphasis]

> Cependant les flammes *s'apaisèrent*, soit que la provision d'elle-même *s'épuisât* ou que l'entassement *fût* trop con-sidérable. L'amour peu à peu *s'éteignit* par l'absence, le regret *s'étouffa* sous l'habitude; et cette lueur d'incendie qui empourprait son ciel pâle se *couvrit* de plus d'ombre et s'effaça par degrés.[24] [my emphasis]

The first passage summarizes duratively in the first three sen-tences, iteratively in the last three; throughout it surveys a psychic syndrome continuing over an extended time period —a narrative approach Flaubert uses quite as frequently for mental as for physical and social situations. The second pas-sage condenses into a discrete event a mutation that takes place over a long period: the adverbs *peu à peu, sous l'habitude*, and *par degrés* convey the gradualness of a process, the *passé simple* the singularity of its occurrence.

This last quotation also contains Flaubert's favorite device for vitalizing summary psycho-narration, the striking image; it often takes the form of a hyperbolic simile:

> From that point on, the memory of Léon was like the

center of her boredom. It sparkled more strongly than in Russian steppes a fire of travelers that has been abandoned on the snow.

As for the memory of Rodolphe, she had buried it in the very depth of her heart; and it remained there more solemn and immobile than the mummy of a king in a subterranean tomb.[25]

At times Flaubert injects an ironic note into these synoptic similes, thereby stressing their authorial origin:

But the anxiety at a new role . . . had been sufficient to make her believe that she finally felt that marvelous passion that until now had been like a great rose-colored bird soaring in the splendor of poetic skies.[26]

Replacing analyses by analogies, such imagistic distillates stand in radical contrast to neutral and patient accounts of the type exemplified in the cited passage from *Emma*. Though Austen's analytic surveys are more typical for Realist novels, Flaubert's imagistic surveys anticipate a technique frequently found in modern psychological novels, when "psycho-analogies" are used to describe a mental instant.

Since all surveys of a temporal span signal the existence of a narrator with a distanced, bird's-eye view, summary psycho-narration is rare in figural novels.[27] If broader inner-time vistas are found in such novels at all, they enter by way of the protagonist's memory. Henry James' novels offer many illustrations of this mnemonic flashback pattern. One of the best

---

* Dès lors, ce souvenir de Léon fut comme le centre de son ennui; il y pétillait plus fort que, dans une steppe de Russie, un feu de voyageurs abandonné sur la neige.

* Quant au souvenir de Rodolphe, elle l'avait descendu tout au fond de son coeur; et il restait là, plus solennel et plus immobile qu'une momie de roi dans un souterrain.

* Mais l'anxiété d'un état nouveau . . . avait suffi à lui faire croire qu'elle possédait enfin cette passion merveilleuse qui jusqu'alors s'était tenue comme un grand oiseau au plumage rose planant dans la splendeur des ciels poétiques.

known occurs in *The Portrait of a Lady*, when the narrator skips silently over the first year of Isabel's marriage, preferring to make it surface in her own mind during her retrospective vigil.[28] This structure is radicalized in stream-of-consciousness novels that follow one or several mental streams through a Woolfian "ordinary day": here years of mental life may weigh on the remembering mind during the brief span of narrated time, but only mental instants are narrated directly. Conversely, when "Time Passes" in the explicitly summary interlude of *To the Lighthouse*, the characters' inner lives during the spanned decade are passed in silence.

But despite the disappearance of the traditional mental survey, psycho-narration itself has by no means disappeared from the modern fictional scene. One reason it continues to exist alongside the modern monologic technique is precisely its temporal elasticity: for if it can contract the long time-span, it can also expand the instant. And, as Nathalie Sarraute has pointed out, the expanded instant—"a disproportionately enlarged present"—is a favorite time-zone of modern novelists.[29]

Psycho-narration is in fact rarely used simply to follow consciousness through its paces, since it can do so only in the form of unadorned indirect quotations—on the pattern "it occurred to him that . . . he asked himself whether . . ."—which easily becomes monotonous. Most often indirect thought quotations quickly give way to the more direct monologic techniques. It is favored only by novelists who like to interrupt their characters' thoughts by expansive glosses: by Jane Austen, George Eliot, Thomas Mann.[30] The prize for this type of psycho-narration must undoubtedly go to Proust, for the extravagant use he makes of it in the third-person narration of *Un Amour de Swann*.

The following typical passage renders Swann's thoughts about the money he habitually sends to Odette, and his paradoxical refusal to consider her as a "kept woman":

And then, suddenly, *he asked himself whether that was not precisely what was implied by "keeping" a woman* (as if, in fact, that idea of "keeping" could be derived from elements not at all mysterious nor perverse, but belonging to the intimate routine of his daily life, such as that thousand-franc note, a familiar and domestic object, torn in places and mended with gummed paper, which his valet, after paying the household accounts and the rent, had locked up in a drawer in the old writing-desk whence he had extracted it to send it, with four others, to Odette) *and whether it was not possible to apply to Odette, since he had known her* (for he never imagined for a moment that she could ever have taken a penny from anyone else, before), *that term, which he had believed so wholly inapplicable to her, of "kept" woman.* He could not explore the idea further, for an access of that mental lethargy which was, with him, congenital, intermittent and providential, came, at that moment, to extinguish all light in his brain, as instantaneously as, at a later period, when electric lighting had been everywhere installed, it became possible, merely by fingering a switch, to cut off all the supply of light from a house. His mind fumbled, for a moment, in the darkness, he took off his spectacles, wiped the glasses, passed his hands over his eyes, and saw light again only when *he found himself face to face with a wholly different idea, namely that he must endeavour, in the coming month, to send Odette six or seven thousand-franc notes instead of five, simply as a surprise for her and to give her pleasure.* [my emphasis][31]

* Alors, tout d'un coup, *il se demanda si cela, ce n'était pas précisément l'"entretenir"* (comme si, en effet, cette notion d'entretenir pouvait être extraite d'éléments non pas mystérieux ni pervers mais appartenant au fond quotidien et privé de sa vie, tels que ce billet de mille francs domestique et familier, déchiré et recollé, que son valet de chambre, après lui avoir payé les comptes du mois et le terme, avait serré dans le tiroir du vieux bureau où Swann l'avait repris pour l'envoyer avec quatre autres à Odette) *et si on ne pouvait pas appliquer à Odette depuis qu'il la connaissait* (car il ne soupçonna pas un instant qu'elle eût jamais pu recevoir d'argent de personne avant lui), *ce mot qu'il avait cru si inconciliable avec elle, de "femme entretenue".* Il ne put approfondir cette

Three rapidly successive moments of narrated inner time are described, marked by the punctual time phrases "suddenly," "at that moment," and "when." It is perhaps not immediately apparent that both the first and the last sentence are syntactically structured as indirect quotation: "he asked himself whether . . . and whether" and "a wholly different idea, namely that. . . ." These sentences—if we disregard for the moment the interrupting parentheses—convey the consecutive words in Swann's mind, and their time of narration therefore approximates the narrated time.

But between these two articulated thoughts there is a sudden blank. Swann's mental light is switched off—"an access of that mental lethargy . . . came, at that moment, to extinguish all light"—and turned on again a few lines later—"and [he] saw light again only when. . . ." This interruption is enlarged by the narrator's analogy, whose vehicle—by anticipating a historically posterior moment ("*at a later period*, when electric lighting had everywhere been installed")—explicitly underlines its authorial origin. The authorial association is then artfully resorbed into the direct description of Swann's mental and physical gestures. The fact that he attends to his physical vision—cleans his glasses, rubs his eyes—suggests his subliminal awareness of his mental blindness. But the momentary hiatus has been extended beyond its natural length by the narrator's exegetic simile.

An even more drastic time dilation is effected by the bracketed asides. The first, a seven-line excursion, is injected between clauses ("he asked himself whether . . . and whether"); the second, briefer in length, separates a verb from its object ("to apply . . . that term"). Both rupture the

---

idée, car un accès d'une paresse d'esprit qui était chez lui congénitale, intermittente et providentielle, vint à ce moment éteindre toute lumière dans son intelligence, aussi brusquement que, plus tard, quand on eut installé partout l'éclairage électrique, on put couper l'électricité dans une maison. Sa pensée tâtonna un instant dans l'obscurité, il retira ses lunettes, en essuya les verres, se passa la main sur les yeux, et ne revit la lumière que quand *il se retrouva en présence d'une idée toute différente, à savoir qu'il faudrait tâcher d'envoyer le mois prochain six ou sept mille francs à Odette au lieu de cinq, à cause de la surprise et de la joie que cela lui causerait.* [my emphasis]

continuity of the mental sentence to explore freely perceptions and events that are not on, nor even in, Swann's mind.
The indirect discourse serves merely as the trigger that sets off
the actual psycho-narration, which sounds those depths that
the discourse itself obliterates. This is entirely in keeping with
views held by Proust and a number of other modern writers
who believe that interior discourse ("l'*oblique* discours intérieur" as Proust pointedly called it) hides more than it reveals.[32]

As suggested by this Proust passage, the same device that
was used in summary narration to distill the essence of mental
events occurring over a long period of narrated time recurs in
punctual narration, but this time with the obverse effect of
expanding time or arresting it. In contrast to Proust, who invariably handles psycho-analogies in an emphatically authorial manner, a number of his contemporaries infused similes
more directly into the thought-streams of their characters. In
the early works of Robert Musil psycho-analogies are so
abundant that they shape a deliberate method for rendering
consciousness, replacing the monologic techniques of other
writers. This is especially true of the story "The Perfecting of
a Love" ("Die Vollendung der Liebe," 1911), one of the most
remarkable, and least remarked, early experiments in
"stream-of-consciousness" fiction.[33]

This story portrays the mind of a woman involved in a
paradoxical experience: during a brief voyage she "perfects"
her love for her husband by way of a sordid affair with a
stranger. Musil's own summation: "an unfaithfulness can be a
union in a deeper inner zone"[34] points to the stratum of the
psyche that is the exclusive site of the story. Its unusual idiom
is exemplified in the following passage:

> She no longer knew what she was thinking, and pleasure
> in being alone with strange experiences now took a quiet
> hold of her; it was *like the play of very faint, scarcely tangible
> inquietudes and of great shadowy stirrings of the soul, groping
> for them.* She tried to remember her husband, but all she

could find of her almost vanished love was a strange notion *as of a room with windows kept shut for a long time.* She
made an effort to get rid of this, but it yielded only a very
little, and remained lurking nearby. And the world was
as pleasantly cool as a bed in which one stays behind alone. . . .
Then she felt as if she were about to be faced with a decision, and she did not know why she felt this, and she was
neither glad nor resentful; all she felt was that she did not
want to do anything or to prevent anything, and her
thoughts slowly wandered into the snow outside, without a backward glance, further and further, *as when one is
too tired to turn back and walks on and on.* [my emphasis]³⁵

This text (the heroine, Claudine, is alone in a train) focuses
exclusively and extensively on inner happenings, and it does
so without recourse to inner discourse, in the form either of
interior or of narrated monologue. As we are twice informed,
the mental activity bypasses not only self-articulation, but
also self-understanding: "She no longer knew what she was
thinking," "she did not know why she felt this." A profusion
of verbs and nouns signals psycho-narration, but of a kind
that evokes and complicates more than it orders or clarifies.
Not only does it underline the vague and contradictory nature
of thoughts and feelings; it also objectifies, animalizes, and
personifies psychic forces. A comparative *like* or *as* introduces
the final clause of nearly every sentence, and the analogues
range from unfathomable abstractions to bold concretions.

* Sie wusste nicht mehr, was sie dachte, nur ganz still fasste sie eine Lust
am Alleinsein mit fremden Erlebnissen; es war *wie ein Spiel leichtester, un-
fassbarster Trübungen und grosser danach tastender, schattenhafter Bewegungen der
Seele.* Sie suchte sich ihres Mannes zu erinnern, aber sie fand von ihrer fast
vergangenen Liebe nur eine wunderliche Vorstellung *wie von einem Zimmer
mit lange geschlossenen Fenstern.* Sie mühte sich, das abzuschütteln, aber es
wich nur ganz wenig und blieb irgendwo in der Nähe wieder liegen.Und die
Welt war so angenehm kühl *wie ein Bett, in dem man allein zurückbleibt* . . . Da
war ihr, als stünde ihr eine Entscheidung bevor, und sie wusste nicht, warum
sie es so empfand, und sie war nicht glücklich und nicht entrüstet, sie fühlte
bloss, dass sie nichts tun und nichts hindern wollte, und ihre Gedanken wan-
derten langsam draussen in den Schnee hinein, ohne zurückzusehen, immer
weiter und weiter, *wie wenn man zu müd ist um umzukehren und geht und geht.*
[my emphasis]

This method is arresting in a literal sense: the similes draw attention to themselves and away from the temporal progression of the narrative. They digress from or impede the sequence of recounted events, slowing the pace by continually expanding the time of narration over the narrated time. The enlargement through similes of each minute inner event is the main stylistic feature that imbues the text with an anti-narrative, nearly stationary quality, making it one of the most "unreadable" stories ever written. The anti-narrative quality of Musil's similes is reinforced by their verbal structure. In all the comparative clauses of the passage, the narrative past gives way either to the present or to noun phrases with participial modifiers: "as when one is too tired to turn back and walks on and on"; "as of a room with windows kept shut for a long time." These verb forms lead the text away from the specific temporal account into a generalized, omnitemporal realm which is further underscored by the use of impersonal pronouns within the comparative clauses: "as pleasantly cool as a bed in which *one* stays behind alone." Unlike Proust's authorial glosses, Musil's similes seem to induce a fusion between the narrating and the figural consciousness by blurring the line that separates them. We can never tell with certainty whether the analogical association originates in the mind of the narrator or in Claudine's own. In the clause "all she could find of her almost vanished love was a strange notion as of a room with windows kept shut for a long time," for example, the comparative conjunction acts as a kind of hinge between authorial evocation and figural imagination, with both partaking of the timeless present that reigns within the simile.

This hypertrophy of analogies prevails throughout the story. Its author likened it to the statue of an unknown deity densely covered with hieroglyphics,[36] a comparison confirmed by one scholar's count of 337 similes in 38 pages (not including other tropes). Musil has clearly used a deliberate psycho-analogical method for rendering consciousness in order to avoid interior discourse techniques, and to reach a sub-verbal stratum in his character's mind, "a life that cannot be expressed in words, and which is my life nonetheless."[37]

Although I know of no other work which uses the analogic approach to consciousness so unrelentingly, many modern novels are interlaced with psycho-analogies. We find them most frequently in works where the narrated monologue is the prevailing method for rendering consciousness, but at moments when an author is for some reason unwilling to entrust the presentation of the inner life to the character's own verbal competence. Here are two examples from Virginia Woolf, the stream-of-consciousness novelist who employs psycho-analogies most copiously:

> But—but—why did she suddenly feel, for no reason that she could discover, desperately unhappy? As a person who has dropped some grain of pearl or diamond into the grass and parts the tall blades very carefully, this way and that, and searches here and there vainly, and at last spies it there at the roots, so she went through one thing and another. . . .[38]

> What then was this terror, this hatred? Turning back among the many leaves which the past had folded in him, peering into the heart of that forest where light and shade so chequer each other that all shape is distorted, and one blunders, now with the sun in one's eyes, now with a dark shadow, he sought an image to cool and detach and round off his feeling in a concrete shape.[39]

In both these passages, the narrated thoughts remain suspended in a question, and the verbal flow is suddenly diverted into tangential vignettes: searches through complicated landscapes of the mind, syntactically too complex to be attributed to inner speech. Whether the simile is explicit, as in the first example, or implicit as in the second, the tense in both instances shifts to the present for the duration of the analogic excursus, and the usual third-person pronouns are replaced by impersonal subjects ("a person," "one"). Then the sentence reverts to the punctual narrative past and the specific figural psyche ("so she went," "he sought").

Whereas Woolf most often uses her imagistic excursions to convey the "moments of vision" that are a hallmark of her novels, Nathalie Sarraute persistently uses striking images for ordinary, everyday inner events. Examples abound in her work, both in conversational scenes (accompanying her characters' *sous-conversations*), and in solo scenes. The following examples are all taken from *The Planetarium*:

> A bell rings . . . it's the kitchen door . . . a traveler lost in the desert, who perceives a light, the sound of footsteps, experiences the same joy mingled with apprehension that rises in her as she runs to open the door. . . . [Sarraute's ellipses]

> As he sits there motionless, he feels it forming inside him: something compact, hard . . . a kernel. . . . But he has become all over like a stone, a silex: things from the outside that knock against him strike brief sparks, little light words which crackle for an instant. . . . [Sarraute's ellipses]

> She has that strange sensation, which comes over her at times . . . of growing huge—a giant in seven-league boots which allow him to walk over rivers, bridges, houses. . . .[40]

Since this entire novel is cast in the present tense, the metaphors blend more smoothly into the narrative context or the narrated monologue than they do in the novels of Musil and Woolf. In the preface to *The Age of Suspicion*, where Sar-

---

* On sonne . . . c'est à la porte de la cuisine . . . Le voyageur égaré dans un désert qui perçoit une lumière, un bruit de pas, éprouve cette joie mêlée d'appréhension qui monte en elle tandis qu'elle court, ouvre la porte . . . [Sarraute's ellipses]

* Assis là immobile, il sent comme cela se forme en lui: quelque chose de compact, de dur . . . un noyau . . . Mais il est devenu tout entier pareil à une pierre, à un silex: les choses du dehors en le heurtant font jaillir de brèves étincelles, des mots légers qui crépitent un instant . . . [Sarraute's ellipses]

* Elle a cette sensation étrange qui la prend par moments . . . de devenir immense—un géant chaussé de bottes de sept lieues qui lui permettent d'enjamber le fleuve, les ponts, les maisons . . .

raute explains the rationale for her method, she explicitly
links this imagistic strain in her psycho-narrations to the
necessity for slowing the narrative rhythm, in order to cap-
ture the extremely rapid "movements" within the mind:
"Since, while we accomplish these movements, no words . . .
not even the words of interior discourse, can express them
. . . it was possible to communicate them to the reader only
by images which render their equivalents and make him feel
analogous sensations. It was also necessary to decompose
these movements, and to unroll them in the consciousness of
the reader in the manner of a film in slow motion."[41] Clearly,
for Sarraute as for Musil, imagistic narration of inner happenings succeeds in depicting aspects of the mind that cannot be
as convincingly rendered by monologic techniques.

Both in theory and in practice, then, the importance that
certain modern novelists give to metaphoric representation of
mental processes suggests that psycho-narration is not the
step-child among modern techniques that theorists of the
stream-of-consciousness novel have regarded it to be. As its
main function evolves from the digest of long-range mental
developments to the dilation of mental instants, it remains
paramount for the novelist, "discovering, lens in hand, the
micro-structure of life."[42]

Narration of Sub-Verbal States

As we have already seen, one of the most important advantages of psycho-narration over the other modes of rendering
consciousness lies in its verbal independence from self-
articulation. Not only can it order and explain a character's
conscious thoughts better than the character himself, it can
also effectively articulate a psychic life that remains unver-
balized, penumbral, or obscure. Accordingly psycho-narration often renders, in a narrator's knowing words, what a
character "knows," without knowing how to put it into
words.

A novel that deliberately sets out to exploit this situation—not only in its ambiguous title—is Henry James' *What Maisie Knew*, about a child who becomes a pawn in her parents' complicated divorce and remarriages. As James indicates in the preface, he had initially planned for Maisie to be the teller of her own tale. But he soon decided that this approach would fail, since "small children have many more perceptions than they have terms to translate them." Instead, he decided to make Maisie into the "ironic center" of the story, whose perceptions "our own commentary constantly attends and amplifies . . . in figures that are not yet at her command."[43] This discrepancy between the child's and the narrator's "figures" is greatest in the earliest sections of the book, when Maisie is youngest:

> She had conceived her first passion, and the object of it was her governess. It hadn't been put to her, and she couldn't, or at any rate didn't, put it to herself, that she liked Miss Overmore better than she liked papa; but it would have sustained her under such an imputation to feel herself able to reply that papa too liked Miss Overmore exactly as much. He had particularly told her so. Besides she could easily see it.[44]

The point of view of this passage is clearly Maisie's, but the language is elaborately Jamesian; with the single exception of the word "papa" not a single phrase corresponds to a child's idiom. The possibility of even the simplest abstraction (the preference for the governess over the father) becoming the subject of quotable thoughts is expressly dispelled: "she couldn't, or at any rate didn't, put it to herself, that. . . ."[45]

Since Maisie is a quick learner, the narrator-figure discrepancy is progressively reduced during the course of the novel, as the child grows into her role of typical Jamesian observer of the gross subtleties that surround her. Before long, Maisie's perceptions become so intricate that the narrator is obliged periodically to remind himself and the reader that she is still in need of his vocal mediation: "She had of course in her mind fewer names than conceptions, but it was only with this drawback that she now made out. . . . ."[46] The narrator comes to play the role of simultaneous translator—or, better, transcriber—of a potentially articulate mind, and his role is justified by Maisie's low verbal factor rather than by the subliminal leval of her mental life.

When narration does descend to the subliminal level, less elaborate justification is needed for authorial intervention. But narrators frequently draw explicit attention to the sub- or unconscious nature of the psychic states they narrate, or to the impossibility of their self-articulation. To mention only two examples, from differing fictional episodes: After Raskolnikov has overheard the conversation in the marketplace that precipitates his decision to murder the old woman, "He thought of nothing and was incapable of thinking; but he felt suddenly in his whole being that he had no more freedom of thought, no will, and that everything was suddenly and irrevocably decided."[47] This compulsive feeling "in his whole being" stands in sharp contrast to Raskolnikov's many ratiocinations about the murder, which are most often rendered in the form of interior monologues. An analogous situation may arise at the opposite end of the psychic spectrum, at moments of climactic vision or cognition. In the famous "Schopenhauer" sequence in *Buddenbrooks*, when Thomas momentarily recognizes the illusory nature of life and is released from the shackles of will and consciousness, we are told that his knowledge came to him "not in words and consecutive thoughts, but in sudden, rapturous illuminations of his inmost being."[48]

The non-verbal quality of certain inner experiences is on occasion stressed after the fact, that is, after lengthy and detailed narration—perhaps for fear that the reader may fail to recognize the circumvention of self-articulation that has just taken place. In Musil's *Young Törless* a prolonged description of the boy's incipient homoeroticism is followed by the words: "But all this was no longer discernable for Törless, and was fused in a single obscure feeling."[49] Similarly in

Lawrence's *Women in Love* an elaborate report of Gudrun's ultimate feelings for Gerald ends with the remark: "All this
Gudrun knew in her subconsciousness, not in her mind."[50]
   As these two last quotations suggest, an inner realm peculiarly in need of narrative mediation is erotic experience, with
its singularly simultaneous involvement of psyche and soma.
Any one of D. H. Lawrence's novels yields a rich metaphoric
complex, made up of all kinds of electromagnetic, igneous,
and meteorological hyperboles. The following are taken from
the early chapters of *Women in Love*: Gudrun is traversed by a
"keen paroxysm, a transport . . . a paroxysm of violent sensation"; Hermione experiences "a flame that drenched down
her body like fluid lightning"; Gerald feels Minette "as if she
were passing into him in a black electric flow . . . like a mag-
netic darkness . . . rapid sensations ran through his blood and
over his brain. . . . Every one of his limbs was turgid with
electric force, and his back was tense like a tiger's with slum-
bering fire."[51] In these early scenes, the most passionate
partners have not even begun their approaches; the climactic
love-scenes between Gudrun and Gerald, Birken and Ursula
will later produce far more spectacular fireworks. Though
other writers may employ less emphatic idioms and images
they generally share Lawrence's preference for psycho-narration over the monologic techniques when they follow their
characters to bed.

   It would be a futile exercise to delimit psycho-narration
sharply from the narration of sensations that impinge on a
character's mind, from within or from without. In figural
novels especially, where the narration of external reality is in-
timately related to subjective perception, there is no clear
borderline between the external and the internal scene. When
they are introduced by perception verbs, the sights a character
sees and the sounds he hears link psyche and scene, and
psycho-narration can then no longer be clearly differentiated
from scenic description. This dovetailing between the inner
and outer realms of fictional reality—which we will encoun-

ter again in connection with the monologic techniques[52]—can only be noted in passing here. More relevant for our focus on consciousness is the fact that purely imaginary perceptions by day- or night-dreaming minds are sometimes introduced by the identical phrases that signal a character's perception of the surrounding world.

Hallucinatory visions introduced by the phrase "He saw . . ." are a case in point, since they conform exactly to the "*Voir*-device" Anna Hatcher has identified as a standard technique used by Realist novelists to present the external reality perceived by a fictional character.[53] When this device is applied in visionary scenes, the context alone can reveal that a sight is present solely to the eye of the mind. During his stroll through a Munich park, Aschenbach hallucinates:

> he *saw, saw* a landscape, a tropical marshland beneath a heavy dank sky, . . . *saw* . . . hairy palm shafts rising up near and far, *saw* strangely mis-shapen trees drop their roots through the air into the ground, . . . *saw* between the knotted stems of the bamboo thicket the lights of a crouching tiger gleaming—and felt his heart throb with terror and inexplicable longing. [my emphasis][54]

The redundancy of the seeing-verb underlines the paradox of mental vision, even as it underlines the momentary inner muteness of the highly verbal mind that "perceives" it. Prefiguring Aschenbach's gravitation to Venice, the Asian cholera, and eros-thanatos, this early vision reveals the later events as objectifications of the suppressed jungle within, and of the crouching tiger that will leap from it. A fascinating counterpart to this prospective revelation is Marcher's retrospective revelation in the closing sentence of James' "The Beast in the Jungle":

---

* er *sah, sah* eine Landschaft, ein tropisches Sumpfgebiet unter dickdunstigem Himmel, . . . *sah* . . . haarige Palmenschäfte nah und fern emporstreben, *sah* wunderlich ungestalte Bäume ihre Wurzeln durch die Luft in den Boden . . . versenken, . . . *sah* zwischen den knotigen Rohrstämmen des Bambusdickichts die Lichter eines kauernden Tigers funkeln—und fühlte sein Herz pochen vor Entsetzen und rätselhaftem Verlangen. [my emphasis]

He *saw* the Jungle of his life and *saw* the lurking Beast; then, while he *looked, perceived* it, as by a stir of the air, rise, huge and hideous, for the leap that was to settle him. His eyes darkened—it was close; and, instinctively turning, in his hallucination, to avoid it, he flung himself, face down, on the tomb. [my emphasis]

Despite their similar appearances, Marcher's and Aschenbach's jungle beasts are very different creatures: the one symbolizes the suppressed presence of all-too-human drives, the other inhuman absence. But the analogy in the presentation of these visions is complete: they both conform to a stylistic pattern that recurs whenever mute visions are engendered in fictional minds.[55]

The narration of dreams in fiction calls for greater diversity of techniques. The mind in vision is paralyzed, whereas the dreaming mind variously interacts with and reacts to the dreamed experience, so that a dream often includes the dreamer's thoughts in his dream. Not surprisingly, novelists generally use the same techniques for thoughts in dreams and for waking thoughts.[56] Dostoevsky has Raskolnikov talk to himself as frequently in the course of his nightmares as in the course of his "real" experiences.[57] Kafka renders his K.'s bafflements in dreamed adventures in the same narrated monologue form he uses during their dream*like* waking lives.[58] Thomas Mann, by contrast, prefers to analyze his dreamers' minds authorially; in Aschenbach's Dionysian dream: "The beginning was fear, fear and desire and a terrible curiosity to know what was to come"; as a result of what actually "comes"—as we are told in the last sentence—"his soul tasted the bestiality and madness of destruction."[59]

While the presentation of the dreamer's consciousness *within* a dream can take these various forms, the dream *as a whole* is most often presented via psycho-narration. Framing it in its third-person context, such prologues as "That night he had a fearful dream,"[60] or "it was while he was asleep in the twilight of a dream"[61]—and analogous epilogues— usually signal the raising and dropping of the curtain on the

oneiric performance.[62] It is not difficult to see why dreams do
not lend themselves to presentation through the monologic
techniques: a dreamer does not tell himself his dream while he
dreams it, any more than a waking person tells himself his
experiences while they are in progress. Within the confines of
third-person fiction, where a narrator's magic power allows
him to see into sleeping minds quite as readily as into waking
ones, dreams are a form of mental life peculiarly in need of
indirect mediation.

  With the narration of visions and dreams, psycho-narration
reaches into the most obscure regions of mental life, momentarily probing the depth. Some modern novelists, however,
have chosen more extensive forays down under, perhaps
none more insistently than Hermann Broch. In his trilogy
The Sleepwalkers he repeatedly descends into a depth of the
psyche almost totally shrouded from self-cognition. The title
concept of sleepwalking signifies a benighted groping and
searching in darkness that has both specifically historical
meaning (the trilogy spans the 30 years preceding and including the First World War) and vast metaphysical or meta-
psychological significance.[63] Almost all the characters in this
novel, while their conscious minds cope with the varied concrete circumstances of their everyday lives, contain and
vaguely sense the existence within them of mystical fears and
desires. This submerged, archetypal, anonymous realm provides the hidden motive for both individual and mass
behavior—not unlike the Jungian collective unconscious. The
novelist's task is, in Broch's view, to represent man in his to-
tality, at all levels of his psychic existence, including that essentially subliminal stratum that cannot be depicted in terms
of a character's conscious thoughts.[64] As a result of this artistic aim, psycho-narration of an emphatically authorial type
has particular importance in Broch's fictions. It enters his
novels most often when he depicts characters of low intellectual or introspective capacity, and it takes the form of intermittent theorizing about the hidden motivations that underlie
figural gestures, words, and feelings.

One example is the moment in the last volume of *The Sleepwalkers* when Huguenau, a thoroughly immoral "realist," has deserted from the army to become a war profiteer. Walking through the streets of a beautiful old town, he is seized by a feeling of aesthetic apprehension quite foreign to his conscious self:

> Huguenau, who had visited many beautiful old towns on previous business trips, but had never noticed them, was seized by a feeling quite unknown to him, which he could neither have named nor traced to any source, but which nonetheless seemed strangely familiar to him; if someone had told him that it was an aesthetic feeling, or a feeling whose origin lies in freedom, he would have laughed incredulously, laughed like a person who has never been touched by a notion of the world's beauty. And he would have been right insofar as no one can determine whether it is freedom that opens the soul to beauty, or whether it is beauty that bestows the notion of freedom upon the soul. And yet he would have been wrong, since there was bound to be even in him a deeper human knowledge, a human longing for freedom in which all the light of the world has its source. . . .[65]

The disparity between authorial and figural psyche could not be greater than it is in this passage: Huguenau is vaguely cognizant of an unfamiliar feeling, but the narrator can label it, explain it, and relate it to a philosophic system—unmis-

---

* Huguenau, der auf seinen Geschäftsreisen schon manch schöne alte Stadt besucht, aber noch keine bemerkt hatte, wurde von einem Gefühl erfasst, einem zwar unbekannten Gefühl, das er weder benennen, noch von irgendeinem Ursprung hätte ableiten können und das ihn dennoch seltsam anheimelte: wäre es ihm als ästhetisches Gefühl bezeichnet worden oder als ein Gefühl, das seine Quelle in der Freiheit besitzt, er hätte ungläubig gelacht, gelacht wie einer, den noch nie Ahnung von der Schönheit der Welt berührt hat, und er hätte insoweit sogar Recht damit gehabt, als niemand entscheiden kann, ob die Freiheit es ist, in der die Seele sich der Schönheit erschliesst, oder ob es die Schönheit ist, die der Seele die Ahnung ihrer Freiheit verleiht, aber er hat trotz alledem unrecht, da auch für ihn ein tieferes menschliches Wissen, ein menschliches Sehnen nach einer Freiheit vorhanden sein muss, in der alles Licht der Welt anhebt . . .

takably Kantian. This incommensurability is underlined by
the incredulous laugh the narrator imputes to Huguenau in
the event that the esoteric nature of his feelings were made
known to him. And it is capped by the initial sentence of the
paragraph immediately following this analysis: "Far removed
from such meditations, Huguenau rented a room in the hotel
in the marketplace."

In another narrative strand woven into the same novel, the
narration of unconsciousness becomes the single, sustained,
and explicit subject. A middle-class woman, Hanna Wend-
ling, responds to the global death-urge of the war by progressive alienation from all the life-sustaining impulses in the self.
This process takes place in the hidden recesses of her psyche,
while the conscious self apprehends only its baffling behavioral symptoms, for "no man knows anything of the microscopic structure of his soul."[66] This non-cognizance is
stressed throughout the text: Hanna is filled with the vaguest
stirrings "of which one wanted to know nothing and indeed
knew nothing"; she has "a very distant and entirely indistinct
thought," she is haunted by images that words can never en-
compass.[67] In one phase of her personality disintegration her
feelings for her absent soldier-husband are reduced to animal
sexuality, her memory of him to an anonymous phallus:

> the first to disappear was his face, then his moveable ex-
> tremities, his hands and feet, but the unmoving rigid
> body, this torso reaching from the breastbone to the
> thighs, that highly obscene image of the male, persisted
> in the depth of her memory. . . . And the further this par-
> tial forgetfulness progressed . . . the more concentric and
> isolated became its indecency, an indecency which
> forgetfulness approached more and more slowly, cutting
> off thinner and thinner slices, paralyzed by the inde-
> cency.

But no sooner has this graphic process been described than
the narrator chides himself for having reduced the psychic
content to a mere metaphor, thereby emphasizing that this

obscene reduction process is an authorial construct rather than a realistic psychological representation. The narrator then proceeds to explain the greater complexity of the "true state of affairs, which always remains shadowy, a mingled flow of unclear images, a flooding of half-remembered memories, half-thought thoughts, half-wished wishes, a river without banks shrouded in a silvery vapor, a silvery mist that reaches all the way to the clouds and to the black stars."[68] Despite the lyric, imagistic idiom, the language of this psycho-narration is meant to elucidate rather than to emulate the figural psyche. The narrator builds a symbolic landscape as a kind of theoretical correlative for a subliminal stratum that can never emerge on the conscious level or the verbal surface of the figural mind. The consciousness is metaphorically *labeled* a stream— "a mingled flow . . . a flooding . . . a river without banks"— but not *rendered* as a stream. In this respect Broch's metaphorical exploration bears closer resemblance to William James' coinage of the term "stream of consciousness" as a psychologist's suggestive conceptual image than to such fictional embodiments of this image as the "Penelope" section of *Ulysses*.

With the exclusive focus on unconscious processes in the two texts from *The Sleepwalkers*, Broch draws near a limit-situation where narrative fiction borders on psychological case study. The narrator's commentary on Huguenau and

---

* zuerst verschwand sein Gesicht, dann alles Bewegte an ihm, Hände und Füsse, aber der unbewegte und starrende Leib, dieser Torso, der vom Brustkorb bis zu den Schenkelstümpfen reicht, dieses höchst laszive Bild des Mannes, das erhielt sich in der Tiefe ihres Gedächtnisses, . . . Und je weiter solch stückweises Vergessen fortschritt . . . , desto konzentrischer und isolierter wurde seine Anstössigkeit, eine Anstössigkeit, an die das Vergessen immer langsamer und langsamer, mit immer schmäleren Schnitten heranrückte,—ohnmächtig vor der Anstössigkeit. Das ist bloss Gleichnis, und wie jedes Gleichnis vergröbert auch dieses den wahren Sachverhalt, der stets im Schattenhaften bleibend, ein Durcheinanderfliessen von unklaren Vorstellungen ist, ein Fluten halberinnerter Erinnerungen, halbgedachter Gedanken, halbgewollter Wollungen, ein Fluss ohne Ufer mit silbrigem Dunst darüber, silbriger Hauch, der bis in die Wolken und zu den schwarzen Sternen reicht.

Hanna, inevitably cast in gnomic present tense, approaches from a different direction the theorizing of the eighteenth- and nineteenth-century authorial tradition, even though its focus has shifted from *inter*personal to *intra*personal relationships, from the manifest social surface of behavior to the hidden depth of the individual psyche.

What this limit-situation underscores concerning the different techniques for rendering consciousness in fiction is that, contrary to a widely held belief, the novelist who wishes to portray the least conscious strata of psychic life is forced to do so by way of the most indirect and the most traditional of the available modes. The correlation drawn by critics of the stream-of-consciousness novel between the relative depth of the levels of consciousness portrayed and the relative directness of the techniques used to portray them is therefore entirely erroneous. When Frederick J. Hoffman, Melvin Friedman, and most recently Erwin R. Steinberg associate psycho-narration with "conscious controls," "the region closest to directed thinking and rational controls," or "the highest level of abstraction," and the more direct "stream-of-consciousness techniques" with less rational, more spontaneous and "unconscious" mental strata,[69] this correspondence is based on a confusion of manner with matter, on the assumption that only disorganized language can render disordered minds. They forget that the most direct of the "stream-of-consciousness techniques," interior monologue, is by definition limited to the linguistic activity of the mind, whereas the unconscious is by definition radically devoid of language. As Leon Edel aptly puts it: "the unconscious cannot be expressed in its own unconscious form, since obviously this is unconscious. *We can only infer it from symbols emerging in the conscious expressions of the person. . . .*"[70] What Edel fails to point out is that a novelist need not limit himself to symbols of the unconscious that appear in his character's consciousness as long as he uses his own language rather than his character's. In this light psycho-narration may be regarded as the most direct, indeed the unique, path that leads to the sub-verbal depth of the mind. The most succinct anticipation of the enduring importance psycho-narration continues to have for the modern psychological novel may well be Schiller's paradoxical adage "Spricht die Seele, ach, so spricht schon die Seele nicht mehr." ("When the soul speaks, alas, it is no longer the soul that speaks.")

2 // Quoted Monologue

Modes of Quotation

The quoted interior monologue became a fully established technique about the middle of the nineteenth century.[1] Many heroes of earlier novels monologize only on exceptional occasions, after elaborate authorial introductions, and in clearly audible voices. One of Tom Jones' rare monologues is featured in a chapter title: "Containing a conversation which Mr. Jones had with himself." Tom's more philosophic German counterpart, Agathon, addresses himself more volubly in a chapter entitled "A Soliloquy." The narrator also prefaces this monologue with a long-winded apology, referring to his ostensible source material: a Greek manuscript based on the hero's own diary. "This evidence," he concludes, "explains how the historian could know what Agathon said to himself on this and other occasions."[2]

The standard inquit phrases we find in pre-Realist novels indicate that the volume of their monologues was normally turned up quite as high as in drama.[3] Tom Jones' monologue is introduced by the words: "and starting up he cried," and concluded by an even clearer sign of audibility: "Here passion stopped his mouth, and found a vent in his eyes." Goethe's Wilhelm Meister "when left alone, exclaimed in rapture."[4] Even nineteenth-century authors continue to allow their characters to speak audibly to themselves. When Dickens presents a self-address at the beginning of *Little Dorrit*, his vantage point is markedly external. As Amy looks at a sleeping lady previously unknown to her, " 'She is very pretty,' she said to herself. 'I never saw so beautiful a face. Oh, how unlike me!' It was a curious thing to say, but it had some hidden meaning, for it filled her eyes with tears."[5] Since what "she said to herself" retains its "hidden meaning," we are forced to assume that it is, like other behavioral symptoms (e.g., her tears), perceptible to the observant narrator without a special amplifying device. Stendhal, whose characters monologize more frequently than those of other writers in his period, is still quite inconsistent in respect to their audibility. Whenever he refers to a tirade Julien addresses to himself as "ce monologue," we can be certain he implies spoken rhetoric, since he was writing at a moment when the coupling of that noun with the adjectives "interior" or "silent" must still have been a contradiction in terms. Julien in fact "calls out" ("s'écria-t-il") at least one of his monologues.[6] And in his longest solo (in prison) his voice again rises as he chides himself for the public posturing of his most private thoughts: "The influence of my contemporaries wins out, he said aloud, and with a bitter laugh. Talking to myself in solitude, two steps away from death, I am still a hypocrite. . . . O nineteenth century!" [Stendhal's ellipsis][7] Historically, an interesting moment: the oratorical leaning of the soliloquy tradition in drama and epic is questioned and deflated by a new Romantic standard of sincerity, still cast, however, in the very form it condemns.

The association of the audibly soliloquizing voice with self-conscious posing occasionally recurs as a fully realistic symptom in later psychological novels. Raskolnikov, in his continuing inner debate before the murder, "from time to time . . . would mutter something, from the habit of talking to himself. . . ."[8] The narrator even names "the monologues in which he jeered at his own impotence and indecision."[9] As Genette has shown, Proust's Swann epitomizes the mendacity of self-address when he intones "those insincere monologues

---

* L'influence de mes contemporains l'emporte, dit-il tout haut et avec un rire amer. Parlant seul avec moi-même, à deux pas de la mort, je suis encore hypocrite . . . O dix-neuvième siècle! [Stendhal's ellipsis]

uttered aloud like a scene, a comedy one plays to oneself."[10]
Gide's Bernard in *The Counterfeiters*, who starts his youthful
revolt with highly rhetorical soliloquizing,[11] gradually un-
learns this form of self-communion as he approaches his and
his author's ideal of sincerity: "I had that habit of constantly
speaking to myself. Now, I couldn't do it any more, even if I
wanted to."[12] As we shall see, rationalization or self-deceit
continues to attend solitary discourse even when it drops
below the audible in modern novels.

   But in Stendhal's time, and in his own novels, exclamation
(or even muttering) in solitary moments is no longer the rule,
and becomes increasingly associated with a strange "habit,"
or with moments of extreme agitation. Realist novelists take
the inner voice entirely for granted, as can be seen from
episodes where they quote the thoughts of characters who are
in the company of others (with silent words often belying
spoken words). Silence is now implied regardless of whether
thinking or saying verbs are used: "he thought (to himself),"
or "he said (to himself)." Sometimes introductory phrases are
even omitted altogether, with the inception of inner speech
signaled merely by quotation marks and other standard
signs.[13] By the mid-nineteenth century, writers who still
apologize elaborately for thought quotations begin to sound
out of date. A notorious example is Victor Hugo, when (in
1862) he interrupts the chapter from *Les Misérables* entitled "A
Tempest in a Brain" by this heavy-handed gloss: "It is certain
that we do talk to ourselves; there is no thinking being who
has not experienced this. . . . It is in this sense only that the
words frequently employed in this chapter, *he said, he
exclaimed*, must be understood. We talk, speak, cry out to
ourselves without breaking the external silence. There is a

---

* Il est certain qu'on se parle à soi-même, il n'est pas un être pensant qui ne
l'ait éprouvé . . . C'est dans ce sens seulement qu'il faut entendre les mots
souvent employés dans ce chapitre, *il dit, il s'écria*. On se dit, on se parle, on
s'écrie en soi-même, sans que le silence extérieur soit rompu. Il y a un grand
tumulte; tout parle en nous, excepté la bouche. Les réalités de l'âme, pour
n'être point visibles et palpables, n'en sont pas moins des réalités. [Hugo's
emphasis]

great tumult; everything speaks within us, excepting the
mouth. The realities of the soul, even if they are not visible
and palpable, are nonetheless realities." [Hugo's emphasis][14]
But even as Hugo betrays the fact that he belongs to a pre-
Realist generation, he also communicates *ex cathedra* the assumptions that underlie the internalization of the monologue
technique, and shows that the novelists who used it tacitly
took its psychological realism for granted.

This silencing of the monologic voice goes hand in hand
with a change in the rhythm of quoted monologue in the
novels of Dostoevsky and other late Realist writers. Direct ci-
tation of a character's thoughts is no longer restricted to isolated moments explicitly set aside for extended contemplation
or inner debate ("A Tempest in a Brain") but accompanies his
successive encounters and experiences. This results in a text
that alternates rapidly between outer and inner scene:

> The paper had come off the bottom of the wall and hung
> there in tatters. He began stuffing all the things into the
> hole under the paper: "They're in! All out of sight, and
> the purse too!" he thought gleefully, getting up and gaz-
> ing blankly at the hole which bulged out more than ever.
> Suddenly he shuddered all over with horror; "My God!"
> he whispered in despair: "what's the matter with me? Is
> that hidden? Is that the way to hide things?"
> He had not reckoned on having trinkets to hide. He
> had only thought of money, and so had not prepared a
> hiding-place.
> "But now, now, what am I glad of?" he thought, "Is
> that hiding things? My reason's deserting me—simply!"
> He sat down on the sofa in exhaustion and was at once
> shaken by another unbearable fit of shivering.[15]

The repeated shifting back and forth between report and quotation produces a proliferation of inquit formulas ("he
thought . . . he whispered . . . he thought") that, together
with the elaborate punctuation, continuously draws attention
to the duality of viewpoints. The result is a discontinuous,

fragmented, jolting rhythm that matches Raskolnikov's inner and outer agitation in this hectic scene, but would be less effective in a less hectic one.

It is no coincidence, then, that the novel that brought the most radical change in the integration of quoted monologue with the surrounding narrative text took for its subject (in Woolf's famous phrase) "an ordinary mind on an ordinary day." A typical passage from one of the Bloom chapters in *Ulysses* reads as follows:

> His hand took his hat from the peg over his initialled heavy overcoat, and his lost property office secondhand waterproof. *Stamps: stickyback pictures. Daresay lots of officers are in the swim too. Course they do.* The sweated legend in the crown of his hat told him mutely: Plasto's high grade ha. He peeped quickly inside the leather headband. *White slip of paper. Quite safe.*
> On the doorstep he felt in his hip pocket for the latchkey. *Not there. In the trousers I left off. Must get it. Potato I have. Creaky wardrobe. No use disturbing her. She turned over sleepily that time.* He pulled the halldoor to after him very quietly, more, till the footleaf dropped gently over the threshold, a limp lid. *Looked shut. All right till I come back anyhow*.[16] [my emphasis]

Here for the first time the inner discourse is no longer separated from its third-person context either by introductory phrases or by graphic signs of any kind. The gain in textual continuity is obvious if we compare this text with the one from *Crime and Punishment*. The narrating and the figural voice now cohere to a point where only close inspection can determine which sentences are Bloom's monologue, which the narrator's report.

But such close inspection also reveals the basic similarity between *Ulysses* and earlier third-person novels that use the quoted monologue. The altered appearance of Joycean monologues tends to make one forget that the most telling *gram-*

matical signals for distinguishing between report and monologue are common to Joyce and to earlier novelists: the
change in basic tense (from past to present) and person (from
third to first). Because of the fundamental sameness of this
grammatical pattern, experimental addition of quotation
marks and introductory tags goes a long way toward giving
the *Ulysses* passage a traditional look:

> On the doorstep he felt in his hip pocket for the latchkey.
> "Not there," he thought. "In the trousers I left off. Must
> get it. Potato I have. Creaky wardrobe. No use disturb-
> ing her. She turned over sleepily that time." He pulled
> the halldoor to after him very quietly . . .

It goes a long way, but not all the way. Even with the addition of explicit quotation signals, the Joycean monologue still
retains an unremittingly "Joycean" quality. But this quality is
a result more of the monologue's idiom and less of its relationship to the surrounding text. Note also that the addition
of the phrase "he thought" gives Bloom's silent words an incongruous, almost an infantile, babbling tone, which may be
explained by our habitual association of that inquit phrase
with more coherent and rational verbal sequences than those
produced by Joyce's characters.

As Breon Mitchell has noted,[17] the presence of quoted
monologues without explicit signals of quotation in a third-
person context is a touchstone for the influence of *Ulysses* on
the novels that followed in its wake. Despite individual variations in the notational systems, the unsignaled quoted monologue became a hallmark for stream-of-consciousness novels.
Döblin's *Berlin Alexanderplatz* (the most famous German offspring of *Ulysses*) constantly alternates between narration and
monologue, and even goes Joyce one better by passing from
one to the other within the same sentence:

> Where should a poor devil like me go, he shuffled along
> the row of houses, there was no end to it. I'm a big ass,
> why shouldn't one be able to walk along here. . . . . He

thrashed his arms about, now my boy here you won't
freeze.[18]

Twice in this passage a mere comma separates quoted monologue from narrative, but tense and person (also when the
impersonal "one" or the second person are used in lieu of the
first) still clearly mark the shift. Sartre's story "Intimité,"
which closely imitates the techniques of *Ulysses* in two of its
four sections, uses a greater variety of punctuation marks to
signal the transition to and from monologue within the same
sentence:

> She heard a gurgling: a singing stomach, I hate it, I can't
> ever tell if it's his stomach or mine.

> She had closed her eyes and blue circles began to turn,
> like at the fair, yesterday, I was shooting at the circles
> with rubber arrows. . . .[19]

At times even these faint signals are omitted:

> She didn't even take the time to comb her hair, she was
> in such a hurry and the people who'll see me won't know
> that I'm naked under my grey coat. . . .[20]

Despite the syntactic continuity, the monologic inception is
again clear from the changes in tense and person.[21]

In modern psychological novels, when thinking verbs are
found at all in the immediate vicinity of interior monologues,
they are used less in a functional than in an incantatory man-

---

* Wo soll ick armer Deibel hin, er latschte an der Häuserwand lang, es
nahm kein Ende damit. Ich bin ein ganz grosser Dussel, man wird sich hier
doch noch durchschlängeln können. . . . Er schlug die Arme umeinander, so
mein Junge, hier frierst du nicht.

* Elle entendit un gargouillis: un ventre qui chante ça m'agace, je ne peux
jamais savoir si c'est son ventre ou le mien.

* Elle avait fermé les yeux et des disques bleus se mirent à tourner, comme
à la foire, hier, je tirai sur les disques avec des flèches de caoutchouc . . .

* Elle ne prit même pas la peine de se peigner, tant elle était pressée et les
gens qui me verront ne sauront pas que je suis nue sous mon grand manteau
gris . . .

ner. Virginia Woolf, for example, dots her texts with the
phrase "he (she) thought": "Oh these parties, he thought;
Clarissa's parties. Why does she give these parties, he
thought."[22] These redundancies serve merely as a kind of
phrasal emphasis, and have little in common with the routine
inquit formulas of pre-Joycean days. In some of his third-
person novels Faulkner uses a similar proliferation of mental
verbs before and within monologue passages, but his repetitions carry weightier meanings than Woolf's. The following
passage from *Light in August* is typical:

> "I don't even know what they are saying to her," he
> thought, thinking *I don't even know that what they are say-*
> *ing to her is something that men do not say to a passing child*
> *believing I do not know yet that in the instant of sleep the*
> *eyelid closing prisons within the eye's self.* . . . [Faulkner's
> emphasis][23]

A sort of stratification of Joe Christmas' consciousness is suggested here, with each successive mental verb ("he thought,
thinking . . . believing") descending into lower depth, less
clear articulation, and more associative imagery.

Finally, we must consider the typologically interesting case
where inquit phrases constitute the sole third-person context
for a quoted monologue. Theoretically, one could conceive of
a fictional text in which the narrator's only function would be
to name the thinker and his mental locution, on the pattern:
"X thought. . . ," followed by a novel-length monologue. I
know of no works that conform to this pattern exactly, but
only some that approach it. Woolf in *The Waves* multiplies the
pattern, with the barest inquit phrases—"Rhoda said: . . . ,"
"Bernard said: . . ."—introducing the alternating monologues of its six characters.[24] Camus' "Renegade" reverses
the pattern: the monologue of its tongueless "speaker," enclosed in quotation marks, begins with the words: " 'What a
stew, what a stew! . . . ,' " and ends 30 pages later, as a narrator enters *in extremis* to explain the halt of the locution: "a

handful of salt filled the mouth of the talkative slave."[25]
These minimal inquit frames, though they draw attention to
the monologic form, leave this form itself intact. Without its
closing sentence, "The Renegade" would be an autonomous
monologue, and thus a first-person, rather than a third-
person, text. Borderline cases of this type highlight the borderline that separates the autonomous monologue from
third-person narration, and at the same time demonstrate the
typological discontinuity between the quoted and the autonomous monologue.

Narrative Context

A monologist in a third-person context is not the uniquely
dominant voice in the text we read. He is always more or less
subordinated to the narrator, and our evalution of what he
says to himself remains tied to the perspective (neutral or
opiniated, friendly or hostile, empathic or ironic) into
which the narrator places him for us. Even a title (*Mr.*
Bloom), or an adjective (*poor* Emma) affects our interpretation of what a character is quoted as thinking. The context of
a monologue is, in short, as important and as variable as its
content. And since the quotation of silent words does not
commit the narrator to the point of view of a character any
more than the quotation of his spoken words, frequent
monologizing is not (as is sometimes thought) a sign of a unified, figural point of view.

Some authors even use interior monologues to reinforce
the ironic gap between their narrator and their protagonist.
When Julien Sorel, faced with the timid advances of Madame
de Rênal, thinks:

before my journey, I took her hand, she withdrew it;
today I withdraw my hand, she grasps and presses it. A
fine opportunity to repay her for all the contempt she had
for me. God only knows how many lovers she has had!
She perhaps chooses me only because it is so convenient
for us to meet. . . .

the narrator instantly places this figural perspective *in* perspective:

> Such, alas, is the misfortune of over-civilization! At twenty, the soul of a young man, if he has any education to speak of, is a thousand miles away from the *laisser-aller* without which love is often only the most tedious of duties.[26]

Such conjunctions of interior monologues and authorial glosses maximize the disparity between the narrator's far-sightedness and his character's myopia. The same holds true when a narrator nods his assent to the thoughts he quotes. Thackeray, never one to let a character steal the show for long, lets Becky monologize only to bend her thoughts his way. Her realistic views of morality, formulated by herself and *pro domo*—" 'It isn't difficult to be a country gentleman's wife,' Rebecca thought. 'I think I could be a good woman if I had five thousand a year. . . .' "—are first evaluated, then swiftly appropriated by her narrator:

> And who knows but Rebecca was right in her speculations—and that it was only a question of money and fortune which made the difference between her and an honest woman? If you take temptations into account, who is to say that he is better than his neighbor? A comfortable career of prosperity, if it does not make people honest, at least keeps them so. An alderman coming from a turtle feast will not step out of his carriage to steal a leg of mutton; but put him to starve, and see if he will not purloin a loaf.[27]

In these texts the narrators' commentaries lead away from psychological characterization toward those generalizations

---

* avant mon voyage, je lui prenais la main, elle la retirait; aujourd'hui je retire ma main, elle la saisit et la serre. Belle occasion de lui rendre tous les mépris qu'elle a eus pour moi. Dieu sait combien elle a eu d'amants! elle ne se décide peut-être en ma faveur qu'à cause de la facilité des entrevues.

Tel est, hélas, le malheur d'une excessive civilisation! A vingt ans, l'âme d'un jeune homme, s'il a quelque éducation, est à mille lieues du laisser-aller, sans lequel l'amour n'est souvent que le plus ennuyeux des devoirs.

about human nature so characteristic of the authorial mode of narration. A different, but no less emphatic, duality of viewpoints can obtain when direct thought-quotations are combined with authorially oriented psycho-narration. We have already glimpsed this dialectic in the passage from *Death in Venice* analyzed in an earlier context. It is further heightened when, toward the end, Aschenbach is allowed to speak his sole extended soliloquy. I quote selectively from the mordantly sarcastic sentence that introduces it:

> He sat there, the master, the artist become dignified . . .
> he whose fame was official, whose name was ennobled,
> and whose style was held up as a model to school
> boys,—he sat there, . . . and his lips, drooping beneath
> their make-up, formed single words out of the strange
> dream logic emerging from his half-slumbering brain.[28]

In the monologue that follows, Aschenbach—in radical reversal of his original apollonian position—ratiocinates on the hopelessly dionysian nature of the artist. In view of the extremely sparing use Mann makes of quoted monologue throughout the story, it is no mere coincidence that, in this moment of maximal distance between the narrating and the figural voices, the former no longer serves as medium or as mediator for the latter, but that the narrator disengages himself completely to let Aschenbach speak for and to himself.[29]

Even when the context of a monologue is less clearly ironic, the mere fact that a narrator stops to quote a figural consciousness introduces a measure of disparity, especially when he shuttles rapidly between quotation and psycho-narration. Depending on the dosage of irony and sympathy, the conjunction can range from dissonance to harmony between the narrating and the figural voices, even within a

---

* Er sass dort, der Meister, der würdig gewordene Künstler, . . . er, dessen Ruhm amtlich, dessen Name geadelt war und an dessen Stil die Knaben sich zu bilden angehalten wurden,—er sass dort, . . . und seine schlaffen Lippen, kosmetisch aufgehöht, bildeten einzelne Worte aus von dem, was sein halb schlummerndes Hirn an seltsamer Traumlogik hervorbrachte.

single work. Two scenes from Tolstoy's *Death of Ivan Ilych*
will illustrate some of the effects.

   The second half of this story focuses on the mental struggle
of the fatally ill hero, oscillating continuously between quotation and narration. At times the narrator distances himself
from his protagonist by injecting a single note of omniscience. This happens when Ivan Ilych first reaches—and instantly represses—the thought that the "correct" life he has
led before his illness may have been meaningless, even evil:

> "Maybe I did not live as I ought to have done," it sud-
> denly occurred to him. "But how could that be, when I
> did everything properly?" he replied, and immediately
> dismissed from his mind this, the sole solution of all the
> riddles of life and death, as something quite impossible.[30]

The brief gnomic comment within the psycho-narration
("this, the sole solution of all the riddles of life and death"), is
sufficient to draw attention to the distance that separates the
unknowing hero from his knowing narrator. When Ivan
Ilych resumes his silent questioning, dramatic irony is fully
operative:

> "Then what do you want now? To live? Live how? Live
> as you lived in the law courts when the usher proclaimed
> 'The judge is coming!' The judge is coming, the judge!"
> he repeated to himself. "Here he is, the judge. But I am
> not guilty!" he exclaimed angrily. "What is it for?"[31]

Having previously received a signal behind Ivan Ilych's back,
the reader knows the answer to the obsessive "riddle" and
continues to be in the know as the text now modulates toward durative psycho-narration:

> And he ceased crying, but turning his face to the wall
> continued to ponder on the same question: Why, and for
> what purpose, is there all this horror? But however much
> he pondered he found no answer.[32]

Here the author-character disparity is no longer explicitly
marked, but since the narrator has now assumed a distant

temporal vantage point, his ironic perspective on the figural
blindness continues to operate.

To some degree, this perspective is maintained to the end
of the story, when Ivan Ilych himself reaches the moment of
truth at his final moment of life. But there are intervening
scenes when the narrator adopts Ivan Ilych's point of view.
As we have seen in discussing Joyce's *Portrait*, psycho-
narration used in this narrative situation readily becomes contaminated by the figural idiom. For the same reason, directly
quoted thoughts in such a context tend to overlap with the
narrator's report. The resultant redundancy can be clearly
seen in the following passage:

> Then again together with that chain of memories
> another series passed through his mind—of how his ill-
> ness had progressed and grown worse. There also the
> further back he looked the more life there had been.
> There had been more of what was good in life and more
> of life itself. The two merged together. "Just as the pain
> went on getting worse and worse, so my life grew worse
> and worse," he thought. "There is one bright spot there
> at the back, at the beginning of life, and afterwards all
> becomes blacker and blacker and proceeds more and
> more rapidly—in inverse ratio to the square of the dis-
> tance from death," thought Ivan Ilych. And the example
> of a stone falling downwards with increasing velocity en-
> tered his mind. Life, a series of increasing sufferings, flies
> further and further towards its end—the most terrible
> suffering. "I am flying. . . ." He shuddered, shifted him-
> self, and tried to resist, but was already aware that resist-
> ance was impossible . . .
>
> "Resistance is impossible!" he said to himself. "If I
> could only understand what it is all for! But that too is
> impossible. . . ."[33]

I list only the most obvious correspondences: "how his illness
had progressed and grown worse" is repeated in "Just as the
pain went on getting worse and worse, so my life grew worse

and worse." The image of life as an object falling toward death, first found in a segment of the monologue, is given greater precision by the narrator's "example of a stone falling downwards with increasing velocity." And the fatal flight— "Life . . . flies further and further towards its end"—is immediately echoed in "I am flying. . . ." Even more literally, "He . . . was already aware that resistance was impossible" is repeated verbatim in direct quotation: "Resistance is impossible."

This passage shows that psycho-narration and quoted monologue do not mesh very effectively in figural narrative situations. They create arbitrary shifts in perspective, discontinuities, redundancies. The creators of the greatest figural novels may have sensed this, more or less consciously. *Madame Bovary, The Ambassadors, The Castle, A Portrait of the Artist*—these novels contain hardly any quoted monologues, but instead long stretches of narrated monologues combined with psycho-narration.

This generalization may well seem absurd in the face of *Ulysses*, where quoted monologues abound in nine of the eighteen sections, always in a strictly figural context,[34] yet continuity between narration and quotation is so perfect that the reader often cannot tell where one ends and the other begins. On closer inspection he discovers that Joyce achieves this symbiosis by casting the narrator into a very different, far more limited, role than Tolstoy does in *Ivan Ilych*. The *Ulysses* narrator omits not only quotational signals before an interior monologue, but also all other forms of psycho-narration, so that we find hardly any verbs of consciousness in his vocabulary. His method may be observed in the following passage from the "Proteus" section:

He [Stephen] lay back at full stretch over the sharp rocks, cramming the scribbled note and pencil into a pocket, his hat tilted down on his eyes. That is Kevin Egan's movement I made nodding for his nap, sabbath sleep. *Et vidit Deus. Et erant valde bona.* Alo! *Bonjour*, welcome as the

> flowers in May. Under its leaf he watched through
> peacocktwittering lashes the southing sun. I am caught in
> this burning scene. Pan's hour, the faunal noon. Among
> gumheavy serpentplants, milkoozing fruits, where on
> the tawny waters leaves lie wide. Pain is far. [Joyce's
> emphasis][35]

Though the narrator in this passage describes Stephen's physical gestures and surroundings, the stream of Stephen's consciousness remains purely subjective, unpolluted by authorial
interference. Significantly, both shifts from narration to
monologue immediately follow mention of Stephen's eyes,
the sensory borderline and link between outer and inner
world. The elements of the reported scene, however, activate
the associations of Stephen's thoughts: as the shared subject of
report and monologue, the narrator's "southing sun," for
example, is transformed by Stephen's literary associations
into "this burning scene. Pan's hour, the faunal noon."[36] The
result is twofold: a purely subjective expression of *internal*
happenings, and a blending of objective and subjective viewpoints on *external* happenings. Note that this is an exact reversal of the method employed in the passage from *Ivan Ilych*. By
excluding the psychological realm from the narration itself,
Joyce avoids redundancy, and achieves continuity.

But narrator and character in *Ulysses* not only share the
field of vision; they also share to some degree the idiom
through which they relate it. Increasingly as narrative sentences approach the inception of monologues they become
colored by the figural idiolect, anticipating its idiosyncrasies
before the grammatical shift to the first person or present
tense actually occurs. Thus "peacocktwittering lashes" in the
above quotation already heralds the lush imagery of Stephen's
self-address. This process is even more clearly displayed by
the following passages (again from "Proteus"):

> In long lassoes from the Cock lake the water flowed
> full, covering greengoldenly lagoons of sand, rising,
> flowing. My ashplant will float away. I shall wait.

flush

> Under the upswelling tide he saw the writing weeds lift languidly and sway reluctant arms, hising up their petticoats, in whispering water swaying and upturning coy silver fronds. Day by day: night by night: lifted, flooded and let fall. Lord, they are weary: and, whispered to, they sigh.
>
> He had come nearer the edge of the sea and wet sand slapped his boots. The new air greeted him, harping in wild nerves, wind of wild air of seeds of brightness. Here, I am not walking out to the Kish lightship, am I?[37]

In each case the sentence preceding the quoted monologue modulates toward Stephen's characteristic lyricism, the style becoming rhythmic, imagistic, alliterative. Note also the a-temporal present participles ("rising, flowing"; "hising . . . whispering . . . swaying . . . upturning"; "harping"), which modulate the past tense of narration toward the present tense of monologue.

Bloom's far more prosaic and colloquial idiom is no less infectious than Stephen's lyricism.

> Mourners came out through the gates: woman and a girl. Leanjawed harpy, hard woman at a bargain, her bonnet awry. Girl's face stained with dirt and tears, holding the woman's arm looking up at her for a sign to cry. Fish's face, bloodless and livid.
>
> The mutes shouldered the coffin and bore it in through the gates. So much dead weight. Felt heavier myself stepping out of that bath. First the stiff: then the friends of the stiff. Corny Kelleher and the boy followed with their wreaths. Who is that beside them? Ah, the brother-in-law.[38]

Here it is even more difficult than in "Proteus" to determine the precise moment when narration stops and monologue starts. Only where finite verbs or personal pronouns appear can we identify the speaker. Where these clues are missing, the text remains ambiguously suspended. Who calls the woman "leanjawed harpy," the corpse "so much dead weight"—the narrator or Bloom? These verbless transitional "sentences" in the Bloom sections weld the narrative to the monologic language even more tightly than the present participles in the Stephen sections.[39]

Since Bloom and Stephen perceive the world about them in a very different light, reflected in the different tone and rhythm of their monologues, it is hardly surprising that their adaptable narrator should sound very different in the Bloom chapters from the way he sounds in the Stephen chapters. Bloom's and Stephen's monologues, far from existing *in vacuo*, are lodged in worlds shaped in their image, by two distinct narrators, a "Bloom-narrator" and a "Stephen-narrator," whose voices differ from each other almost as much as do those of their protagonists.[40]

In post-Joycean stream-of-consciousness novels, quoted monologue and narrative context mesh even more closely. The narrator of Döblin's *Berlin Alexanderplatz* submerges in the demotic milieu of Berlin, adopting the slang of his lower-class characters before and after quoting their silent (as well as their spoken) language:

> Der Franz Biberkopf aber,—Biberkopf, Lieberkopf, Zieberkopf, keinen Namen hat der—, die Stube dreht sich, die Betten stehen da, an einem Bett hält er sich fest. Da liegt Reinhold drunter, der Kerl, der liegt da mit Stiebeln und macht een Bett dreckig. Wat hat der hier zu suchen? Der hat doch seine Stube. Den hol ick raus, den setzen wir raus, machen wir, . . .[41]

This passage simultaneously modulates from High German to dialect and from narration to quotation, with the dividing line between the language levels quite as hard to draw as that between the narrative voices. Already the first sentence contains elements of figural jargon (the name-game, the colloquialism "keinen Namen hat der"). The second sentence could be attributed to the narrator as well as to Franz Biberkopf, though the vocabulary begins to lapse into slang (*Stiebeln* for *Stiefel, een* for *ein*). Only in the following sentences, first the syntax and finally the first-person pronouns clearly signal inner speech.

In the above passage, moreover (as in much of the novel), Döblin narrates in the present tense. This eliminates one of the clearest clues for distinguishing between the narrating and the figural voices, enhancing their fusion (and confusion). A similar equivoque is created when a text shifts to a gnomic or a descriptive present in the immediate vicinity of a quoted monologue. This happens in one of the Peter Walsh sections in *Mrs. Dalloway*:

> As a cloud crosses the sun, silence falls on London; and falls on the mind. Effort ceases. Time flaps on the mast. There we stop; there we stand. Rigid the skeleton of habit alone upholds the human frame. Where there is nothing, Peter Walsh said to himself; feeling hollowed out, utterly empty within. Clarissa refused me, he thought. He stood there thinking, Clarissa refused me.[42]

Though the identification tags—"Peter Walsh said to himself . . . he thought . . . thinking"—pinpoint the inception of quotation at "Where . . . ," the preceding sentences remain unassigned. As happens occasionally throughout this novel, a sort of disincarnated narrator-consciousness has entered the scene with a statement cast in a gnomic present. Yet Peter's thoughts pick up where this anonymous voice leaves off, and deal with the identical theme of inner hollowness. The semantic continuity, supported by the continuity of tense, then creates a sense of unity between the two voices, suggesting that Peter may be the silent speaker of the entire passage.[43] This kind of equivocation (who is speaking?) could not have arisen within an authorial narrative situation, but only in a context where the distance between narrator and character has already been reduced by other means. A present-tense statement that leaves the reader uncertain as to its origin is therefore a certain sign of a successful merger.

We may conclude that the effect of quoted monologues in third-person novels depends very largely on the context in which they are lodged. In authorial narrative situations, especially where they are accompanied by explicit quotation signals, monologues tend to increase the distance that separates a narrator from his character, to induce ironic remove by dramatizing figural fallacies. In figural narrative situations monologues are most effective when special devices are brought into play to insure the smooth blending of the narrating and the figural voices: omission or discreet use of inquit signals, espousal of the character's vantage point on the surrounding scene, omission of psycho-narration, syntactic ambiguity, or coloration of the narrator's language by a character's idiolect.

Psychological Implications

Within the medium of third-person narration, monologues take on the meaning of mimetic reproductions of figural language, with the narrator lending the quotation of his characters' silent thoughts the same authority he lends to the quotation of the words they speak to others. As a rule interior monologues are therefore quite as closely bound to the norms of psychological realism as fictional dialogues: just as dialogues create the illusion that they render what characters "really say" to each other, monologues create the illusion that they render what a character "really thinks" to himself.

This rule is most convincingly proved by its exceptions. Certain mental quotations are introduced by warnings that they are to be understood not as literal reproductions, but as authorial transcriptions of inchoate figural thoughts. Dostoevsky, who elsewhere quotes reams of monologues without apologies, prefaces one lengthy sample by the following disclaimer: "It is well known that whole trains of thought sometimes pass through our brains instantaneously as though they were sensations without being translated into human speech, still less into literary language. But we will try to translate these sensations of our hero's, and present to the reader at least the kernel of them, so to say, what was most essential and nearest to reality in them. For many of our sensations when translated into ordinary language seem absolutely unreal."[44] Such "unreal" or "anti"-monologues even show up in the age of the stream-of-consciousness novel. Faulkner, who seems to have shared Dostoevsky's view that some thoughts are too rapid to pass into words, repeatedly preludes Joe Chistmas' quoted thoughts by paradoxical phrases: "It was not thinking. It was too fast, too complete," or "thinking too fast for even thought."[45] These concerns with psychological credibility stand in striking contrast to Faulkner's autonomous monologues: the self-address of a speechless idiot (Benjy in *The Sound and the Fury*) or of a dead woman (Addie in *As I Lay Dying*) are radical departures from monologic verisimilitude that are difficult to imagine in the context of a third-person novel, where we expect figural language to be as real as its fictional speaker.

But if the quoted-monologue technique implies the mimesis of a real language, the model for that language in the real world is strangely elusive. Unlike fictional dialogue, which imitates a readily observable aspect of human behavior, fictional monologue purports to imitate a concealed linguistic activity whose very existence cannot be objectively attested. This does not mean, however, that inner language is purely imaginary: writers and readers alike know it exists, even though they have heard it spoken only by their own inner voices. The *audition* of another voice in another head is one of the conventions of third-person fiction, and partakes in the larger convention of the transparency of fictional minds. But that inner voice *itself* is a generally accepted psychological reality, and by no means a literary invention. Before we survey its diverse fictional modulations, we must therefore glance briefly at its basis in psychological reality.

The phenomenon that interior monologue imitates is, contrary to its reputation, neither the Freudian unconscious, nor the Bergsonian inner flux, nor even the William Jamesian stream of consciousness, but quite simply the mental activity psychologists call interior language, inner speech, or, more learnedly, endophasy. Though many thinkers since Plato had alluded to it, it was first given expert attention surprisingly late, in a study by the French psychologist Victor Egger, entitled *La parole intérieure* (1881). Less surprisingly, its author was an entirely traditional psychologist, concerned solely with the workings of the conscious mind, and without the least pretensions to depth psychology. This is how he introduces his subject: "At every instant the soul speaks its thoughts internally. This fact, disregarded by the majority of psychologists, is one of the most important aspects of our existence: it accompanies nearly all our activities; the series of internal words forms a quasi-continuous sequence, parallel to the sequence of other psychic facts; it alone therefore represents a major part of each person's consciousness."[46] Without employing the term "interior monologue," Egger at one point acknowledges that his insight was anticipated by novelists, and that such phrases as "il se dit en lui-même" introduce imitations of interior speech.[47] He could not have known that novels would before long be filled with "souls" that literally speak their thoughts internally "at every instant."

Like the novelists who preceded and followed him, Egger relied entirely on the introspective method; and even though introspection is to this day the main evidence for internal language, most modern psychologists regard it as a standard component of a normal adult's mental life.[48] There is less agreement about its continuity and its importance: not all experts would agree with Egger that all persons speak to themselves all the time. William James, for example, despite the fact that he knew and admired Egger's work, did not conceive of his "stream of consciousness" as purely or necessarily verbal, but discerned in it other "mind stuff" as well, notably visual images[49]—a fact that has generally been ignored by critics, who use the terms "interior monologue" and the Jamesian term interchangeably. A number of modern philosophers of the mind went considerably further than James in divorcing thinking from language: notably Bergson, who believed that "pure" thought is unrelated to, and even distorted by, verbal formulations—for which reason the link between interior monologue and Bergson's conception of the mind is even more tenuous than the link with James' "stream of consciousness."[50] There are, in short, considerable variations among theorists in regard to the relationship between thought and language, ranging between two extreme positions which a recent study of the subject sums up as follows: "One can find proponents of, and evidence for, two distinct views of the relationship between language and thinking. One school says that thinking consists of verbalization, that the thought and the words in which it is expressed are one and the same thing. The other says that thought takes shape independent of language and that language is merely the vehicle, the container of an already accomplished thought."[51] Clearly, internal language plays a far more important and more positive role in the first of these schools than in the second.

Novelists don't as a rule belong to schools of psychology, but their choice of technique for rendering their characters' consciousness is probably not unrelated to these two main tendencies. A writer like Joyce, who gives us Bloom's mind almost entirely in Bloom's own words, reveals that he conceives of thought largely as verbalization, whereas a novelist who shuns interior monologues as steadfastly as Musil manifests an opposite view. A passing comment on *Ulysses* in Musil's diaries confirms this divergence: Joyce, says Musil, presents thought-processes "naturalistically," as though they were merely abbreviated speech processes.[52] Proust, as his well-known Bergsonian affinities also suggest, belongs in this respect to the same camp as Musil: his polemic against Realist art in *Le Temps retrouvé* includes some harsh words against the technique that imitates what he pointedly calls "l'oblique discours intérieur," "oblique" because it invariably draws attention away from more significant psychic realities.[53] In very much the same spirit, Nathalie Sarraute speaks of "the thin

curtain of the interior monologue," which conceals far more
than it reveals, namely "an immense profusion of sensations,
images, sentiments, memories, impulses, little larval actions
that no inner language can convey, that jostle one another on
the threshold of consciousness, gather together in compact
groups and loom up all of a sudden, then immediately fall
apart, combine otherwise and reappear in new forms, while
unwinding inside us, like the ribbon that comes clattering
from a telescriptor slot, is an uninterrupted flow of words."[54]
The eloquent, typically Sarrautean imagery of this passage
clearly opposes the inarticulate depth of the mind to its auto-
matically verbal surface. For Sarraute, as for Musil and
Proust, the interior monologue technique therefore offers an
entirely deceptive solution to the problem of exploring what
she calls—in a phrase taken from Virginia Woolf—"the
obscure places of psychology."[55]

Not all writers who hold such views exclude monologues
from their works altogether. But those who perceive as deep
a cleavage between mental language and other mental realities
as Musil, Proust, or Sarraute bring to the technique entirely
different assumptions from writers who have a more monisti-
cally verbal conception of consciousness. The former tend to
use quoted monologue to expose the mendacity of a character's thinking language, rather than to depict searchingly introspective minds. Stendhal offers early examples of self-
serving mental posturings, which his narrator always duly
deflates.[56] In later writers interior lies are more often left to
speak for themselves. Thus in Sartre's "Intimité," where the
quoted-monologue technique deliberately catches a mind in
its *réflexion complice*. Throughout the story, Lulu fabricates
arguments to camouflage her erotic drives and to safeguard
her ethereal self-image. At one point, as the memory of her
reactions in her lover's bed threatens to destroy one of her favorite myths—that she is constitutionally frigid—she tries to
destroy the evidence with a torrent of words:

> Lulu bit her lip and shuddered because she remembered
> that she had moaned. It isn't true, I didn't moan, I simply
> breathed a little hard, because he's so heavy, when he's
> on me he cuts off my breath. He said: "You're moaning,
> you're coming;" I hate when they talk while they're
> doing it. . . . I didn't moan, in the first place, I can't feel
> any pleasure, it's a fact, the doctor said so, unless I do it
> myself.[57]

The mendacity of this monologue is evident both from its
tone and its context, where Sartre suggests by numerous contradictions between thoughts and acts that Lulu uses silent
language primarily to hide the self from the self.

But if some writers employ the monologue technique to
demonstrate how the conscious mind habitually fends off
disturbing truths, others reserve it for those special occasions when this defense mechanism breaks down in the course
of a momentous inner crisis. Not surprisingly, these moments of sudden awareness, when the consciousness is released from what Ibsen called the life-lie, are often associated
with approaching death. Such diverse characters as Andrej
Bolkonsky, Gail Hightower, and Georg Bendemann silently
articulate their diverse last truths; and even Proust breaks his
own rule against internal language—as well as the logic of
first-person narration—to quote Bergotte's famous last
thought about the "petit pan de mur jaune" on the Vermeer
painting.[58] Poignant as these monologues *in extremis* are, we
may wonder in passing whether their eloquence is not surpassed by the mute deaths of a Bazarov, a Joe Christmas, or
an Emma Bovary.

Other characters are allowed to survive their moments of

---

* Lulu se mordit la lèvre et frissonna parce qu'elle se rappelait qu'elle avait
gémi. C'est pas vrai, je n'ai pas gémi, j'ai seulement respiré un peu fort, parce
qu'il est si lourd, quand il est sur moi il me coupe le souffle. Il m'a dit: "Tu
gémis, tu jouis"; j'ai horreur qu'on parle en faisant ça. . . . Je n'ai pas gémi,
d'abord, je ne peux pas prendre de plaisir, c'est un fait, le médecin l'a dit, à
moins que je ne me le donne moi-même.

truth, and indeed to save their lives by reaching them: Hans
Castorp's pivotal *"For the sake of goodness and love man shall not
allow death domination over his thoughts*," though italicized by
its author, stands in the middle of the long self-address that
follows Hans' "Snow"-dream. Levin's marathon monologue, woven through the last eight chapters of *Anna
Karenina*, starts with the contemplation of suicide, and arrives at a life-giving truth quite similar to Hans Castorp's. It
(and Tolstoy's novel) ends with the words: "my life now, my
whole life apart from anything that can happen to me, every
minute of it is no more meaningless, as it was before, but it
has the positive meaning of goodness, which I have the power
to put into it." Less explicit, but no less intense, is Peter
Walsh's final epiphany at Clarissa's party: "What is this terror? What is this ecstasy? he thought to himself. What is it
that fills me with this extraordinary excitement? It is Clarissa,
he said. For there she was."[59] Many other novels peak or
close with such flourishes of monologic authenticity, even
some where the technique is sparingly used on less climactic
occasions.

Between the lies by which a character lives and the truths
by which he dies or is revived quoted monologues run the
gamut, often within a single work, and the degree of their authenticity is not always easy to determine. But one situation
in which quoted monologue invariably acquires a candid air is
when it is used against the backdrop of dialogue. For no matter how insincere we are with ourselves, we are always *more*
insincere with others. Stendhal was one of the first to exploit
this counterpoint between intimacy and social behavior, in
the famous hand-grasping episode in *Le Rouge et le noir*, and
many similar scenes. It has assumed thematic centrality in the
stream-of-consciousness novel and the *nouveau roman*, where
it is often worked with great technical virtuosity.[60] In conversational contexts interior monologues often stretch time out of
all realistic proportions, as in this moment from Stephen's conversation with Mr. Deasy in the "Nestor" section of *Ulysses*:

[Mr. Deasy is speaking]
 —I paid my way. I never borrowed a shilling in my life.
Can you feel that? *I owe nothing.* Can you?
 Mulligan, nine pounds, three pairs of socks, one pair
brogues, ties. Curran, ten guineas. McCann, one
guinea. Fred Ryan, two shillings. Temple, two lunches.
Russell, one guinea, Cousins, ten shillings, Bob Reyn-
olds, half a guinea, Kohler, three guineas, Mrs. McKer-
nan, five weeks' board. The lump I have is useless.
 —For the moment, no, Stephen answered.[61] [Joyce's
emphasis]

The comic effect depends on the interpolation of the
monologue between Mr. Deasy's question and Stephen's answer: the sheer number of Stephen's debts and his compulsion
to silent itemizing, followed by the spoken understatement.
 The drama of contrapuntal scenes of this type is greatly
heightened when the monologizing character has a horrific
secret to hide. In *Crime and Punishment* the quotation of Raskolnikov's thoughts during his interviews with Porfiry and
others continuously secures the reader's sympathy for the
murderer whose secret he shares. At the same time the contrast between Raskolnikov's silent and spoken words helps to
build the almost unbearable tension, which can be relieved
only when secret thought becomes audible speech in the act of
confession. In a novella by Arthur Schnitzler, this counterpoint is epitomized when an interior monologue, by a special
kind of *lapsus linguae*, leads directly to self-betrayal. Under
the ironic title "Dead Men are Silent" ("Die Toten
schweigen") it tells of an adulterous wife who survives a
traffic accident that kills her lover. Returning home to her
husband, and in his presence, her directly quoted thoughts
revolve obsessively around the accident, finally finding relief
in the idea that her affair will never come to light, since "dead
men are silent." At this moment she hears her husband say:
"Why do you say that?" and realizes that she has spoken these

words aloud. Interior language here becomes the agent of a
faulty verbal gesture, revealing that conscious reflection is
powerless against the unconscious compulsion to confess.
Somewhat melodramatically this Schnitzler scene points up
that language for oneself, caught between a threatening world
within and a threatening world without, is an all too precarious refuge from both worlds.

In most of the instances we have considered to this point,
quoted monologues have taken the form of an organized *suite
des idées*, no matter whether rational faculties were put at the
service of rationalization, of the discovery of difficult truths,
or of self-defensive maneuvers. But the technique is most
notorious, of course, for its ability to mime less controlled,
more passive states of mind, for following the meandering
current of random thoughts we associate with the stream-of-
consciousness novel, and particularly with *Ulysses*. It has by
now become a commonplace of literary history that many instances of such undirected thinking patterns can be found in
both the spoken and silent language of pre-Joycean characters.[62] This long ancestral line is surprising only if one regards
the difference between directed and undirected thinking as an
absolute rather than a relative one, and believes that free
association and inner flux were invented—rather than observed—by twentieth-century psychologists. Novelists, at
any rate, had used fragmentary syntax, staccato rhythms, non
sequiturs and incongruous imagery when quoting minds in a
state of agitation or reverie long before Jamesian, Freudian,
Bergsonian, or Jungian ideas became fashionable. Conversely, novelists who know all about mental incongruities
continue to include moments of discursive rhetoric and logical reasoning in their monologues when their characters'
minds or moods incline to such forms of self-address. This is
not to deny the obvious shift in emphasis toward freely associative patterns in the quoted monologues of modern psychological novels, but rather to see this shift as occurring on a
continuous range of possibilities inherent in the technique itself.

As several critics have noted, Tolstoy's quoted monologues on occasion move remarkably close to the pole of free association. The most famous instance is Anna's monologue during her carriage ride to and from Dolly's house, when she mingles in her thoughts the fleeting sights she passes and the obsessive concerns of her final hours.[63] But her brother Stepan Arkadyevitch's moment of drowsiness in Lidia Ivanovna's drawing room—introduced by the words "The most incongruous ideas were in confusion in his head"—contains even more discontinuous associations: "Maria Sanin is glad her child's dead. . . . How good a smoke would be now! . . . To be saved, one need only believe," and so forth.[64] Nicolai Rostov's somnolent battlefield thoughts, as Gleb Struve has suggested, even anticipate "Joycean verbal play," though probably without the implication of unconscious motivation underlying such language patterns in *Ulysses*.[65] Seeing a white patch in the distance, Nicolai freely associates as follows:

"I expect it's snow . . . that spot . . . a spot—*une tache*," he thought. "There now . . . it's not a *tache* . . . Natásha . . . sister, black eyes . . . Na . . . tásha. . . . (Won't she be surprised when I tell her how I've seen the Emperor?) Natásha . . . take my sabretache. . . ." [Tolstoy's emphasis and ellipses][66]

Further verbal associations follow ("hussar with mustaches") clustering around *tache* in word plays that are only imperfectly translatable into English.

As the ellipsis marks in these passages indicate, Tolstoy seems to envision states of drowsiness as a spasmodic inner voice, periodically silenced. But the thought-fragments themselves are explicitly presented as verbatim quotations, as the verbal residue remaining in a mind that loosens or loses its control over logical syntax. Joyce clearly places the verbal threshold lower down in the psyche, so that language flows in a continuous stream even on the borderline of sleep. This is how Bloom's mind looks during a paragraph of somnolence (on the beach, following the long-distance love scene with Gerty):

O sweety all your little girlwhite up I saw dirty bracegir-
dle made me do love sticky we two naughty Grace darling she him half past the bed met him pike hoses frillies
for Raoul to perfume your wife black hair heave under
embon *señorita* young eyes Mulvey plump years dreams
return tail end Agendath swoony lovey showed me her
next year in drawers return next in her next her next.[67]

Bloom momentarily loses his hold even over his customarily
truncated syntax here, and Joyce renders this by abandoning
the dense punctuation that paces most other passages of
Bloom's monologue. But even at this moment of maximal
undirectedness his consciousness is presented exclusively
through the language it produces, without even an elliptic
suggestion that his thought stream contains any other
"mind-stuff" except words.

It would hardly seem necessary to insist that every quoted
interior monologue, no matter how disjointed its syntax, attributes linguistic activity to fictional minds, were it not for
the assertion found throughout the literature on the stream-
of-consciousness novel that it renders primarily "preverbal"
thoughts or the "prespeech level of consciousness." Applied
to *Ulysses*, this view implies that Bloom's and Stephen's
monologues are something on the order of prespeech
speeches made of preverbal words.[68] These contradictions
pervade Erwin Steinberg's recent study of the "stream-of-
consciousness technique" in *Ulysses*. Since Steinberg conceives of this technique as a "simulation" of pre- or non-
verbal psychic phenomena,[69] he understands the words of a
typical Bloomian monologue as "symbolic printed analogues
of Bloom's visceral sensations," rather than as direct quotations of Bloom's internal language.[70] His non-verbal conception of the stream of consciousness, in other words, blinds
him to Joyce's primary purpose in choosing the quoted-
monologue technique over the other available techniques for
depicting the inner life, namely to record his characters' *verbal*
responses to their experience. Joyce's protagonists, hardly
ever speechless, may even be said to suffer from a kind of

chronic logorrhea. The term "stream-of-consciousness" therefore applies to the monologues of *Ulysses* only if one equates the word "consciousness" with interior language, as Joyce himself seems to have done. For in their entire range, from logical reasoning to stray associations, the thought streams he creates are plausible imitations of mental language, no less "in character" with the characters through which they run than is the language they speak to others.

A corollary and even more fallacious misconception has been that interior monologues in stream-of-consciousness novels present a character's psyche simultaneously at different levels of awareness.[71] This is an ambition the interior monologue technique is even less able to fulfill than any other, for reasons related both to the nature of the psyche and to the nature of literary texts. However many sensations, perceptions, or images we may imagine as coexisting in a mind at one moment in time, words can be thought only one at a time, no matter how asyntactically they are interrelated.[72] But since this consecutiveness applies quite as strictly to the language of fiction (the words a writer writes and a reader reads) as it does to the language of consciousness, the correspondence creates for the reader a peculiarly convincing illusion of reality: a sense that he is "mind-reading," which may amply compensate him for the linearity of the mental events he follows.

Moreover, despite its restriction to what is uppermost in fictional minds, the interior monologue can indirectly suggest the psychic depth beneath the verbal surface. In this respect the technique can be compared to—and may, in its post-Freudian phase, have been influenced by—the psychoanalytic technique of free association, the "method according to which voice must be given to all thoughts without exception which enter the mind."[73] It is as though the reader were placed in the position of a psychiatrist whose patient would execute the psychoanalytic compact to the letter, in a manner the person on the couch is rarely willing or able to do. But this analogy by no means implies that quoted monologues are recitations of unconscious thoughts. Even perfectly executed

free association would, in Freudian theory, reflect the unconscious only symptomatically, by way of revealing fissures and
irregularities in the texture of the discourse—incongruous associations, slips of the tongue, repetitions, omissions, and
other forms of over- or under-emphasis. It is well-known
that post-Freudian novelists liked to lard their interior
monologues with tell-tale lapses when, as Scholes and Kellogg put it, repressed thoughts "evade the censor and leap
into the verbalized stream."[74] How intricately Joyce imprints
Stephen's internal language in *Ulysses* with unconscious
motivations and obsessions has recently been demonstrated
by Margaret Solomon's Lacanian analysis of a passage from
"Proteus."[75] In this indirect fashion the monologic technique
can realistically suggest psychic depth, even as it draws attention to the shallowness of the language stratum it quotes
directly.

The Freudian unconscious itself, by contrast, can never be
quoted directly, since its "language" presents only features
that are, as a modern linguist says, "both infra- and su-
pralinguistic," and "absolutely specific and different" from
verbal language.[76] Modern novelists who know their Freud,
therefore, would be the last to resort to direct quotation in
order to express their characters' unconscious processes. That
Joyce, for one, was fully aware of the difference between
interior discourse and the "language" of the unconscious is
confirmed by his abandonment of the realistic monologue
technique in favor of a distinctly surrealistic dramatic phantasmagoria when he ventured into the arena of the unconscious in "Circe." Most other writers, as we have seen in the
preceding chapter, prefer to tell rather than to show those
psychic happenings that their characters cannot plausibly verbalize, employing analyses, analogies, and other authorial in-
directions to penetrate the speechless nether realm.

Stylistic Tendencies

Since interior monologue purports to render a real psychological process, the mimetic norms that apply to its content apply

equally to its form: like the language a character speaks to others, the language he speaks to himself will appear valid only if it is "in character": if it accords with his time, his place, his social station, level of intelligence, state of mind, and other fictional facts and circumstances. But although the monologic technique shares in the "formal mimeticism" of all figural language in realistic fiction,[77] it occupies in this respect an entirely peculiar position. Everyday reality offers both writers and readers an almost unlimited empirical basis for assessing the verisimilitude of dialogues in fiction. But how can a writer know, or a reader judge, the plausibility of a language for which no audible models exist in his non-literary experience? This is perhaps why the greatest stylistic experiments with this technique had to come from writers who generally relied at least as much on introspection and imagination as on camera-eye and eavesdropping.

With the obvious exception of Joyce and his most important progeny, novelists have taken little advantage of the potential freedom interior monologue offers for stylistic experimentation. Instead, ever since the "Conversation which Mr. Jones had with Himself" at the beginning of the Realist era, countless characters in third-person novels have conversed with themselves in a volubly colloquial idiom.[78] This is as true for modern writers like Lawrence, Malraux, or Hemingway—no matter how avant-gardist they may be in other respects—as it is for nineteenth-century Realists like Austen, Stendhal, or Dostoevsky. One reason for this conservatism is obvious: the more the language of monologue deviates from communicative language, the less readily will it be communicable to readers. Novelists who do not want to take risks with the readability of their works will instinctively avoid this deviation.

Like the dialogic language that served as its model, monologic language did of course go through considerable changes as the Realist tradition evolved: it became progressively less formal, more spontaneous and "vulgar," even as it developed greater accuracy in reproducing dialects, jargons, and personal idiosyncrasies. We will never know whether middle-

class women in Austen's time talked to themselves as formally as they talked to each other: all we know is that Austen's women do. And if Hemingway's men monologize more
frankly, this frankness reflects the altered norms of his society
and the enlarged social compass of modern fiction rather than
an altered conception of internal language itself. Stylistically,
at any rate, interior monologue is interesting only to the degree that it departs from the colloquial model and attempts
the mimesis of an unheard language.

Before we discuss the special style that comes into being
with the modern monologue, we must consider a number of
distinctive features that differentiate monologue from
dialogue generally, even in texts that do not deliberately cast
monologue in a special language.

The most important of these is a frequently noted semantic
pattern peculiar to self-address: the free alternation of first and
second person pronouns in reference to the same subject. Col-
lapsing the normal dichotomy of speech, in which "you" always refers to the person spoken to, "I" to the person speaking,[79] monologic language makes these two persons coincide,
each pronoun containing the other within itself. Paradoxically, therefore, when the grammar of monologue most resembles dialogue, its semantics are most characteristically
monologic. This structure is most clearly in evidence when an
interior monologue takes the form of a dialogue with an internalized partner. Here is a particularly clear example from
The Death of Ivan Ilych:

> Then he grew quiet and not only ceased weeping but
> even held his breath and became all attention. It was as
> though he were listening not to an audible voice but to
> the voice of his soul, to the current of thoughts arising
> within him.
> "What is it you want," was the first clear conception
> capable of expression in words, that he heard.
> "What do you want? What do you want?" he repeated
> to himself.

And again he listened with such concentrated attention
that even his pain did not distract him.
"To live? How?" asked his inner voice.
"Why, to live as I used to—well and pleasantly."
"As you lived before, well and pleasantly?" the voice
repeated.[80]

This passage presents a dialogue-variant of a recurring pattern
discussed earlier, where a buried truth emerges verbally in a
consciousness approaching death. Ivan Ilych's mind is split
between a familiar, habitual internal voice, and another,
stranger "voice of his soul . . . arising within him" that he
strains simultaneously to hear and to articulate. It is this alien
voice that addresses socratic questions to the self as second
person.

Such internal dialogues have not gone out of style in the
stream-of-consciousness novel. When Stephen at Sandy-
mount contemplates his aptitude for life-saving, the I-you alternation carries analogous (if less momentous) meaning:

He [Mulligan] saved men from drowning and you shake
at a cur's yelping. . . . Would you do what he did? A boat
would be near, a lifebuoy. *Natürlich*, put there for you.
Would you or would you not? . . . The truth, spit it out.
I would want to, I would try.[81]

The immediately following association with his mother's
death—"I could not save her. Waters: bitter death: lost."—
proves that Stephen's central guilt lurks behind these jibes.
Here again, then, as in the Tolstoy passage, the second-
person form is associated with the voice of conscience.
This peculiar rhetoric of self-addressed chiding, judgment,
or interrogation would seem to confirm Freud's notion that
the voice of conscience (the superego) is constituted through
the internalization of the parental voice, or the voices of other
authority figures.[82] The second-person form in fictional
monologues accords, at any rate, with a phenomenon widely
known from self-observation and noted by many psychologists: that the self tends to take itself for an audience. It is im-

portant to distinguish this rhetoric of "an 'I' addressing its 'me' " (as G. H. Mead calls it)[83] from the audience-directed rhetoric of pre-Realist monologues: the latter jars with the norms of the Realist third-person novel, the former aims at psychological credibility.

This brings us to a second pervasive tendency of monologic language. As the Prague linguist Jan Mukařovskí has pointed out, the dialogic pattern of monologues in literature may be regarded as a special, and specially clear, stylistic display of the coexistence of "different semantic contexts" within the mind.[84] Vying for simultaneous linguistic expression, these many voices are forced by the temporal dimension of language to wait and take their turns. They cancel, support, variously interrupt, or interfere with each other, and generally shape for interior monologues a highly discontinuous syntax. Though this syntax, as long as self-address follows the colloquial model, does not differ in kind from the syntax of spoken address in dialogues, it tends to differ in its degree of fragmentation and variegation. The contrast is most pronounced between an extended monologue (say, Mosca's during his attack of jealousy in *La Chartreuse de Parme*) and an extended dialogue speech that shapes a persuasive argument. Monologues generally contain flurries of unanswered questions, exclamations, invocations, invectives, or curses addressed to various absent persons, human and divine. They also teem with unfinished sentences, graphically marked by suspension points—and although aposiopesis appears in the dialogues of Realist novelists as well, it tends to be more frequent and more radical in their monologues, where mental hesitation has less momentous causes and effects. Cumulatively, therefore, these various discontinuous speech patterns distance monologue from dialogue even before the laws of communicative language are broken in any single sentence. Nonetheless, there is little in the thinking idiom of Mosca or Raskolnikov to prepare us for Bloom and Stephen.

The monologues of *Ulysses* may be regarded as a particu-

larly clear instance of the historical dimension of realism
Roman Jakobson defined in his essay "On Realism in Art":
the revolutionary artist deforms the existing artistic canons
for the sake of closer imitation of reality; the conservative
public misunderstands the deformation of the canon as a dis-
tortion of reality.[85] The first generation of *Ulysses* readers,
conditioned by a long tradition of monologues modeled on
dialogues, could only have experienced Bloom's and
Stephen's mental productions as radical departures from
realistic representation. Most "sentences" Stephen says to
himself on the first pages of "Telemachus"—"As he and
others see me"; "Cranley's arm. His arm"; "To ourselves . . .
new paganism. . . . Omphalos"—or those Bloom produces at
the beginning of "Calypso"—"Cup of tea soon. Good.
Mouth dry"; "Cruel. Her nature. Curious mice never
squeal. Seem to like it"—are not sentences at all, at least not in
the usual sense of word-combinations spoken with "intelligible purpose."[86] Yet it seems likely that Joyce himself aimed at
an accurate representation rather than an artful stylization of
mental language. Today's reader is more likely than his
grandparents to take Joyce's conception of verbal thought for
granted, to accept the notion that it differs from communicative speech in a number of significant respects, and to accept
the monologues of *Ulysses* as supremely convincing achieve-
ments of formal mimeticism.

One consequence of Joyce's break with the speech-minus-
sound conception of verbal thought is that his characters
speak to themselves a far more idiosyncratic language than
they speak to others. Several recent studies have shown how
Stephen's and Bloom's interior idioms reflect their complementary personalities, and have pointed out significant
differences in their grammar and their vocabulary.[87] After following Stephen and Bloom through hours of self-communion, it almost comes as a surprise to find them speaking
the same King's English when they finally commune in the
cabmen's shelter. This high individualization of monologic
language was emulated by many of Joyce's followers (Döblin

and Faulkner, among others), and resulted in a wide variety of different figural idioms. But despite this diversity, all interior monologues transform colloquial language along essentially similar lines. To a greater or lesser degree they all conform to two principal tendencies: syntactical abbreviation and lexical opaqueness.

It could be argued that the abbreviated syntax of Joycean monologues merely exaggerates the tendency to elision inherent in spoken language itself, and that they are in this respect more, rather than less, colloquial than realistic dialogues. But abbreviation has its limits in language aimed at communication, a limit beyond which it impedes the prime function of speech: communication of meaning. Both fictional and real characters who go beyond this limit become comic figures: Dickens' Mr. Jingle or Mann's Mynheer Peeperkorn. The former, as Harry Levin pointed out, may be regarded as a forerunner of Leopold Bloom.[88] But what is presented as an odd mannerism in Dickens' eccentric is presented as a standard manner in Joyce's everyman. Inner language as Joyce conceived it is a language freed from syntactical completeness, a language that suppresses elements that are customary, and often even indispensable, in language aimed at communicating meaning to an interlocutor. In Bloom's language the word classes most regularly eclipsed are articles, subject pronouns, prepositions, and copulas:

> Ba. What is that flying about? Swallow? Bat probably. Thinks I'm a tree, so blind. Have birds no smell? Metempsychosis. They believed you could be changed into a tree from grief. Weeping willow. Ba. There he goes. Funny little beggar. Wonder where he lives. Belfry up there. Very likely. Hanging by his heels in the odour of sanctity. Bell scared him out, I suppose.[89]

This reduction of sentences to bare bones has often reminded readers of the money-saving shortcuts of telegrams, or the time-saving shortcuts of diaries. Here, as so frequently in

Bloom's monologues, the most fully furnished sentence is the one in which he mounts a ready-made cultural reference into his language: "They believed you could be changed into a tree from grief"; and these longer, "cultured" sentences heighten by contrast the startling brevity and fragmentation, the almost atavistic freedom of Bloom's other sentences.[90]

This castrated grammar brings to mind early forms of speech, the single-word exclamations (Fire!) philologists attribute to primitive man, or the rudimentary sentences of small children. Could it be that child-language is a neglected source of *Ulysses*? One might almost think so when one reads the Russian psycho-linguist Vygotsky's study of egocentric speech, which Joyce could not have known.[91] This study provides the only empirical confirmation (outside personal introspection) that Bloom's silent language is indeed everyman's. Vygotsky's views seem to me so relevant to the stylistics of interior monologue that I shall summarize them briefly.

Continuing Piaget's well-known early experiments with egocentric speech—the "thinking aloud" of small children that gradually wanes and disappears completely around the age of six—Vygotsky arrived at results that tended to disprove Piaget's assumption that egocentric speech simply dies out as the child learns to use speech socially. By systematically observing egocentric speech in its waning phases Vygotsky found that it becomes increasingly differentiated from a child's developing social speech, and less and less comprehensible as its frequency decreases. He therefore concluded that Piaget had been wrong in assuming that egocentric speech simply becomes converted into social speech. Rather, he maintained, this linguistic activity becomes internalized as the maturing child develops a "new faculty to 'think words' instead of pronouncing them."[92]

But if the vocal egocentric speech of children evolves into the inner speech of adults, then it opens a window on a realm that had previously been totally closed to observation. This is

how Vygotsky sums up what he saw: "Our experiments
convinced us that inner speech must be regarded, not as
speech minus sound, but as an entirely separate speech function. Its main distinguishing trait is its peculiar syntax. Compared to external speech, inner speech appears disconnected
and incomplete."[93] Vygotsky defines this syntactical peculiarity as "a tendency toward an altogether specific form of abbreviation: namely, omitting the subject of a sentence and all
words connected with it, while preserving the predicate."[94]
This radical ellipsis has the simplest reason: it is because we
already know what subject we are thinking about that we can
condense verbal thought to pure predication.

So that we may understand how accurately this description
of interior speech fits Joyce's interior monologues, it must be
pointed out that Vygotsky uses the words "subject" and
"predicate" not in a grammatical, but in a psychological
sense. The subject is the known, topically neutral part of a
statement, the predicate is its "carrier of topical emphasis."[95]
If predication is understood in this sense, all Bloom's abbreviated sentences conform to Vygotsky's description: the
purely nominal sentences that focus on objects perceived, remembered, or imagined ("Creaky wardrobe." "Strings."
"Metempsychosis."),[96] no less than the purely verbal sentences that focus on actions or states ("Seem to like it."
"Looked shut." "Makes you want to sing after.")[97] Both
types of sentences concentrate single-mindedly on the single
new moment that comes to mind, building what Vygotsky
paradoxically calls "speech almost without words."[98]

The correspondence between Vygotsky's findings and the
Joycean monologue extends also to the second principal transformation of the technique from its colloquial model: its
tendency to lexical opaqueness. Vygotsky observed that the
impoverishment of syntax in the egocentric speech of children is counteracted by a semantic enrichment of each individual word. In inner speech words don't just stand for the
common (dictionary) meaning they have in spoken language,
but they siphon up additional meaning—he speaks of an "in-

flux of sense"[99]—from the thought-context in which they
stand. Consequently words mix and match far more freely
and creatively than in ordinary speech, forming heterodox
clusters, neologisms, and agglutinations. Again the psycho-
linguist's empirical description sounds every bit like a stylistic
analysis of the *Ulysses* monologues. The special meanings that
tie certain common words into "knots of privacy"[100] for
Bloom (home, sun, perfume, etc.) and for Stephen (sea,
snotgreen, etc.) have often been noted, as have their obsessions with rare words (Bloom's parallax, Stephen's omphalos), their neologisms, word games, and agglutinations
(portmanteau words).[101]

What are we to make of these remarkable correspondences?
We can hardly suppose that Joyce listened to children talking   *why not?*
to themselves, nor even that he consciously drew the analogy
between endophasy and egocentric speech. But if we assume
that Joyce, like William James, Freud, or other great pioneer
psychologists, had extraordinary powers of introspection,
we may suppose that he might well have derived from
self-observation the same conception of inner speech that
Vygotsky deduced from his experiments with children.

At the same time it is highly unlikely that Joyce addressed
himself in an idiom like Bloom's—probably he used one
closer to the more autobiographical Stephen's. Obviously, introspection cannot be the sole source for the stylistic invention of a characteristic monologic style. The second and
equally important source of that style must be the mimetically
crafted language a character is made to utter in conversations.
It is this characteristic colloquial idiom that inner speech ab-
breviates and charges with private meanings, and with which
it must dovetail when silent thoughts pass into spoken utter-
ances (or vice versa). In respect to its genesis, then, Bloom's
monologues might be regarded as a kind of confluence between Joyce's self-knowledge and his knowledge of the
world, including Dubliners of Bloom's ilk.

For the creators of *post*-Joycean monologues one must, of
course, add yet another model when one speculates on the

origins of their characters' monologic idioms: *Ulysses*. In this,
as in all other aspects of the technique we have examined—the
dropping of inquit signals, the devices for inducing consonance, the lowered verbal threshold—Joyce's novel brought
crucial innovations. Their importance is not reduced when
one relates them (as I have done) to the pre-Joycean history of
the form, and understands them as brilliant exploitations of
the potential inherent in direct thought-quotation. Still, no
matter how far the technique has evolved from the simple
"He said to himself" model, it has not overcome the basic
limitations that quotation of language imposes in the presentation of the inner life. Compared to psycho-narration, what
the quoted monologue gains in directness it loses in—depth?
mystery? complexity? It is not easy to label the missing dimension. Musil's previously mentioned diary reaction to
Ulysses hints at it: "Question: How does one think? His
[Joyce's] abbreviations are: shortened formulas for orthodox
speech formulas. They copy . . . the speech-process. Not the
thought-process." As Musil knew all too well, the opposite
approach through psycho-narration has the opposite disadvantages: what it gains in depth it loses in directness. The
third, narrated monologue technique is, in this and other respects, a kind of synthesis of antitheses.

3 / Narrated Monologue

Initial Description

In a German Naturalist story entitled *Papa Hamlet* (1889), which recounts the mental and physical decay of a Shakespearean actor, one finds the following passage:

He had of late—but wherefore he knew not—lost all his mirth, forgone all custom of exercises; and indeed it went so heavily with his disposition that this goodly frame, the earth, seemed to him a sterile promontory; this most excellent canopy, the air, this brave o'erhanging firmament, this majestical roof fretted with golden fire, why it appeared no other thing to him than a foul and pestilent congregation of vapours. What a piece of work was a man! how noble in reason! how infinite in faculty! in form and moving how express and admirable! in action how like an angel! in apprehension how like a god! the beauty of the world! the paragon of animals! And yet, to him, what was this quintessence of dust? man delighted him not; no, nor woman neither.[1]

* Er hatte seit kurzem—er wusste nicht wodurch—all seine Munterkeit eingebüsst, seine gewohnten Übungen aufgegeben, und es stand in der Tat so übel um seine Gemütslage, dass die Erde, dieser treffliche Bau, ihm nur ein kahles Vorgebirge schien. Dieser herrliche Baldachin, die Luft, dieses majestätische Dach mit goldnem Feuer ausgelegt: kam es ihm doch nicht anders vor als ein fauler, verpesteter Haufe von Dünsten. Welch ein Meisterwerk war der Mensch! Wie edel durch Vernunft! Wie unbegrenzt an Fähigkeiten! In Gestalt und Bewegung wie bedeutend und wunderwürdig im Handeln, wie ähnlich einem Engel; im Begreifen, wie ähnlich einem Gotte; die Zierde der Welt! Das Vorbild der Lebendigen! Und doch: was war ihm diese Quintessenz vom Staube? Er hatte keine Lust am Manne—und am Weibe auch nicht.

With the assistance of Shakespeare (Hamlet, II, 2) the translation is my own; it is no less exact than the "German Shakespeare" (the celebrated Schlegel-Tieck translation) which dic-
tated every detail of this passage in the original. Every detail,
that is, except its person and tense. For, as is immediately apparent, this is *Hamlet* with a difference: third-person pronouns
have replaced first-person pronouns, the past tense has replaced the present. The result is not "Shakespeare" (a *quotation* of Hamlet's monologue[2]), but "narrated Shakespeare" (a
narration of Hamlet's monologue). What is the meaning of
this transformation?

The Shakespearean language in this passage cannot be attributed to the narrator of *Papa Hamlet*, who speaks—in the
purely narrative portions of the text—the neutrally reportorial language typical for the narrator of a Naturalist story. His
protagonist, by contrast, habitually declaims Shakespeare to
himself and others, and by this professional deformation feeds
his need to dramatize and euphemize his sordid experiences.
Even a reader of this story who has never heard of the technique of the "narrated monologue" will recognize that the
above passage renders what Papa Hamlet thinks to himself
rather than what his narrator reports about him. He will instinctively "redress" this text to mean that Papa Hamlet
"thought to himself: 'I have of late—but wherefore I know
not—lost all my mirth. . . .' "

A transformation of figural thought-language into the narrative language of third-person fiction is precisely what characterizes the technique for rendering consciousness that will
occupy us throughout this chapter, and that I call the narrated
monologue. It may be most succinctly defined as the technique for rendering a character's thought in his own idiom
while maintaining the third-person reference and the basic
tense of narration. This definition implies that a simple transposition of grammatical person and tense will "translate" a
narrated into an interior monologue. Such translations can
actually be applied as a kind of litmus test to confirm the

validity of a reader's apprehension that a narrative sentence belongs to a character's, rather than to a narrator's, mental domain.[3]

But before I discuss this and other critical problems attending the narrated monologue, I will add to the rather far-fetched initial illustration others taken from the mainstream of the modern narrative tradition. They will show that, even when fictional characters have less idiosyncratic thinking styles than Papa Hamlet's, their narrated monologues are easy to identify. I provide a minimal context in each case, and italicize the sentences in narrated monologue form.

1. Woolf's Septimus in Regent's Park, after Rezia has removed her wedding ring:

"My hand has grown so thin," she said. "I have put it in my purse," she told him.

He dropped her hand. Their marriage was over, he thought, with agony, with relief. *The rope was cut; he mounted; he was free, as it was decreed that he, Septimus, the lord of men, should be free; alone (since his wife had thrown away her wedding ring; since she had left him), he, Septimus, was alone, called forth in advance of the mass of men to hear the truth, to learn the meaning, which now at last, after all the toils of civilisation—Greeks, Romans, Shakespeare, Darwin, and now himself—was to be given whole to.* . . . "To whom?" he asked aloud. [Woolf's ellipsis][4]

2. Kafka's K. walking through the night with Barnabas (the messenger from the castle):

At that moment Barnabas stopped. *Where were they? Was this the end of the road? Would Barnabas leave K.? He wouldn't succeed.* K. clutched Barnabas' arm so firmly that he almost hurt himself. *Or had the incredible happened, and were they already in the Castle or at its gates? But they had not done any climbing so far as K. could tell. Or had Barnabas taken him up by an imperceptibly mounting road?* "Where are we?" asked K. in a low voice, more of himself than of Barnabas.[5]

3. Joyce's Stephen Dedalus waiting for confession:

The slide was shot to suddenly. The penitent came out. He was next. He stood up in terror and walked blindly into the box.

At last it had come. He knelt in the silent gloom and raised his eyes to the white crucifix suspended above him. *God could see that he was sorry. He would tell all his sins. His confession would be long, long. Everybody in the chapel would know then what a sinner he had been. Let them know. It was true. But God had promised to forgive him if he was sorry. He was sorry.* He clasped his hands and raised them towards the white form, praying with his darkened eyes, praying with all his trembling body, swaying his head to and fro like a lost creature, praying with whimpering lips.[6]

What the italicized portions of these passages most obviously share is that they cannot be read as standard narration. Narrative language appears in them as a kind of mask, from behind which sounds the voice of a figural mind. Each of its sentences bears the stamp of characteristical limitations and distortions: of Septimus' manic obsessions, K.'s ignorance of present and future circumstance, Stephen's self-serving religiosity. Far more than in ordinary narrative passages, their language teems with questions, exclamations, repetitions, overstatements, colloquialisms. In short, neither the content nor the style of these sentences can be plausibly attributed to their narrators. But both their content and their style become

---

* Da blieb Barnabas stehen. *Wo waren sie? Ging es nicht mehr weiter? Würde Barnabas K. verabschieden? Es würde ihm nicht gelingen.* K. hielt Barnabas' Arm fest, dass es fast ihn selbst schmerzte. *Oder sollte das Unglaubliche geschehen sein, und sie waren schon im Schloss oder vor seinen Toren? Aber sie waren ja, soweit K. wusste, gar nicht gestiegen. Oder hatte ihn Barnabas einen so unmerklich ansteigenden Weg geführt?* "Wo sind wir?" fragte K. leise, mehr sich als ihn. [my emphasis]

entirely plausible if we understand them as transposed thought-quotations—which is why the "translation" test (as the willing reader can verify) will "work" in each case.

But the point is, of course, that the language a "translation" yields is *not* in the text. Nor are there other indications that someone is thinking. We are told not "Stephen said to himself: 'God can see that I am sorry. I will tell all my sins,' " but simply "God could see that he was sorry. He would tell all his sins." Stephen's personal rapport with the Divinity is treated *as if* he were formulating it in his mind, but the words on the page are not identified as words running through his mind.[7] By leaving the relationship between words and thoughts latent, the narrated monologue casts a peculiarly penumbral light on the figural consciousness, suspending it on the threshold of verbalization in a manner that cannot be achieved by direct quotation. This ambiguity is unquestionably one reason why so many writers prefer the less direct technique.

Another is the seamless junction between narrated monologues and their narrative context. Note how, in the Joyce passage, the text weaves in and out of Stephen's mind without perceptible transitions, fusing outer with inner reality, gestures with thoughts, facts with reflections, as report of posture and gaze—"he knelt . . . and raised his eyes"—gives way to the purely imaginary "God could see . . . God had promised," which in turn gives way to factual report—"He clasped his hands and raised them." By employing the same basic tense for the narrator's reporting language and the character's reflecting language, two normally distinct linguistic currents are made to merge.

The Kafka text alternates more rapidly, but no more perceptibly, between report and reflection: "At that moment Barnabas stopped. *Where were they?* . . . K. clutched Barnabas' arm so firmly that he almost hurt himself. *Or had the incredible happened. . . ?*" By contrast when the very same question that begins the narrated monologue—"*Where were they?*"—is repeated at its end—"Where are we?"—it cuts off the unified current by direct quotation. Such sudden shifts to directly

quoted discourse (silent or spoken) underline the potential-
actual relationship between narrated monologue and verbal
formulation, creating the impression that a mind's vague
ruminations have irresistibly led to conceptual expression.
We get the same pattern at the end of Septimus' narrated
monologue, when an unfinished thought-sentence breaks
into a quoted question: *"was to be given whole to . . .* 'To
whom?' he asked aloud."

The beginning of the Woolf passage illustrates a different
junction between narration and narrated monologue. In
another standard pattern, a sentence of psycho-narration—
"Their marriage was over, he thought, with agony, with
relief"—shapes the transition from the preceding report to
the narrated monologue, even as it sets the tone (of agony and
relief) that reigns in Septimus' thoughts. As we already noted
in the villanelle passage from Joyce's *Portrait* (in Chapter 1),
psycho-narration flows readily into a narrated monologue,
and the latter clinches the narrator-figure cohesion that the
former approximates.

We can now profile the narrated monologue more sharply
by examining its linguistic relationship with its closest relatives: first with the two rival techniques for rendering consciousness, second with the narration of fictional reality generally.

The demarcation between the narrated monologue and the
two other techniques for rendering consciousness is generally
easy to draw. Tense and person separate it from quoted
monologue, even when the latter is used in the Joycean manner, without explicit quotation or introduction; the absence of
mental verbs (and the resulting grammatical independence)
separates it from psycho-narration. The following schema
shows how the same thought-phrase would appear in the
three techniques:

> *quoted monologue*
> (He thought:) I am late
> (He thought:) I was late

> (He thought:) I will be late
>> *narrated monologue*
> He was late
> He had been late
> He would be late
>> *psycho-narration*
> He knew he was late
> He knew he had been late
> He knew he would be late

A typical narrated-monologue sentence stands grammatically *between* the two other forms, sharing with quoted monologue the expression in the principal clause, with psycho-narration the tense system and the third-person reference. When the thought is a question, the word-order of direct discourse is maintained in the narrated monologue, increasing its re-semblance to quoted monologue and its distinction from psycho-narration:

>> *quoted monologue*
> (He thought:) Am I late?
>> *narrated monologue*
> Was he late?
>> *psycho-narration*
> He wondered if he was late.

Minute as these differences may appear when schematized in this fashion, they reflect in simplest grammatical terms the basic relationship between the three techniques: in its meaning and function, as in its grammar, the narrated monologue holds a mid-position between quoted monologue and psycho-narration, rendering the content of a figural mind more obliquely than the former, more directly than the latter. Imitating the language a character uses when he talks to himself, it casts that language into the grammar a narrator uses in talking about him, thus superimposing two voices that are kept distinct in the other two forms. And this equivocation in turn creates the characteristic indeterminateness of the narrated monologue's relationship to the language of consciousness, suspending it between the immediacy of quotation and the mediacy of narration. Accordingly, its function fluctuates when it is found in the immediate vicinity of the other techniques: when it borders on psycho-narration, it takes on a more monologic quality and creates the impression of rendering thoughts explicitly formulated in the figural mind; when it borders on spoken or silent discourse, it takes on a more narratorial quality and creates the impression that the narrator is formulating his character's inarticulate feelings.

The problem of delimiting the narrated monologue from narration generally is far more complex, since purely linguistic criteria no longer provide reliable guidelines. Cloaked in the grammar of narration, a sentence rendering a character's opinion can look every bit like a sentence relating a fictional fact. In purely grammatical terms "He was late" (our sample sentence) could be a narrator's fact, rather than a character's thought. Within a broader context it might become possible to attribute it to a figural mind: for instance, if the next sentence belied the idea that "he was late"; or if the statement were embedded in a recognizable thought sequence. Woolf's "The rope was cut; he mounted; he was free" (in the passage quoted above) could, when taken out of context, be read as a narrator's description of a balloonist taking off for a flight. But in its context—the insane Septimus sitting on the Regent's Park bench, misinterpreting his wife's removal of her wedding ring—we understand these statements as the author means us to understand them, even before the following sentences more clearly signal monologic language. Obviously, an author who wants his reader to recognize a narrated monologue for what it is will have to plant sufficient clues for its recognition. These clues may be contextual, semantic, syntactic, or lexical, or variously combined.[8] A narrated monologue, in other words, reveals itself even as it conceals itself, but not always without making demands on its reader's intelligence. The critic who suggested that the trial against Flaubert for *Madame Bovary* would not have taken place if the prosecutor had recognized that the "immoralities" it contained were Emma's narrated monologues rather than Flaubert's authorial statements may have overstated his case.[9] But there is no doubt that this kind of confusion is responsible for innumerable misreadings—including some in print—of works that employ the technique.

In sum, the narrated monologue is at once a more complex and a more flexible technique for rendering consciousness than the rival techniques. Both its dubious attribution of language to the figural mind, and its fusion of narratorial and figural language charge it with ambiguity, give it a quality of now-you-see-it, now-you-don't that exerts a special fascination. Even dry scholars wax poetical when they describe its effects. Here is an early German theorist's description: "It lights up with vivid hues a realm that the reporting and describing narrator deliberately tones down by keeping it at a distance from himself. And it creates this effect far more readily than a narrative containing occasional monologues, where a more perceptible contrast exists between pure report and quoted thought. Its stirring effect depends on the fact that it is barely discernible to the naked eye: the device is irresistible precisely because it is apprehended almost unconsciously."[10]

Theoretical and Historical Perspective

In both France and Germany—where it goes respectively by the names *style indirect libre* and *erlebte Rede*—the narrated monologue has been the subject of intensive discussions ever since it was first identified around the turn of the century.[11] The first students of the technique were grammarians and linguists, but—since literary scholarship in both these countries maintained a close relationship with philological studies —the phenomenon was soon discussed by such eminent literary scholars as Leo Spitzer, Oskar Walzel, and Albert Thibaudet.[12] In the fifties there was a marked revival of interest in the phenomenon in Germany, this time in the context of more theoretical discussions, as *erlebte Rede* came increasingly to be regarded as a key concept for generic definitions of fiction, typologies of the novel, the nature of narrative language, and the development of modern narrative practices. [13] In the recent writings of the French structural narratologists *style indirect libre* has played a less central role, perhaps because they have been more preoccupied with macro- than with micro-structures, and more with first- than with third-person forms of fiction. Still, it is a standard concept in French criticism today. Todorov, Genette, and others have variously related it to their central categories of *mode, aspect*, and *voix*, even if they have not yet given it the close attention it deserves in a systematic study of narrative discourse. [14]

An entirely different situation exists in Anglo-American criticism, where the narrated monologue has until recently been virtually ignored, and where it bears no standard name. [15] This neglect is especially surprising when we consider that an English writer was the first extensive practitioner of the form (Jane Austen), and that it has been the preferred mode for rendering consciousness in the works of James, Lawrence, the early Joyce, Virginia Woolf, Thomas Wolfe et al. Even such sensitive theorists and historians of fiction as David Daiches, Ian Watt, or Scholes and Kellogg seem unaware of its existence, and Wayne Booth—though acquainted with the German term *erlebte Rede*—dismisses it as an unwonted stylistic nicety. [16] Not that the phenomenon has gone entirely unnoticed in individual texts: in a number of stylistically oriented studies one finds it aptly described, but always only as an idiosyncrasy of the particular writer or text under consideration. Here are three examples from James, Joyce, and Woolf criticism: For Gordon O. Taylor the method for rendering Isabel's thoughts in Chapter 42 of *The Portrait of a Lady* "although still cast in the third-person, [is] divested of most authorial trappings," and the "third-person intrusions approximate convincingly, though they fail to reproduce exactly, the links in her own train of thought." [17] William M. Schutte, citing what is clearly a narrated-monologue passage from Joyce's *Portrait*, describes it as a combination of "the unselected stream of Stephen's consciousness" and a "traditional third person summary account."[18] For David Daiches, Woolf's use of the technique in *Mrs. Dalloway* is a very special "compromise between reported thought and direct, unedited transcription of consciousenss."[19] The similarity in the foregoing quotations is obvious, and should of itself suggest that James', Joyce's, and Woolf's specimens belong to the same species. Is it perhaps because he has no name for the beast that each critic assigns it to the special fauna of the text he is examining? A common label for so widespread a stylistic phenomenon would, at any rate, clarify critical discourse: the heuristic value of a standard literary term is precisely to identify an individual occurrence as an instance (and variation) of a general norm.

In recent years, British and American linguists, using mostly the translated French term "free indirect style," have given mounting attention to this literary technique, with some even regarding it as the most fertile meeting ground between linguists and literary scholars.[20] A number of less technical essays now exist in English as well, by literary critics familiar with the German and French background.[21] But the concept—no matter by which of its names—has yet to enter the everyday language of criticism in English.

My own term "narrated monologue" as an English equivalent for *style indirect libre* and *erlebte Rede* calls for some justification and qualification. The French and German terms have generally designated not only the rendering of silent thought in narrated form, but also the analogous rendering of spoken discourse, which displays identical linguistic features.[22] I have deliberately chosen a term that excludes this analogous employment of the technique, because in a literary—rather than a strictly linguistic—perspective the narration of silent thoughts presents problems that are quite separate, and far more intricate and interesting than those presented by its more vocal twin. "Narrated discourse" involves neither the ambiguity concerning the actual - potential status of language that characterizes the narrated monologue, nor the difficulties of recognizing it within its narrative context. It has seemed to me that so special a phenomenon deserves a separate name, a name that relates it to the other techniques for rendering consciousness, more nearly and more clearly than other, more inclusive terms.[23] For the purposes of the present study, at any rate, the overarching concern with the presentation of figural minds prompted the more restrictive term.[24]

But the term "narrated monologue" is purposefully restrictive in yet another, more important sense: the denotative field of the French and German terms—and of their English equivalents—has, in recent years, grown far beyond the bounds of figural thought (and discourse) to include the entire realm of figural narration. Todorov has sketched its range of meanings as follows: "This term has been used to designate a family of phenomena which have common traits, but which nonetheless cannot be encompassed by a single definition. All cases of *style indirect libre* range between two limits: on the one side, a reported discourse that has the syntactic forms of indirect discourse, but that maintains certain characteristics of pragmatic speech; on the other side, a vision of reality that is not the narrator's own, but that of a fictional character, the so-called '*vision avec*,' which does not necessarily conform to precise linguistic criteria."[25] In its broadest meaning, then, at the second limit Todorov mentions above, *style indirect libre* becomes an alternate term for an entire mode of narration (*vision avec*—the term originally proposed by Pouillon—being roughly identical to figural narrative situation). It is this broad denotation that my more narrowly conceived term "narrated monologue" purposely excludes.[26] By implying the correspondence to a (potential) quoted monologue, the more specific name pinpoints a more specific "thing." And even though the line of demarcation between figural thought and its immediate context may not always be easy to draw in practice, the term "narrated monologue" suggests a method for discerning its location—or for explaining its effacement.

The terminological separation of this technique for rendering consciousness from the narrative situation with which it has become associated seems to me important for at least three different reasons. 1. Narrated monologues can—as we shall see—also occasionally be very ironically used in authorial narrative contexts, and though its effect varies with its surroundings, its basic structure remains the same. 2. Conversely, figural narration can be used for quite different purposes than can the narration of consciousness: even Henry James and Kafka often use their protagonists merely to reflect (but not to reflect *on*) the external events they witness. Other devices then come into play, such as "narrated perception," and related techniques.[27] 3. Finally, the narrated monologue is by no means the only method used for rendering consciousness in a figural context: we have already seen that the consonant type of psycho-narration and the unsignaled quoted monologue often supplement, and sometimes supplant, the narrated monologue form.

It is only when we have drawn this distinction between narrated monologue and figural narration that we can describe the very special relationship between them. It is one not only of part to whole, but of mutual affinity and enhancement: figural narration offers the narrated monologue its optimal habitat, and the narrated monologue caps the climax of figural narration. The first is true because the narrated monologue—in contrast to the quoted monologue—suppresses all marks of quotation that set it off from the narration, and this self-effacement can be achieved most perfectly in a milieu where the narrative presentation adheres most consistently to a figural perspective, shaping the entire fictional world as an uninterrupted *vision avec*. The narrated monologue itself, however, is not *vision avec*, but what we might call *pensée avec*: here the coincidence of perspectives is compounded by a consonance of voices, with the language of the text momentarily resonating with the language of the figural mind. In this sense one can regard the narrated monologue as the quintessence of figural narration, if not of narration itself: as the moment when the thought-thread of a character is most tightly woven into the texture of third-person narration.

Critics have called on a variety of metaphors to describe this narrator-figure coincidence: optic, acoustic, geometric, textile, erotic, and so forth. It matters little which image we use, so long as it stresses the very special two-in-one effect created by this technique, without overstressing either its dualism or its monism. To speak only of a *dual* presence (perspective, voice, etc.) seems to me misleading: for the effect of the narrated monologue is precisely to reduce to the greatest possible degree the hiatus between the narrator and the figure existing in all third-person narration.[28] But to speak simply of a *single* presence (perspective, voice, etc.,) is even more misleading: for one then risks losing sight of the difference between third- and first-person narration; and before long the protagonists of figural novels (Stephen, K., Strether) become the "narrators" of their own stories.[29] In narrated monologues, as in figural narration generally, the continued employment of third-person references indicates, no matter how unobtrusively, the continued presence of a narrator. And it is his *identification*—but not his *identity*—with the character's mentality that is supremely enhanced by this technique.[30]

If the narrated monologue is defined and understood in the manner outlined in the preceding pages, then the main stages of its historical development also becomes clear: its occasional occurrence in eighteenth-century "Histories" (of *Tom Jones* or *Agathon*), despite their over-all authorial-ironic cast; its upsurge in the nineteenth-century Realist novel, in rough correspondence with the rise of objective over obtrusive narrators, and of the inner over the outer scene; its expansion in the twentieth-century psychological novel, prompted by the unprecedented importance given to the language of consciousness, but with the narrated monologue now competing with the rival technique of the unsignaled "Joycean" monologue. Its evolution thus differs considerably from that of the quoted monologue and of psycho-narration: since the narrated monologue blurs the line between narration and quotation so dear to the old-fashioned authorial narrator, it makes its appearance rather late in the history of narrative genres. Its growth is also closely tied to a specific moment of the novel's development: the moment when third-person fiction enters the domain previously reserved for first-person (epistolary or confessional) fiction, and begins to focus on the mental and emotional life of its characters.

It is not at all surprising, then, that Jane Austen should have been one of the first writers to use the narrated monologue frequently and extensively: for it is in her work—as Ian Watt suggests in the epilogue to *The Rise of the Novel*—that the "divergent directions" of Richardson and Fielding were first brought together, launching the novel on its way toward their full-fledged "reconciliation" in Henry James.[31] In her narrated monologues Austen seems precisely to cast the spirit of epistolary fiction into the mold of third-person narration. This happens at moments of inner crisis in several of her novels, as in the following example from *Emma*:

> How could she have been so deceived! He protested that he had never thought seriously of Harriet—never! . . .
> The picture! How eager he had been about the picture! And the charade! And a hundred other circumstances; how clearly they had seemed to point at Harriet! To be sure, the charade, with its "ready wit"—but then, the "soft eyes"—in fact it suited neither; it was a jumble without taste or truth. Who could have seen through such thick-headed nonsense?[32]

And so forth, for a few more paragraphs, with the rhythm of inner debate—no matter how rhetorical and self-conscious— exactly transposed into narrative language, without explicit quotation or authorial explication. Most Victorian novelists, notably Eliot and Meredith, continued to use narrated monologues in this fashion, without altogether banishing the authorial tone from their novels as a whole.[33]

The decisive turning-point for the narrated monologue came, of course, with Flaubert. Perceptive students of his style agree that his systematic employment of the *style indirect libre* is his most influential formal achievement. Proust said, in a famous essay, that this device "completely changes the appearance of things and beings, like a newly placed lamp, or a move into a new house."[34] Flaubert himself, when he comments on his "impersonal" narrative method, employs phrases that come close to pinpointing the narrated monologue itself, especially in the following passage from a letter to Georges Sand: "I expressed myself badly when I told you that 'one should not write with one's heart.' I meant to say: one should not put one's personality on stage. I believe that great Art is scientific and impersonal. One should, by an effort of the spirit, *transport oneself into the characters, not draw them to oneself.* That, at any rate, is the method." [my emphasis][35] Translating this kinetic image into linguistic terms would yield an exact description of the narrated monologue—as would the theological image Flaubert used elsewhere, when he referred to his "faculté panthéiste."[36]

After Flaubert, as Thibaudet remarks, the *style indirect libre* enters "into the common current of novelistic style, abounds in Daudet, Zola, Maupassant, everyone."[37] Whenever Naturalist novels focus on individual lives and on instantaneous experiences—say in Maupassant's *Une Vie*, or Zola's *Le Docteur Pascal*, or the Gervaise scenes of *L'Assommoir*—their pages teem with narrated monologues, hardly ever lapsing into directly quoted ones. Yet, in view of the Naturalists' predilection for mass scenes, wide temporal vistas, manifest behavior and dialogues, they created relatively few extended occasions for the employment of narrated monologues. Such occasions had to await the "inward turning" of the novel: those writers who believed with Henry James that "what a man thinks and what he feels are the history and the character of what he does."[38] In James' own theoretical pronouncements, which so persistently revolve around the axis of the narrator-protagonist relationship, we find images that come even closer than Flaubert's to describing the narrated monologue. Given James' general reticence in erotic matters, it is both amusing and significant to find him using in this connection what is probably the most direct allusion to the sexual act in his entire oeuvre: "A beautiful infatuation this, always, I think, the intensity of the creative effort to get into the skin of the creature; the act of personal possession of one being by another at its completest."[39] This espousal of a character by his narrator "at its completest" is precisely what James attains in moments when he uses the narrated monologue.

The pattern set by Jane Austen thus unfolds throughout the nineteenth century: precisely those authors who, in their major works, most decisively abandoned first-person narration (Flaubert, Zola, James), instituting instead the norms of the dramatic novel, objective narration, and unobtrusive narrators, were the ones who re-introduced the subjectivity of private experience into the novel: this time not in terms of direct self-narration, but by imperceptibly integrating mental reactions into the neutral-objective report of actions, scenes, and spoken words.

When the Impressionist and Expressionist writers in Germany, and the stream-of-consciousness writers in England began to shape more slowly paced novels dominated by their characters' fluid mental responses to momentary experience, they found in the narrated monologue a ready-made technique that could easily be adapted to the new aims. Unlike the quoted monologue, it needed no Joycean revolution to make it a workable instrument for recording the minutiae of the inner life. Hence it acted as a kind of stylistic bridge that led from nineteenth- to twentieth-century fiction. Far from being a mark of modernity, the narrated monologue is a device that the novelists of our century who are most conservative in matters of form (Thomas Wolfe, Mauriac, or Lawrence) share with such experimental novelists as Virginia Woolf, Broch, Sarraute, or Robbe-Grillet. The difference lies only in the quantitative relationship of the narrated monologue to its narrative context: in *Mrs. Dalloway, The Death of Virgil, The Planetarium, The Voyeur*, the narrative text appears as the adjunct of the narrated monologue, rather than the other way around.

This brief historical synopsis of the technique must now be supplemented by closer study of its various functions and effects.

Irony and Sympathy

The narrated monologue, unlike the quoted monologue, does not readily shape itself into an independent fictional text, for by referring to the character whose thoughts it renders in the third person it includes the narrative voice in its language, and the monologic effect it creates vanishes the moment fictional facts reappear. As we have seen in the *Portrait* passage quoted earlier, when we read the sentence sequence: "But God had promised to forgive him if he was sorry. He was sorry. He clasped his hands and raised them towards the white form . . . ," the moment Stephen's manual gesture appears, the monologic impression is dispelled. The narrated monologue is thus essentially an evanescent form, dependent on the narrative voice that mediates and surrounds it, and is therefore peculiarly dependent on tone and context.

Many novels that use the narrated monologue as the predominant technique for rendering their characters' consciousness start from a neutral and objective narrative stance—typically the description of a specific site or situation—and only gradually, often by way of minimal exposition, narrow their focus to the figural mind. The first sentence of *L'Education sentimentale* reads as follows: "On the 15th of September 1840, about six o'clock in the morning, the Ville de Montereau was ready to sail from the quai Saint-Bernard, and clouds of smoke were pouring from its funnel." From this soberly informational base, Flaubert's text then imperceptibly gravitates, within a few pages, to the emotive speculations with which Frederic reacts to Madame Arnoux's "appari-

* Le 15 septembre 1840, vers six heures du matin, *la Ville de Montereau*, près de partir, fumait à gros tourbillons devant le quai Saint-Bernard.

* Quels étaient son nom, sa demeure, sa vie, son passé? . . . Il la supposait d'origine andalouse, créole peut-être; elle avait ramené des îles cette négresse avec elle?

tion": "What was her name, her home, her life, her past? . . .
He supposed her to be of Andalusian origin, perhaps a creole.
Had she brought the negress back with her from the West In-
dies?"[40] From here on the narrator will glide in and out of
Frederic's mind at will, adopting his protagonist's inner language at crucial moments, but always free to return to his
objective narrative base, to describe minutely the protagonist's actions and his surroundings, or to sketch with broader
strokes changes of circumstance occurring over longer
periods.

But no matter how "impersonal" the tone of the text that
surrounds them, narrated monologues themselves tend to
commit the narrator to attitudes of sympathy or irony. Precisely because they cast the language of a subjective mind into
the grammar of objective narration, they amplify emotional
notes, but also throw into ironic relief all false notes struck by
a figural mind. A narrator can in turn exploit both possibilities, even with the same character, and Flaubert exploits
them both with Frederic, alternately stressing the pathos of
his love for Madame Arnoux and the blunders of his social
and professional choices. Sympathy predominates in this passage that renders Frederic's thoughts after the Arnoux bank-
ruptcy:

> And afterwards? What would become of her? Would she
> be a schoolmistress, a companion, or even a lady's maid?
> She had been abandoned to all the perils of poverty. His
> ignorance of her fate tormented him. He should have
> prevented her flight, or else followed her. Was he not her
> real husband?[41]

and irony predominates in this passage where he decides on
his "future":

---

* Et après? que deviendrait-elle? Institutrice, dame de compagnie, femme
de chambre, peut-être? Elle était livrée à tous les hasards de la misère. Cette
ignorance de son sort le torturait. Il aurait dû s'opposer à sa fuite ou partir
derrière elle. N'était-il pas son véritable époux?

> He wondered, seriously, if he was to be a great painter,
> or a great poet; and he decided in favour of painting, for
> the demands of this profession would bring him closer to
> Madame Arnoux. So he had found his vocation! The aim
> of his existence was now clear, and the future infallible.[42]

In the first quotation the narrator creates the impression that
he is seriously identifying with Frederic's anguish; in the
second he mockingly seems to identify with his inauthentic
decision.

In *L'Education sentimentale* these alternating attitudes of empathy and parody are applied by the narrator to a single protagonist. But the narrated monologue also enables a narrator
to weave in and out of several characters' minds. Virginia
Woolf is the master-weaver of such multi-figural novels.
From Clarissa to Peter, from Rezia to Septimus, from Mrs. to
Mr. Ramsay, narrated monologues pass from hers to his and
back again, often without intervening narrative sentences.[43]
But in transit the tone can change, and it often does when the
gender of the pronoun changes. In *To the Lighthouse* a lyric
climax is reached with the narration of Mrs. Ramsay's
"wedge of darkness" meditation, a parodistic climax with the
narration of Mr. Ramsay's "He reached Q" rumination.[44]
The fertile feminine mind and the arid masculine mind are
both relayed by the same narrator's grammar, but the
former's language is heightened by the transposition, the latter's is abated.

The ironic pole of this tonal range is most clearly in evidence when narrated monologues show up in a pronouncedly
authorial milieu, framed by explicit commentary. Here is
how the Stendhal narrator presents Fabrice's reactions to the
filching of his horse by his own comrades at the Battle of
Waterloo:

* Il se demanda, sérieusement, s'il serait un grand peintre ou un grand
poète;—et il se décida pour la peinture, car les exigences de ce métier le rap-
procheraient de Mme Arnoux. Il avait donc trouvé sa vocation! Le but de son
existence était clair maintenant, et l'avenir infaillible.

> He could find no consolation for so great an infamy, and,
> leaning his back against a willow, began to shed hot
> tears. He abandoned one by one all those beautiful
> dreams of a chivalrous and sublime friendship, like that
> of the heroes of the *Gerusalemme Liberata*. To see death
> come to one was nothing, surrounded by heroic and ten-
> der hearts, by noble friends who clasp one by the hand as
> one yields one's dying breath! But to retain one's en-
> thusiasm surrounded by a pack of vile scoundrels!!!
> Like all angry men Fabrizio exaggerated. After a quarter
> of an hour of this melting mood. . . .[45]

A character's illusions and a narrator's worldliness, romance
and realism clash head-on here, with the triple exclamation
mark signaling the "exaggeration" of Fabrice's language even
before it is spelled out after the fact. Framed in this fashion by
markedly dissonant psycho-narration, a narrated monologue
appears as though it were enclosed in tacit quotation marks,
creating an effect of mock-impersonation. The metaphor of
an actor playing a role, which a number of critics have applied
to the narrator-character relationship created by the narrated
monologue,[46] is valid here only if we expand it to include the
actor schooled in Brechtean alienating techniques.

Even abrupter alienation is achieved when authorial remarks are enclosed *within* a narrated monologue. An interesting instance of this kind occurs in *The Magic Mountain*, when
the amorous Hans Castorp catches himself singing a love
ditty from the lowlands, turns a critical glance on its banal
language, and in turn prompts his narrator to turn a critical
glance on his hero's language:

> This kind of sentimental ditty might very well satisfy

---

* Il ne pouvait se consoler de tant d'infamie, et, le dos appuyé contre un
saule, il se mit à pleurer à chaudes larmes. Il défaisait un à un ses beaux rêves
d'amitié chevaleresque et sublime, comme celle des heros de la *Jérusalem déliv-
rée*. Voir arriver la mort n'était rien, entouré d'âmes héroiques et tendres, de
nobles amis qui vous serrent la main au moment du dernier soupir! mais gar-
der son enthousiasme, entouré de vils fripons!!! Fabrice exagérait comme tout
homme indigné. Au bout d'un quart d'heure d'attendrissement . . .

and please some young man who had quite legitimately, peacefully, and optimistically "given his heart," as the saying goes, to some healthy little goose down there in the flatlands. . . . But for him and his relationship with Madame Chauchat—the word "relationship" must be charged to his account, we refuse to take the responsibility for it—this kind of ditty was decidedly inappropriate. . . .[47]

Note that the narrator, even as he dissociates himself from his character, draws attention to the fact that it is not he, but his character, who here engenders the vocabulary of the narrative text. He is actually teaching his reader an instant lesson in narrative technique, as much as to say: don't be deceived by appearances, this passage may look like my narration, but it is really a monologue that I am narrating—verbatim.[48]

Such explicitly ironic narrators play easier games with the narrated monologue than those who pretend sympathy for their characters in the surrounding text, creating what might be called mock-figural narrative situations. In Sartre's *Bildungsnovella* of a budding fascist, "L'Enfance d'un chef," the narrator adopts, from beginning to end, the point of view of Lucien, his *salot*-protagonist. Inauthenticity stands most clearly revealed not in the purely narrative sections of the work, but at those moments when Lucien's own language appears in the guise of narration. The following narrated monologue toward the end of the story tells how he discovers in anti-Semitism a long-searched-for identity and virility:

He absolutely had to find words to express this extraordinary discovery. Quietly, cautiously, he raised his hand to his forehead, like a lighted candle, then collected him-

---

* An solchem innigen Liedchen mochte irgendein junger Mann Genüge und Gefallen finden, der "sein Herz", wie man zu sagen pflegt, erlaubter-, friedlicher- und aussichtsreicherweise irgend einem gesunden Gänschen dort unten im Flachlande "geschenkt" hatte . . . Für ihn und sein Verhältnis zu Madame Chauchat—das Wort "Verhältnis" kommt auf seine Rechnung, wir lehnen die Verantwortung dafür ab—schickte sich ein solches Gedichtchen entschieden nicht; . . .

self, for an instant, thoughtful and sacred, and the words
came of themselves, he murmured: "I HAVE RIGHTS!"
Rights! Something in the nature of triangles and circles: it
was so perfect that it didn't exist, no matter how many
thousands of rings you traced with a compass, you could
never make a single circle. In the same way generations
of workers could scrupulously obey the commands of
Lucien, they would never exhaust his right to command,
rights were beyond existence, like mathematical objects
or religious dogmas. And Lucien was precisely that: an
enormous bouquet of responsibilities and rights.[49]

This language creates its own distancing effects from within;
exaggerations, pompously narcissistic imagery, the false
analogy between mathematical, religious, and social abso-
lutes: all build up the devastating portrait of an inauthentic
man.

The first half of the "Nausicaa" section of *Ulysses* uses narrated monologues in a similar context, melted into mock-
figural narration.[50] The narrator's style is at times so strongly
"infected" by Gerty's own mental idiom that it is difficult to
draw borderlines between narration and narrated monologue—even more difficult than in the *Ulysses* sections that
quote Bloom's or Stephen's thoughts directly, since no help is
offered by changing person or tense. Yet a narrator is distinctly present, and it is his burlesque of sentimental *kitsch* that
molds the common denominator between his narration and
Gerty's thoughts:

* Il fallait absolument trouver des mots pour exprimer son extraordinaire
découverte. Il éleva doucement, précautionneusement sa main jusqu'à son
front, comme un cierge allumé, puis il se recueillit un instant, pensif et sacré,
et les mots vinrent d'eux-mêmes, il murmura: "J'AI DES DROITS!" Des
Droits! Quelque chose dans le genre des triangles et des cercles: c'était si par-
fait que ça n'existait pas, on avait beau tracer des milliers de ronds avec des
compas, on n'arrivait pas à réaliser un seul cercle. Des générations d'ouvriers
pourraient, de même, obéir scrupuleusement aux ordres de Lucien, ils
n'épuiseraient jamais son droit à commander, les droits c'était par delà l'existence, comme les objets mathématiques et les dogmes religieux. Et voilà
que Lucien, justement, c'était ça: un énorme bouquet de responsabilités et de
droits.

> She gazed out towards the distant sea. . . . And while she
> gazed her heart went pitapat. Yes, it was her he was look-
> ing at and there was meaning in his look. His eyes
> burned into her as though they would search her through
> and through, read her very soul. Wonderful eyes they
> were, superbly expressive, but could you trust them?
> People were so queer.[51]

From "Yes" on, the sentences lend themselves to translation
into quoted monologue. But the preceding sentences—
"pitapat" and all—are purely narrative even as they speak of
Gerty as she would speak of herself.

   The satirical force of both Joyce's and Sartre's narrative
style in these texts relies in part on the shock effect created by
the parody of a norm: the normal milieu for narrated
monologue is *serious* figural narration. The empathic pole of
this technique's tonal scale can be observed in all the more celebrated novels of this type: James' *Ambassadors*, Joyce's *Portrait*, Lawrence's *Plumed Serpent*, the three Kafka novels,
Robbe-Grillet's *Voyeur*. Their protagonists—no matter how
distorted or benighted they may be—are presented to the
reader's understanding "from within," through a profusion
of narrated monologues.
   One of the most poignant instances is a frequently quoted
passage from the penultimate paragraph of *The Trial*. It renders Josef K.'s thoughts instants before he is slaughtered by
his two executioners:

> His glance fell on the top storey of the house adjoining
> the quarry. With a flicker as of a light going up, the
> casements of a window there suddenly flew open, a
> human figure, faint and insubstantial at that distance and
> that height, leaned abruptly far forward and stretched
> both arms still farther. Who was it? A friend? A good
> man? Someone who sympathized? Someone who
> wanted to help? Was it one person only? Or was it man-
> kind? Was help at hand? Were there arguments in his

favour that one had overlooked? Of course there must be. Logic is doubtless unshakable, but it cannot withstand a man who wants to go on living. Where was the Judge whom he had never seen? Where was the High Court, to which he had never penetrated? He raised his hands and spread out all his fingers.[52]

This is the moment of his novel where Kafka perhaps comes closest to "giving away" the existential implications of *The Trial*, or at least the fact that the work *has* existential implications. And it is not coincidental that this moment takes the form of a narrated monologue: had it been quoted directly, signaled as K.'s mental language, fenced off from the surrounding narration, it could not have implicated the narrator (and the reader) in K.'s anguish to nearly the same degree. The cumulative interrogations—a syntactic pattern typical of Kafka's narrated monologues—bring to a climax *in extremis* all the unknowns that have been gathering throughout the novel. Prompted by the vision of the lone figure in the window—perhaps a projection of the self—this crescendo of narrated questions leads from the specific and concrete "Who was it?" to the general and abstract "was help at hand? . . . Where was the Judge . . . ? the High Court . . . ?" The impersonal forms (one, a man) further underline the "everyman" status K. acquires here. And the gnomic present tense in the sentence "Logic is doubtless unshakable . . ."—a rare occurrence in Kafka's third-person works—further suggests that this penultimate moment of the novel builds a deliberate stylistic (as well as thematic) climax. By contrast, the direct

* Seine Blicke fielen auf das letzte Stockwerk des an den Steinbruch angrenzenden Hauses. Wie ein Licht aufzuckt, so fuhren die Fensterflügel eines Fensters dort auseinander, ein Mensch, schwach und dünn in der Ferne und Höhe, beugte sich mit einem Ruck weit vor und streckte die Arme noch weiter aus. Wer war es? Ein Freund? Ein guter Mensch? Einer, der teilnahm? Einer, der helfen wollte? War es ein einzelner? Waren es alle? War noch Hilfe? Gab es Einwände, die man vergessen hatte? Gewiss gab es solche. Die Logik ist zwar unerschütterlich, aber einem Menschen, der leben will, widersteht sie nicht. Wo war der Richter, den er nie gesehen hatte? Wo war das hohe Gericht, bis zu dem er nie gekommen war? Er hob die Hände und spreizte alle Finger.

quotation of K.'s dying words—" 'Like a dog!', he said"—
abruptly cuts the empathic communication.

Hermann Broch's *Death of Virgil*—a novel he himself called
a stretched-out lyric poem—shows what happens when this
kind of stylistic pitch is extended over hundreds of pages. The
formal experiment is entirely in keeping with the daring subject: a verbal artist's lone mental crisis during the last eighteen
hours of his life.[53] Adhering closely to Virgil's feverish mind,
the text's more than five hundred pages minutely render the
continuous flow of his hyper-consciousness until it comes to a
halt with words that signal and signify passage into death: "it
was the word beyond speech." The work's time structure
thus approaches that of autonomous monologues like "Penelope," in which a character's mental language simultaneously determines the forward movement of fictional time
and text, without elision or summary.

Broch's own description of his work indicates his precise
awareness of the technique he used to render this continuous
mental experience: "Even though it is presented in the third
person, it is the interior monologue of a poet."[54] Yet, techni-
cally, this description is something of an overstatement: even
this work, taken *as a whole*, cannot be regarded as an uninterrupted narrated monologue. For one thing, it begins with an
omniscient prelude that, after describing Augustus' fleet approaching the harbor of Brundisium, introduces the protagonist with solemn formality: "on the ship that immediately followed was the poet of the Aeneid and death's signet
was engraved upon his brow."[55] But even after the marathon
of narrated monologues begins in the following paragraph,
the narrative voice occasionally reappears to report internal
and external changes, inner visions and outer sights, and especially Virgil's own physical gestures. If the novel nonetheless creates the impression of absolute homogeneity, of a poetic monologue from beginning to end, it is because the narrative voice is tuned to exactly the same pitch as the figural
voice; or, phrased in terms of the acting metaphor applied earlier, the narrated monologue here casts the narrator in a role

that coincides with his own "real" self. It becomes the choice
medium for the mental portraiture *of* a verbal artist *by* a verbal
artist, both joined in a language flow of sustained poetic
prose.

Because the method works cumulatively, by huge "ser-
pent-sentences" and tightly woven imagistic-ideational com-
plexes, quotation can only faintly suggest the effect. Here is a
minimal illustration (from the opening section; Virgil is observing the gluttony of the courtiers on board ship):

> Everywhere there was someone putting something into
> his mouth, everywhere smouldering avarice and lust,
> rootless but ready to devour, all-devouring, their fumes
> wavered over the deck, carried along on the beat of the
> oars, inescapable, unavoidable; the whole ship was lap-
> ped in a wave of greed. *Oh, they deserved to be shown up
> once for what they were! A song of avarice should be dedicated
> to them! But what would that accomplish? Nothing avails the
> poet, he can right no wrongs; he is heeded only if he extols the
> world, never if he portrays it as it is. Only falsehood wins re-
> nown, not understanding! And could one assume that the
> Aeneid would be vouchsafed another or better influence?* [my
> emphasis][56]

The passage contains two typical devices for melding the narrating and the figural voices. First, by rendering what Virgil
sees in Virgil's own emotive-lyrical idiom, scenic description
(the first sentence) flows uninterruptedly into the narrated
exclamations that follow. But whereas a conjunction of poetic

---

* Überall gab es einen, der etwas in den Mund steckte, überall schwelte
Begehrlichkeit, schwelte Habsucht, wurzellos, schlingbereit, alles-
verschlingend, ihr Brodem flackerte über das Deck hin, wurde im Rucktakte
der Ruder mitbefördert, unentrinnbar, unabstellbar: das ganze Schiff war von
Gier umflackert. Oh, sie verdienten es, einmal richtig dargestellt zu werden!
Ein Gesang der Gier müsste ihnen gewidmet werden! Doch was sollte dies
schon nützen?! nichts vermag der Dichter, keinem Übel vermag er abzuhel-
fen; er wird nur dann gehört, wenn er die Welt verherrlicht, nicht jedoch,
wenn er sie darstellt, wie sie ist. Bloss die Lüge ist Ruhm, nicht die Er-
kenntnis! Und wäre es da denkbar, dass der Aneis eine andere, eine bessere
Wirkung vergönnt sein sollte?

description and monologue is not itself unusual in novels that
adopt the *vision avec*, it is rarely so effective and convincing:
here the perceiving mind belongs to a creative poet, who
would naturally (professionally) transmute the reality he perceives into poetic language—at the very moment when he
perceives it.

The second device is more special to Broch, and he uses it
perennially: when Virgil formulates generalizations in his
mind, the tense of the narrated monologue shifts from past to
present: "Nothing avails the poet, he can right no wrong; he
is heeded only if he extols the world, never if he portrays it as
it is. Only falsehood wins renown, not understanding." Note
that these statements sound identical to a narrator's *ex cathedra*
statements in gnomic present tense. But since they continue
(and are continued by) the statements of the narrated
thought-sequence, they must be interpreted as quotations of
Virgil's monologic language. Clearly Broch has created this
equivocation of vocal origins systematically, in order to fuse
narrator and character inextricably in the language of philosophic commentary.[57] This gnomic language later reaches
climactic density and intensity in long passages of versified
poetry that grow out of and merge back into Virgil's narrated
monologues.[58]

In Broch's *Death of Virgil*, then, the narrated monologue
reaches both quantitatively and qualitatively an extreme limit.
The near-continuous employment of the technique in its most
empathic form, inducing a radical fusion of narrating and
figural voices, leads third-person narration to the frontiers
where it borders at once on lyric poetry and philosophic discourse.

Dimensions and Conjunctions

The narrated monologue is a choice medium for revealing a
fictional mind suspended in an instant present, between a remembered past and an anticipated future. All three of these
time-zones converge in Lily Briscoe's mind the morning after
her return to the Ramsay's summer cottage:

> Suddenly she remembered. When she had sat there last *ten years ago* there had been a little sprig or leaf pattern on the table-cloth, which she had looked at in a moment of revelation. There had been a problem about a foreground of a picture. Move the tree to the middle, she had said. She had never finished that picture. She would paint that picture *now*. It had been knocking about in her mind *all these years*. Where were her paints, she wondered? Her paints, yes. She had left them in the hall *last night*. She would start *at once*. She got up quickly, before Mr. Ramsay turned. [my emphasis][59]

Both the tenses and the adverbs in this passage underline the temporal fluidity the narrated monologue can achieve. The sudden moment of remembrance is the "now" that revives the decade-old "moment of revelation" after "all these years" have intervened; "last night" has brought her—and her paints—to the site of remembered experience. But the moment of memory also opens to the future, and as it moves the mind to decision—"She would paint that picture now. . . . She would start at once"—Lily anticipates that other moment of revelation when she will draw in the middle of her canvas the line with which the novel ends. Lily's mind thus momentarily spans the entire decade of narrated time contained in *To the Lighthouse*. The tenses she employs to reach backward and forward are the standard tenses for memory and anticipation in narrated monologues: the pluperfect and the conditional which correspond to the simple past and future in direct quotation.

The adverbs in this passage point up another distinctive feature of the narrated monologue form: its adoption of the temporal orientation of the figural consciousness, for whom the day of the fictional action is *today*, and the previous and following days are *yesterday* and *tomorrow*. As Käte Hamburger was the first to point out, when this "deictic" adverbial system prevails in a text, the past tense loses its retrospective function, and becomes the tense that creates a fictional reality before our eyes.[60] The consistent adjustment of temporal adverbs in narrated monologues is therefore one of the most powerful tools available to the novelist for locating the narrative perspective within the psyche of his characters.[61] It is from their vantage point that we can then experience the past as a realm that can be reached through memory, and the future as a realm essentially unknown, open only to conjecture and fantasy.

Narrated memories (as flashbacks by means of narrated monologues may be called[62]) can be far more extended than Lily's, and can perform expository, as well as mnemonic, functions. Like several other narrated memories in the final "Lighthouse" section (James' recall of his Oedipal feelings, for example[63]) Lily's memory repeats exactly an inner and outer scene that had been recounted in the earlier "Window" section. But narrated memories often refer to moments that predate the narrated time of a novel, replacing the authorial exposition of more traditional fiction.[64] Clarissa's memory of Peter at Bourton in the second paragraph of *Mrs. Dalloway* is typical. Its first sentences also illustrate the fact that narrated memories, though they must begin in the pluperfect if they are to be recognized, may shift to the simple past tense before long:

> What a lark! What a plunge! For so it *had* always *seemed* to her, when, with a little squeak of the hinges, which she could hear now, she *had burst open* the French windows and *plunged* at Bourton into the open air. How fresh, how calm, stiller than this of course, the air *was* in the early morning; . . .[65] [my emphasis]

Though "plunged" may still be subordinate to "had," the "was" of the next sentence initiates the simple past that prevails to the end of the page-long memory. Once the anterior time-level of a narrated memory has been established, the text can, and often does, safely lapse into the less cumbersome tense without causing temporal confusion.

In some instances, however, one finds narrated memories that create intricate puzzles of tense and Chinese-box effects.

Chapter 42 of James' *Portrait of a Lady* provides a remarkably complex instance. In this entire twenty-page chapter Isabel Archer is "given up to her meditation"[66] about the first years of her marriage—a period that, in the chronological progress of the novel, had been skipped earlier (between chapters 35 and 36). But the function of Isabel's flashback is not primarily to fill in this gap; her remembering psyche does not focus on the elided events themselves, but engages in a kind of retrospective self-analysis. This is how Isabel's early (and now lost) illusions about her husband are presented at one point:

> during those months she had imagined a world of things that had no substance. She had had a more wondrous vision of him, fed through charmed senses and oh such a stirred fancy!—she had not read him right.[67]

The narrated monologue form is clearly signaled here, most clearly in the exclamation "and oh such a stirred fancy!" The entire passage translates readily into a direct interior monologue: "during those months I imagined . . . I had a more wondrous vision of him . . . I did not read him right." This remembrance of thoughts past, however, soon acquires a new grammatical dimension, and new semantic complications:

> She had felt at the same time that he was helpless and ineffectual, but the feeling had taken the form of a tenderness which was the very flower of respect. He was like a sceptical voyager strolling on the beach while he waited for the tide, looking seaward yet not putting to sea. It was in all this she had found her occasion. She would launch his boat for him; she would be his providence; it would be a good thing to love him. And she had loved him, she had so anxiously and yet so ardently given herself—[68]

The simple past of the second sentence can be understood as a normal lapse from the pluperfect of the narrated memory. But the conditional of the third sentence ("she would . . . she would . . . it would") can only be a narrated monologue of Isabel's past illusions about the future: a future that, at the moment of her retrospection, already lies in her disillusioned past. We have here, to be precise, a narrated fantasy within a narrated memory. Translation into direct quotations at both time levels yields: (She thought:) "It was in all this I found my occasion. I thought to myself: 'I will launch his boat for him; I will be his providence; it will be a good thing to love him.' And I have loved him. . . ." To complicate matters further, the preceding sentence in simple past ("He was like a sceptical voyager . . ."), which on first reading looked like a lapsed pluperfect, can now be interpreted with equal validity as a narrated monologue to the second degree, nested *within* the narrated memory: (She thought:) "I thought: 'He is like a sceptical voyager. . . .' "

Such Chinese-box effects occur repeatedly in James' narrated monologues. They seem to correspond exactly to the *esprit en escalier* of his protagonists, who are forever "gazing at a remembered vision," "seeing things afterward," "remembering in subsequent meditation," or recalling things "in that belated vision."[69] But James never shaped an entire text as a narrated memory. This peculiar structure was explored by Robert Musil in a novella entitled *Tonka* (1924): it shows a nameless central consciousness vainly struggling to disentangle a mystery lodged in his past, and since he is largely concerned with his own past responses, it creates astonishingly complex effects of time and tense.[70]

The grammar of narrated monologues anticipating the future does not present the same complications and fascinations as do narrated monologues digesting the past. Because of the cumbersome conditional tense, narrated fantasies tend rather to extreme stylistic tedium. The prize for this variant of the narrated monologue must go to Thomas Wolfe, for the "golden fantasies" he spins with George in the chapter "Alone" in *The Web and the Rock*. I quote only one of the racier paragraphs:

Lying beside her now, wound in her long arms, he would pass his hand along her silken, swelling hips, down the silken seam of her calf, and gently up her thigh below her skirt, lingering for a moment upon the tender, heavy flesh of her under leg. Then he would loosen one breast over the neck of her gown, holding its tender weight and teat gently and lovingly in one hand. The nipples of her firm breasts would not be leathery, stained brown, and flaccid, like those of a woman who has borne children; they would end briefly in a tender pink bud, as did those of the ladies in old French paintings—those of Boucher, for example.[71]

This syntax continues for an unbelievable fifteen pages, with the verb form of every sentence unremittingly cast in would-plus-infinitive form.

Wolfe's "Alone" is interesting for an additional reason: George's narrated monologue is embedded not in a scenic, but in a summary, context. Both its introduction and its conclusion[72] suggest that George ruminates the identical thoughts again and again throughout "a lone and desperate year." Other writers have used narrated monologues with iterative or durative meaning more economically. Many passages in *Madame Bovary* render Emma's habitual thoughts over an extended period in narrated monologues that conform to this type. Kafka is another writer who employs them with consumate artistry, particularly in those of his shorter pieces that are largely structured on an iterative pattern. In "A Hunger Artist," when the narrator explains the ritual that regularly ends the fasting period on the fortieth day, the protagonist's reluctance to leave his cage is rendered as follows:

And that was the moment when the hunger artist always resisted. True, he was still willing to place his bony arms into the helpfully extended hands of the ladies bending over him, but stand up he would not. Why stop now, of all times, after forty days? He could have held out much longer, infinitely long; why stop now, of all times, when he was in his best, no, not yet even in his best fasting form?[73]

Several further narrated questions follow, all of which the hunger artist asks himself not just on a single occasion but "always" when the identical occasion recurs, and apparently always in the same words. Used iteratively, the narrated monologue is thus a highly effective means for pointing up the mental rigidity of a character caught in a seemingly inescapable predicament. Note, however, that its iterative meaning can only be deduced from the summary context in which it is embedded. The monologue passage itself creates the singular mental instant within the repetitive series, and thereby enlivens the eternal return of the same with scenic immediacy.

In narrated memories and fantasies the scene, whether real or imagined, is wholly contained within the figural mind, and clearly separated from the character's present surroundings. But narrated monologues can also cross this inner-outer boundary, and can reflect sites and happenings even as they show a character reflecting *on* these sites and happenings. At such moments, as one critic puts it, "conscious awareness flickers between words and pictures, between speech and sense data,"[74] effacing the demarcation between narrated monologue and its narrative context.

Take the following passage, again from *To the Lighthouse*, where Lily is watching Mr. Ramsay:

Heaven could never be sufficiently praised! She heard sounds in the house. James and Cam must be coming. But Mr. Ramsay, as if he knew that his time ran short,

* Und in diesem Augenblick wehrte sich der Hungerkünstler immer. Zwar legte er noch freiwillig seine Knochenarme in die hilfsbereit ausgestreckten Hände der zu ihm hinabgebeugten Damen, aber aufstehen wollte er nicht. Warum gerade jetzt nach vierzig Tagen aufhören? Er hätte es noch lange, unbeschränkt lange ausgehalten; warum gerade jetzt aufhören, wo er im besten, ja noch nicht einmal im besten Hungern war?

> exerted upon her solitary figure the immense pressure of
> his concentrated woe; his age; his frailty; his desolation;
> when suddenly, tossing his head impatiently, in his
> annoyance—for after all, what woman could resist
> him?—he noticed that his boot-laces were untied. Re-
> markable boots they were too, Lily thought, looking
> down at them: sculptured; colossal; . . .[75]

This text gives us Lily's thoughts and interpretations, but it
simultaneously describes objects that exist in narrated space,
and events that move the action forward in narrated time.
Here the function of the narrated monologue seems to be less
to render a character's consciousness than to narrate a fictional
scene: Mr. Ramsay waiting for his children, his gestures, his
boots. Is this passage, in fact, a narrated monologue at all? We
find, on closer examination, that it oscillates constantly between monologic and narrative language. Certainly the initial
exclamation is Lily's, as is the conjecture concerning James'
and Cam's arrival, and the final hyperbolic description of the
"remarkable boots"—explicitly identified, this time, as Lily's
thought. The long middle sentence concerning Mr. Ramsay,
on the other hand, is a narrative, reportive sentence. Yet its
language is inoculated with Lily's subjectivity: in the initial
"But," the speculative "as if" clause, the apposite "his concentrated woe; his age; his frailty; his desolation." Most remarkable of all, it contains a narrated question ("—for after
all, what woman could resist him?—"), which can be interpreted only as a question Lily imagines running through Mr.
Ramsay's mind at that moment: a narrated monologue within
a narrated monologue that, in direct quotation, would read:
(She thinks) "He thinks: 'what woman can resist me?' " This
sentence, then, contains contradictory signals, and remains
ambiguously suspended between narration and narrated
monologue.

There are two different ways for describing the topography
of this hazy region where inner and outer fictional realities are
intertwined in the figural mind. R. J. Lethcoe, a critic who
has studied this territory with great care, suggests the term

"narrated perception," which he defines as "the report of a
character's conscious perceptions . . . presented in such a
manner that they resemble objective report, but on careful
consideration can be shown to be transcriptions of consciousness rather than reality."[76] This definition points to the difficulty of deciding whether a specific passage should be understood as a narrated monologue, a narrated perception, or an
objective report.

Another way to describe this overlap between narrated
monologue and narration is provided by Ludomír Doležel's
concept of a "diffuse" type of narrated monologue, which in
contrast to the "compact" type does not contain a sufficient
number of discriminating features to distinguish it clearly
from "narrator discourse," or to assign it clearly to "character
discourse."[77] Doležel's idea of diffusion, therefore, accounts
for the presence within a narrative passage of "just a tinge,"
of figural language, even if this passage as a whole cannot be
convincingly transposed into an interior monologue by shifting its pronouns and tenses. This way of looking at the region
between inner reflection and outer reality in no sense invali-
dates the concept of narrated monologue itself, but—though
limiting it to the "compact" type of represented discourse—
allows for traces of this technique for rendering a character's
consciousness to pervade the surrounding narrative text.

More important for the internal focus of our survey of
techniques is the conjugation of the narrated monologue with
the two alternative techniques for rendering consciousness.
Most often we find the narrated monologue dovetailing
neatly with one, the other, or both, as a text plays up and
down the gamut of consciousness.

The permutations that can result are extremely varied. The
clearest, most standard sequence is the triad psycho-narra-
tion-narrated monologue-quoted monologue, as in the following passages from Flaubert:

Then she tried to calm down; she remembered the let-

ter. *It had to be finished, but she didn't dare. Besides, where? How? She would be seen.*
—No, she thought, here I'll be alright.

She looked all around her, wishing that the earth would crumble. *Why not end it all? Was there anyone holding her back? She was free.* She moved forward, looking at the pavement, saying to herself:—Go ahead! Go ahead![78]

A quarter of an hour later he had a longing to go into the coach yard, as if by chance. *Would he perhaps see her again?*
"What's the use?" he said to himself.

He left his friends; he wanted to be alone. His heart was overflowing. *Why had she offered him her hand? Was it a thoughtless gesture, or an encouragement?* "Come, I must be mad!"[79]

In every instance the inner happenings are presented in "ascending" order, with the narrated monologue (as emphasized), wedged between the other two techniques, bridging the gap between wordless emotion and emotional words. Each technique assumes its most standard function: psychonarration summarizes diffuse feelings, needs, urges; narrated monologue shapes these inchoate reactions into virtual questions, exclamations, conjectures; quoted monologue distills moments of pointed self-address that may relate only dis-

---

* Alors elle voulut se calmer; elle se rappela la lettre; il fallait la finir, elle n'osait pas. *D'ailleurs, où? comment? On la verrait.*
—Ah! non, ici, pensa-t-elle, je serai bien. [my emphasis]
* Elle jetait les yeux tout autour d'elle avec l'envie que la terre croulât. *Pourquoi n'en pas finir? Qui la retenait donc? Elle était libre.* Et elle s'avança, elle regarda les pavés en se disant:
—Allons! allons! [my emphasis]
* Un quart d'heure après, il eut envie d'entrer comme par hasard dans la cour des diligences. *Il la verrait encore, peut-être?*
"A quoi bon?" se dit-il. [my emphasis]
* Il quitta ses amis; il avait besoin d'être seul. Son coeur débordait. *Pourquoi cette main offerte? Était-ce un geste irréfléchi ou un encouragement?* "Allons donc! Je suis fou!" [my emphasis]

tantly to the original emotion. In writers like Flaubert, who shun quoted monologues for extended meditations, these triads customarily end in brisk colloquialisms, even when the other two techniques are spun out at much greater length.

The same general preference for narrated over quoted monologues often prompts the reverse sequence of techniques in Woolf's novels. The passage that recounts Mrs. Ramsay's vision of herself as "a wedge-shaped core of darkness" begins with a cliché lodged at the surface of her mind: "No, she thought, . . . children never forget." Now, by way of the narrated monologue, Woolf prepares the descent into psychic depth, at first still with causal syntax, and a realistic domestic theme: "For this reason it was so important what one said and what one did, and it was a relief when they went to bed." In the following sentences, the language becomes increasingly introspective, and then more and more imagistic, until it finally reaches the essential visionary image:

> For now she need not think about anybody. She could be herself, by herself. And that was what now she often felt the need of—to think; well, not even to think. To be silent; to be alone. All the being and the doing, expansive, glittering, vocal, evaporated; and one shrunk, with a sense of solemnity, to being oneself, a wedge-shaped core of darkness, something invisible to others. Although she continued to knit, and sat upright, it was thus that she felt herself;[80]

Unlike Flaubert's triads, where the lines between the techniques are clearly marked, here the passage from narrated monologue to psycho-narration is almost imperceptible. Since Mrs. Ramsay is thinking about thinking, her vocabulary becomes dotted with the very words that usually signal psycho-narration. Or is it the narrator whose language becomes contaminated by the figural idiom (the "stylistic contagion" noted earlier in connection with the villanelle scene from Joyce's *Portrait*[81])? All we can say is that the two techniques merge, before psycho-narration clearly emerges in the final sentence of the quotation.

This insensible shading of narrated monologue into psycho-narration, or vice versa, is very frequent in figural narrative situations. The narrated monologue and the quoted monologue, on the other hand, overlap only under very special circumstances: when a text shifts or adheres to the present as a narrative tense.[82] Thus one finds that novelists who like to employ the narrative present to depict vivid scenes also like to shift to the present when they narrate vivid monologues.[83] And those who follow the New French mode of casting entire third-person novels in the present tense give the narrated monologue a new look as well: Nathalie Sarraute's *Planetarium*, for example, a novel built almost entirely of narrated monologues attributed to half a dozen different characters. Here, in a typical passage, a woman named Giselle momentarily looks behind the façade of her "happy" marriage to Alain:

> She runs to her room and drops face down on her bed. *. . . To let oneself sink, farther, still farther down . . . voluptuousness of going down . . . to arrive all the way on the bottom. . . . It's all fake . . .* she gets up and sits down on her bed: *it's fake, Alain and her. A sham, a deceit, pictures to represent happiness, and there's something in back . . . those laughs of the old witches. . . .* [Sarraute's ellipses, my emphasis][84]

Only when third-person reference occurs—"it's fake, Alain and her"—do these monologues give away their "narrated" structure. Elsewhere they look exactly like unsignaled quoted monologues in the manner of *Ulysses*, a resemblance rein-

---

★ Elle court dans sa chambre et se laisse tomber à plat ventre sur son lit . . . *Se laisser couler, plus bas, encore plus bas . . . volupté de la descente . . . arriver jusqu'au fond . . . Tout est faux . . .* elle se redresse et s'assoit sur son lit: *c'est faux, Alain et elle. Du toc, du trompe-l'oeil, des images pour représenter le bonheur, et derrière il y a quelque chose . . . ces rires des vieilles sorcières . . .* [Sarraute's ellipses, my emphasis]

forced by their abbreviated syntax. And yet, since they never include first-person references, they maintain the relationship of latency between words and thoughts so characteristic of the narrated-monologue technique. This may well be the reason that Sarraute chose to narrate, rather than to quote, her *sous-conversations*. The resultant contrast between the quotation of spoken words and the narration of silent thoughts helps to create what she describes as "a close, subtle game, which is also a savage game . . . between the conversation and the sub-conversation."[85]

With these virtuoso performances on the keyboard of consciousness our tour of the narrated monologue ends, as does our tour of the different techniques in third-person narrative context. A few summary correlations can be made, none simple, all tentative.

First, the relation between technique and narrative situation: since all three main techniques can mix and match in various ways at both ends of the authorial-figural scale, there is obviously no one-to-one correspondence. Still, narrative situation is an important consideration in analyzing why one technique is used in preference to another, and how different techniques combine with each other and with the narrative context. There is clearly affinity between authorial narration and pyscho-narration, between figural narration and the narrated monologue. Each of the other two techniques entering these territories assimilates (is assimilated)—one would like to use active and passive forms simultaneously when discussing this relationship—in various ways. In an authorial milieu both monologic forms take on an ironic tonality. In a figural milieu psycho-narration and quoted monologue move toward each other (and toward the narrated monologue): psycho-narration by coloration from the figural language, quoted monologue by camouflaging itself as best it can. Here, listed in order of frequency, are the two groups of modified techniques:

Authorial

1. dissonant psycho-narration
2. ironically quoted monologue
3. ironically narrated monologue

Figural

1. empathically narrated monologue
2. consonant psycho-narration
3. unsignaled quoted monologue

Historically the evolution from authorial to figural narration brings with it an evolutionary development of the second group of modified techniques. These are also the techniques that work toward the effacement of the line of demarcation between authorial and figural language. As a result, these techniques themselves become increasingly difficult to differentiate: psycho-narration may adopt the figural vocabulary, narrated monologue may be cast in the present tense, quoted monologue may be unsignaled. We have not followed these developments far enough into modernity to show what happens in those experimental texts where the systems of tense and pronoun become unstable, and the "logic" of literature is perceived only through its absence.

A second, equally complex relationship exists between techniques and levels of consciousness. Most generally, one can say that the more direct the technique, the more evidently verbal the activity of the mind, and therefore the more clearly conscious the mind that is exposed. To adopt an approximate Freudian continuum, this would be an oversimplified diagram of the relationship:

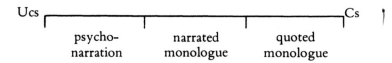

Ucs ——————————————————————————————— Cs

| psycho-narration | narrated monologue | quoted monologue |

This diagram would be more accurate:

	Ucs	Cs
psycho-narration	———————————————————
narrated monologue	————————————————
quoted monologue	—————————

The reach of the quoted monologue in the direction of the unconscious depends on a novelist's conception of the relationship between language and thought. For the narrated monologue, the language-thought problem is less crucial, because its language is less firmly committed to the figural origin. Psycho-narration, finally, is the technique that can range most freely through the mental strata, but in the age of the interior monologue it has been favored by novelists who aim for the nether depth.

Part II

*Consciousness in
First-Person Texts*

4 // *Retrospective Techniques*

Robinson Crusoe, as Coleridge noted with a touch of envy, has "the instant passing on without the least pause of reflex consciousness."[1] The same could be said of many picaresque narrator-heroes and of some deadpan narrators in modern American novels as well. But few first-person narrators dispense with inside views altogether, and many prefer them to all other vistas; whence the aptness of the title Jean Rousset gave to his recent book on first-person narrative: *Narcisse romancier.*[2]

In some respects a first-person narrator's relationship to his past self parallels a narrator's relationship to his protagonist in a third-person novel. The kind and extent of the distance between subject and object, between the narrating and the experiencing self,[3] here also determines a whole range of possible styles and techniques, analogous to those I defined in the chapter on psycho-narration in third-person novels. To one side there is the enlightened and knowing narrator who elucidates his mental confusions of earlier days, and this wide disparity between the two selves corresponds to the distance that separates the narrator from his protagonist in such third-person texts as *Death in Venice*. To the other side there is a narrator who closely identifies with his past self, betraying no manner of superior knowledge, and this near-cohesion between the two selves corresponds to the near-cohesion of the narrator with his protagonist in such third-person texts as *A Portrait of the Artist*. Like psycho-narration in the third-person novel, self-narration can articulate inarticulate states of consciousness, or summarize long-range psychological situations and their slow mutations. Under special circumstances a first-person narrator can even call on more direct methods for reproducing his past consciousness, by verbatim quotation and narration of thoughts that passed through his mind.

But these analogies between third- and first-person narration should not obscure the obvious and crucial differences between them: even when a narrator becomes a "different person" from the self he describes in his story, his two selves still remain yoked by the first-person pronoun. Their relationship imitates the temporal continuity of real beings, an existential relationship that differs substantially from the purely functional relationship that binds a narrator to his protagonist in third-person fiction.[4] Contrary to what one might have expected, therefore, the first-person narrator has less free access to his own past psyche than the omniscient narrator of third-person fiction has to the psyches of his characters. His retrospection depends on a fundamentally different optics: there is no magic mirror corresponding to the magic lens, only the "telescope leveled at time" of which Proust speaks, and by which he means a "real" psychological vision conditioned by memory. This frequently prompts a first-person narrator to mention the plausibility of his cognition, particularly when it involves the most inchoate moments of his past. When James tells about Maisie's early childhood feelings, he does not and need not explain how he found out. When David Copperfield does the same, he refers to his source: "if it should appear from anything I may set down in this narrative that I was a child of close observation, or that as a man I have a strong memory of my childhood, I undoubtedly lay claim to both of these characteristics."[5] But if a narrator with "a strong memory" can tell us what he thought at his life's beginning, no narrator can tell us what he thought at its ending. The thoughtful *Death of Ivan Ilych*, the even more thoughtful *Death of Virgil* cannot be imagined in realistic first-person form. Infancy and death point up the most obvious limitations imposed on self-narration by the figural identity of hero and historian.

This limitation imposed by mnemonic credibility is obviously not the feature of first-person narration Henry James had in mind when he called it "a form foredoomed to looseness," and rejected "the terrible *fluidity* of self-revelation." Yet it is this same dimension of figural identity—"the double privilege of subject and object"—that motivates his negative critique.[6] Though it has often been understood differently, the context suggests that James meant by "fluidity" the variable relationship of the narrating and the experiencing self along the *temporal* axis that connects them. If Strether had narrated his own story, we are told, he could not have been *"encaged* and provided for as 'The Ambassadors' encages and provides."* The word "encaged" is crucial here: as the center of consciousness in a figural novel Strether is fettered to his present moment of experience; he cannot know his future self, nor how that self will be affected by its present experience. The experiencing self in first-person narration, by contrast, is always viewed by a narrator who knows what happened to him next, and who is free to slide up and down the time axis that connects his two selves.

These special restraints and freedoms of autobiographical retrospection result in tensions and ambiguities that variously affect the techniques to be explored in this chapter.

Dissonant Self-Narration

A lucid narrator turning back on a past self steeped in ignorance, confusion, and delusion: we recognize here the basic design of "the most extensive exercise in the first-person singular," as Harry Levin has called *A la Recherche du temps perdu*. But Proust was not only the supreme practitioner of this type of retrospective mental narration; he was also its most committed advocate. Its justification is an integral aspect of his aesthetic theory in *Le Temps retrouvé*. These famous pages have often been read as an anti-intellectual aesthetic that prizes involuntary memory above all else;[7] and the creative act certainly depends for Proust on the miraculous contingencies that trigger the knowledge of the "essence of things."[8] But he makes equally clear that involuntary memory is merely the precondition—necessary, but insufficient—for recreating the past through narration. The narrative process itself, by contrast, is emphatically conscious, deliberate, and intellectual. Marcel stresses this repeatedly, most succinctly in the following passage:

> One experiences, but what one has experienced is like these negatives which show nothing but black until they have been held up before a lamp, and they, too, must be looked at from the reverse side; one does not know what it is until it has been held up before the intelligence. Only then, when one has thrown light upon it and intellectualized it can one distinguish—and with what effort!— the shape of what one has felt.[9]

The imagery of light and darkness in this passage underlines the mental antinomies: "intelligence" and "intellectualize" as opposed to "experience" (*éprouver*) and "feel" (*sentir*). Clearly this polar relationship corresponds to the one pertaining between the narrating and the experiencing self. Elsewhere in these pages Proust uses different images—a diver sounding the depth, a cryptographer deciphering hieroglyphics.[10] But all define the narrative process as the retrospective cognition of an inner life that cannot know itself at the instant of experience. It is therefore essentially a method for rendering past consciousness that Proust has in mind in the frequently cited sentence: "True life, life at last discovered and illuminated, the only life therefore really lived, that life is literature."[11]

---

* On éprouve, mais ce qu'on a éprouvé est pareil à certains clichés qui ne montrent que du noir tant qu'on ne les a pas mis près d'une lampe, et qu'eux aussi il faut regarder à l'envers: on ne sait pas ce que c'est tant qu'on ne l'a pas approché de l'intelligence. Alors seulement quand elle l'a éclairé, quand elle l'a intellectualisé, on distingue, et avec quelle peine, la figure de ce qu'on a senti.

* La vraie vie, la vie enfin découverte et éclaircie, la seule vie par conséquent réellement vécue, c'est la littérature; . . .

We must note in passing that this entire *art poétique* is itself an instance of self-narration: it is the Marcel who is waiting in the library of the Guermantes before he enters the *matinée* who *thinks* the aesthetic theory, not the Marcel who writes this scene years later. Significantly, this is the only moment in the entire *Recherche* where the thoughts of the experiencing self reach the lucid omniscience that the narrating self has manifested throughout its two thousand pages. And this juncture between the narration of past thoughts and the thoughts that give rise to the narration—the very illumination that brings about the narrator's vocation as a writer and the decision to write the book we hold in our hands—is one important aspect of the well-known structural circularity of Proust's novel.[12]

A la Recherche is an inexhaustible source-book for the type of self-narration in which the benighted past self is "lit up" by a sovereignly cognizant narrator. The hundreds of passages that could be cited fall into two essential groups: those that depict Marcel's inner life over an extended period of time, and those that render his reactions during specific episodes.

Given Proust's general predilection for iterative and durative narration, some of the most extended passages of self-narration survey a mental state during a certain summer, a certain year, or even an entire biographical era.[13] Manner is perfectly adapted to matter here, since such panoramic views are dependent on a distanced and discerning eye. The two-page paragraph that relates Marcel's awakening to panerotic feelings in early adolescence is a typical and beautiful example, from which I can quote only the beginning:

> Sometimes to the exaltation that solitude gave me, a second exaltation would be added that I could not separate clearly from the first, stimulated by the desire to see rise up before me a peasant-girl whom I might clasp in my arms. Coming abruptly, and without giving me time to trace it accurately to its source, among so many ideas of a

different kind, the pleasure which accompanied it seemed
to me only a degree superior to that given me by my
other thoughts.[14]

The initial adverb and the imperfect tense immediately create
the sense of an extended time-frame, which will be reinforced
by later adverbial phrases. From the start, the cognitive defi-
ciency of the past self is stressed, especially its incapacity to
analyze ("separate clearly") discrete emotions, cause, and effect. This incapacity eventually culminates in the paragraph's
central sentence: "And between the earth and its creatures I
made no distinction." From the start also the erotic delight is
associated with delusion ("seem" will appear twice more in
the passage, and alternate with "appear" and "believe"). But
the most emphatic distancing of the present from the past self
occurs toward the end of this passage, with one of those digressions in gnomic present tense that are Proust's trademark,
and that so often display all the disillusioned wisdom the narrator has culled from his iterative past.

   The same distancing techniques are employed by the
Proustian narrator when he focuses on a specific moment of
his past. I select for close scrutiny the scene in *Du Côté de chez
Swann* where the young Marcel catches his first glimpse of the
fabled Duchesse de Guermantes in the church of Combray.[15]
It is one of those many moments in the novel when Marcel
has a "ce n'est que cela" experience: when he apprehends a
drastic discrepancy between an ideal image, deeply implanted
in his mind, and a reality that threatens to destroy it. Circumstantial evidence having convinced him that the woman
he sees in the church must indeed be the legendary duchess,
the account of his reaction begins:

   * Parfois à l'exaltation que me donnait la solitude, s'en ajoutait une autre
que je ne savais pas en départager nettement, causée par le désir de voir surgir
devant moi une paysanne que je pourrais serrer dans mes bras. Né brusquement, et sans que j'eusse eu le temps de le rapporter exactement à sa cause, au
milieu de pensées très différentes, le plaisir dont il était accompagné ne me
semblait qu'un degré supérieur de celui qu'elles me donnaient.
   * Et la terre et les êtres, je ne les séparais pas.

it was she! My disappointment was great. It arose from my not having borne in mind, when I thought of Mme de Guermantes, that I was picturing her to myself in the colours of a tapestry or a painted window, as living in another century, as being of another substance than the rest of the human race. Never had I taken into account that she might have a red face, a mauve scarf like Mme Sazerat; and the oval curve of her cheeks reminded me so strongly of people whom I had seen at home that the suspicion brushed against my mind (though it was immediately banished) that this lady in her creative principle, in the molecules of her physical composition, was perhaps not substantially the Duchesse de Guermantes.

A brief phrase renders the perception ("it was she"); a brief sentence summarizes the decisive reaction ("My disappointment was great"); and now the analysis sets in, with a profusion of verbs of consciousness linked in multiple subordination. "It arose from my not having borne in mind, *when* I thought . . . *that* I was picturing . . . ," etc. A sovereign narrator, a master psychologist, moves back and forth in time, from effect to cause to further effect, bringing to bear on the instant conflict an expansive capacity to detail, to dissect, and to elucidate. One could hardly imagine a language further removed from interior monologue, or any other form of instant rendering of consciousness.

The subsequent pages tell of the complicated mental operation Marcel performs to reconcile the ideal and the real images of the duchess, and here even more pronounced distancing factors come into play. To explain the difficulty of the opera-

* c'était elle! Ma déception était grande. Elle provenait de ce que je n'avais jamais pris garde, quand je pensais à Mme de Guermantes, que je me la représentais avec les couleurs d'une tapisserie ou d'un vitrail, dans un autre siècle, d'une autre manière que le reste des personnes vivantes. Jamais je ne m'étais avisé qu'elle pouvait avoir une figure rouge, une cravate mauve comme Mme Sazerat, et l'ovale de ses joues me fit tellement souvenir de personnes que j'avais vues à la maison que le soupçon m'effleura, pour se dissiper d'ailleurs aussitôt, que cette dame, en son principe générateur, en toutes ses molécules, n'était peut-être pas substantiellement la duchesse de Guermantes, . . .

tion the narrator calls on a simile: "onto this quite recent un-
changeable image, I tried to apply the idea: 'It is Mme de
Guermantes,' succeeding only to make the idea move in front
of the image, like two discs separated by an intervening
space." The spatial vehicle of the comparison is used as a kind
of demonstrating device, emphasizing the ironic distance between narration and experience by the very fact that it demonstrates an attempt that fails.[16] The subsequent success of
the operation is ushered in by an even more ironic technique,
direct quotation of the ritual phrases Marcel says to himself to
dispel the threat of the real duchess's ordinary physique:

> my imagination, which, paralyzed for a moment by con-
> tact with a reality so different from anything that it had
> expected, began to react and to say to me: "Great and
> glorious before the days of Charlemagne, the Guer-
> mantes had the right of life and death over their vassals;
> the Duchesse de Guermantes descends from Geneviève
> de Brabant. She does not know, nor would she consent
> to know, any of the people who are here."[17]

The invocation works, the duchess is successfully transfig-
ured, as the narrator explains in a sentence which contains the
most emphatic of all marks of narratorial disparity, a gnomic
generalization:

> And now that all the thoughts I brought to it made me
> find that face beautiful—and especially perhaps that de-
> sire one always has to avoid disappointment, a form of
> the instinct for preserving what is best in ourselves— . . .
> I grew indignant when I heard people saying around me:

---

* sur cette image toute récente, inchangeable, j'essayais d'appliquer l'idée:
"C'est Mme de Guermantes", sans parvenir qu'à la faire manoeuvrer en face
de l'image, comme deux disques séparés par un intervalle.

* mon imagination qui, un moment paralysée au contact d'une réalité si
différente de ce qu'elle attendait, se mit à réagir et à me dire: "Glorieux dès
avant Charlemagne, les Guermantes avaient le droit de vie et de mort sur leurs
vassaux; la duchesse de Guermantes descend de Geneviève de Brabant. Elle
ne connaît, ni ne consentirait à connaître aucune des personnes qui sont ici."

"She is better looking than Mme Sazerat, than Mlle Vinteuil," as though she had been in any way comparable to
them.

The generalization, though parenthetical and hedged by a
"perhaps" (as so often in Proust),[18] raises the momentary experience to a higher plane, even as it exposes it as a case of
ordinary human inauthenticity. Note that the gnomic "that
desire one always has to avoid disappointment" relates back
specifically to the starting point of the inner drama: "My disappointment was great." The "eternal truth" thus interrupts
the narration to recapitulate the meaning of the entire episode.

There follows a kind of postscript to the self-narrative
scene in which the narrator draws attention, suddenly, to his
own narrating self at its present post of observation: "And the
attention with which I illuminated her face isolated it so completely that *today, if I think back* to this ceremony, I find it impossible to visualize a single person who was present, except
for her." [my emphasis] Adverb and tenses underline the
clear (though unspecified) temporal distance that separates the
narrating from the experiencing self. Such reminders of the
memory process are another hallmark of the type of self-
narration this scene exemplifies.

In sum, Proust's method for rendering Marcel's past consciousness is essentially one of elucidation and interpretation:
the elaborate mental vocabulary, the hypotactic style, the expansive concern with psychological motivation, the occasional ironic self-quotation, and finally the recourse to imagistic and theoretical glosses all stress the cognitive privilege of
the narrating over the experiencing self.[19]

---

* Maintenant que me le faisaient trouver beau toutes les pensées que j'y
rapportais—et peut-être surtout, forme de l'instinct de conservation des meil-
leures parties de nous-mêmes, ce désir qu'on a toujours de ne pas avoir été
déçu—. . . je m'irritais en entendant dire autour de moi: "Elle est mieux que
Mme Sazerat, que Mlle Vinteuil", comme si elle leur eût été comparable.

* Et l'attention avec laquelle j'éclairais son visage l'isolait tellement *qu'aujourd'hui, si je repense* à cette cérémonie, il m'est impossible de revoir une seule
des personnes qui y assistaient sauf elle.

Proust brought to its culmination a long tradition of self-analytic retrospection in the novel, and in many ways he carried it to a limit. Many of the most serious novelists in his own and following generations were more apt to use this form of self-narration parodistically, if they used it at all: Mann in *Felix Krull*, Kafka in his animal stories, Grass in *The Tin Drum*, Beckett in *Molloy*.

No wider disparity between a narrating and an experiencing self can be imagined than the anthropogenic distance in Kafka's "Report to an Academy." Its self-consciously urbane narrator himself calls this distance "infinite":

> Honored Gentlemen of the Academy!
> You grant me the honor, to invite me to deliver to the Academy a report about my early life as an ape.
> In this sense I am unfortunately unable to answer the request. Nearly five years separate me from apehood, a period which may seem short when measured by a calendar, but infinitely long when one gallops through it, as I have done. . . .[20]

The very change that makes the narration possible has erased the experience to be narrated. The "old ape truth" can no longer be reached by one who has attained "the average education of a European"—"let no one say it was not worth the trouble." All the speaker can do is underscore the antinomies between past and present, and he does so with equal measures of pride and nostalgia: now, in possession of human language, he can reproduce only by a neat syllogism his decision to enter the human world, "a clear and beautiful mental process that I somehow hatched out with my belly, for apes think with their bellies."

---

* Hohe Herren von der Akademie!

Sie erweisen mir die Ehre, mich aufzufordern, der Akademie einen Bericht über mein äffisches Vorleben einzureichen.

In diesem Sinne kann ich leider der Aufforderung nicht nachkommen. Nahezu fünf Jahre trennen mich vom Affentum, eine Zeit, kurz vielleicht am Kalender gemessen, unendlich lang aber, durchzugaloppieren, so wie ich es getan habe . . .

In one of its meanings Kafka's story may therefore be taken as a parody of retrospective self-narration, pointing up the paradox of the form: the present, verbal act that can never recapture the non-verbal reality of past experience. To some degree all of us "think with our bellies" in our most intense moments, and our true past selves can never be revived in language. Beckett's Molloy entirely agrees with the realism of Kafka's ape, though hardly with his *nouveau riche* pride in words:

> I say that now, but after all what do I know now about then, now when the icy words hail down upon me, the icy meanings, and the world dies too, foully named. All I know is what the words know, and the dead things, and that makes a handsome little sum, with a beginning, a middle and an end as in the well-built phrase and the long sonata of the dead.[21]

But Molloy's words, in turn, read almost like a deliberate reversal of Proust's credo quoted earlier: "True life, life at last discovered and illuminated, the only life therefore really lived, that life is literature."

Consonant Self-Narration

The counter-movement to this tradition of distanced self-narration was already reigning supreme when Proust wrote his novel, and Henry James' critique of first-person novels was one of its early symptoms. When, in *The Craft of Fiction*, Percy Lubbock in turn vetoed first-person novels that attempt to depict the detailed workings of a mind, it was precisely on account of their delayed and distanced presentation of consciousness. Granting that Lubbock stacked his cards rather heavily by choosing the lame example of Meredith's *Henry Richmond*, what he said about this novel is applicable—*toute proportion gardée*—to the entire tradition of retrospective self-analysis: "Harry, speaking of himself, can only report; he can only recall the past and *tell* us what he was, only *describe* his emotion; and he may describe very vividly, and he does, but it would necessarily be more convincing if we could get behind his description and judge for ourselves." [Lubbock's emphasis]²² This critique of self-narration introduces Lubbock's well-known "next step": the presentation of the psyche "made immediately visible" in the Jamesian manner. Twenty-five years later, Nathalie Sarraute leveled an almost identical charge at self-narration, this time directing it at Proust himself. Speaking of the subliminal conflicts that are for her (as they were for Proust) the essential subject of fiction, she says: "But . . . to us it appears already as though he had observed them from a great distance, after they had run their course, in repose and, as it were, congealed in memory. He tried to describe their respective positions as though they were stars in a motionless sky. He considered them as a sequence of causes and effects which he sought to explain. He rarely—not to say never—tried to relive them and make them relive for the reader in the present, while they were forming and developing, like so many tiny dramas, each one of which has its adventures, its mystery and its unforeseeable ending."²³ Having entered the age of suspicion, Sarraute is far less confident than Lubbock in legislating a "next step." Since third-person narration has, as she believes, lost its "credibility" for the modern reader, the figural dramatization of consciousness cannot carry the same supreme value for her that it bore for the Jamesian critic. Though she uses the Jamesian method on occasion (as in *The Planetarium*), Sarraute does not—in either theory or practice—dismiss first-person forms altogether as a vehicle for depicting the inner scene.²⁴ Like other twentieth-century novelists she prefers to search for more direct methods within the first-person mode itself— notably to experiment with "simultaneous" forms that abandon past-tense narration altogether in favor of present-tense discourse.

But a more immediate depiction of the inner life within the autobiographical mode itself has actually been around almost as long as the Jamesian central consciousness has. This type has generally been ignored by theorists of the novel, who have continued to conceive of first-person narration according to the "classical" model of the distanced memorialist who "retraces from the point of view of a later time the earlier course of his life."[25] Yet typologically this distanced, wise, discursive narrator stands only at one end of the autobiographical spectrum. His opposite number is the unobtrusive narrator who identifies with his earlier incarnation, renouncing all manner of cognitive privilege.[26] When this consonance is applied to self-narration, the result is entirely different from the analytic elucidations in *A la Recherche.*

One of the earliest and most sustained examples of consonant first-person narration is Knut Hamsun's *Hunger* (1890). Not once in this entire novel does its narrator draw attention to his present, narrating self by adding information, opinions, or judgments that were not his during his past experience.[27] But at the same time the novel is wholly self-centered, indeed self-obsessed, depicting as it does a mind hyperactivated by starvation. Hamsun himself said of his novel that it "deliberately plays on a single string, but with an attempt to draw from that string hundreds of tones."[28] Some of these tones can be heard in the following passage:

> Suddenly one or two high notes of a clarinet drifted up to me from the concert and started my thoughts off in a new direction. Depressed at not being able to do my article, I poked the papers in my pocket and leaned backward over the bench. In this instant my head is so clear that I can follow the most difficult train of thought without effort. Lying in this position, letting my eyes float down over my chest and legs, I notice the tiny leaping movements my foot is making every time my heart beats. I sit up part way and gaze down at my feet. At that moment a strange and fantastic mood comes over me which I have never felt before; a delicate and wonderful shock ran through all my nerves as though a stream of light had flowed through them. As I stared at my shoes I

felt as if I had met an old friend, or got back some part of
me that had been torn off: a feeling of recognition goes
through me, tears come to my eyes, and I experience my
shoes as a soft whispering sound coming up toward me.
Getting weak! I said fiercely to myself and closed my fists
and said, Getting weak. I was furious with myself for
these ridiculous sensations, which had overpowered me
even though I was fully conscious of them. I spoke harsh
and sensible phrases, and closed my eyes tightly to get
rid of the tears. Then I begin, as though I had never seen
my shoes before, to study their expression, mimelike
movements when I move my toes, their shape and the
worn-out leather they have; and I discover that their
wrinkles and their white seams give them an expression,
provide them with a face. Something of my own being
had gone into those shoes, they struck me as being a
ghost of my "I," a breathing part of myself. . . .[Ham-
sun's ellipsis][29]

A dynamic inner life emerges here, with complete spontaneity and immediacy: Sarraute could hardly have wished
for a "tiny drama" observed at closer range. Yet it is a
drama that is *narrated*, not directly enacted before our eyes.
The manifold psychological vocabulary (*thoughts, train of
thought, mood, shock, nerves, feeling, sensations*, etc.) clearly indicates this indirection, as do, by contrast, the brief references
to direct discourse ("Getting weak," and the other "harsh and
sensible phrases"). But, though the retrospective narrative
stance is maintained, the narrator never draws attention to his
hindsight: neither analyzing nor generalizing, he simply records the inner happenings, juxtaposing them in incongruous
succession, without searching for causal links. A series of
temporal adverbs (*suddenly, in this instant, at that moment*) introduces each new shade of feeling: depression, illumination,
anger, sobriety, pathos. Where Marcel would have searched
for a law, or at least for a pattern, Hamsun's narrator leaves
his "strange and fantastic mood" intact, merely recording it
with the same seismographic accuracy with which he records

the "tiny leaping movements" of his feet. Both gnomic digressions and explicatory similes, so habitual in *A la Recherche*, are lacking in *Hunger*. When Hamsun uses similes, he uses them not to explain, but to underline the absurdity of the experience: in his shoe-ecstasy, what first appears as a simile—"*as if* I had met an old friend, or got back some part of me that had been torn off"—in fact *becomes* a reality— "Something of my own being *had gone* into those shoes, they struck me as *being* a ghost of my 'I,' a breathing part of myself." Simply accepting these incongruities, Hamsun's narrator displays no increment in intellectual powers over his past self; he is as reflective and enlightened during his mental antics as he is when he records them, ironically removed from them not by time and maturation but by a coeval tension: "I was furious with myself for these ridiculous sensations, which had overpowered me even though I was fully conscious of them."

The absence of self-exegesis and of all references to the narrating self excludes from Hamsun's text the entire temporal zone for which the present tense is normally employed by a dissonant narrator like Proust's Marcel. When Hamsun shifts from past to present—as he does with remarkable frequency in our passage, and sometimes in mid-sentence—the present tense he uses is of an entirely different nature: not a "true" present that refers to the speaker's present moment, but a narrative present that refers to the same past moment as the past tense does. The ease with which this narrative present alternates with the customary narrative past indicates the degree of consonance Hamsun has achieved in his text: he evokes the past as though it were present, no matter whether he uses the past or the present tense.

This quasi-annulment of the narrative distance appears as the formal correlative for a narrator's fascination with psychological incongruities, and for his endeavor to present them without corrective hindsight. The consonant type of self-narration thus presupposes a relationship between sentience and intellect entirely different from Proust's *ex post facto* analysis. Though Hamsun never explained his method as ex-

tensively as Proust did—and it would have been unthinkable
for him to do so *within* his narrative—the essays he wrote in
the same year as *Hunger* present some highly relevant glosses
on his novel. "I want to take 'contradictions' in man's inner
being for granted," he said; "I dream of a literature peopled
with characters for whom inconsistency is literally a fundamental trait."[30] It is this fascination with the psychic in-
choateness that brings Hamsun at times, in theory as well as
in practice, into amazing proximity to Woolfean and Sarrautean ideas: "What if literature began to concern itself more
with spiritual states than with engagements, dances, excursions to the country and accidents for their own sake? . . . We
would get to know a little more about the secret stirrings that
go on unnoticed in the remote parts of the mind, the incalcu-
lable chaos of impressions, the delicate life of the imagination
seen under the magnifying-glass; the random wandering of
thoughts and feelings, untrodden trackless journeyings by
brain and heart. . . ."[31] The link between these concerns and
the exclusive focus on the experiencing self in the confines of
first-person narration is evident. Even Henry James, had he
known Hamsun's work, would no doubt have found its hungry protagonist sufficiently "encaged and provided for" to
forgive him the fact (if not the content) of his self-revelation:
in this strictly controlled consonant form the first-person
novel moves into close proximity to the figural third-person
form.[32] But *Hunger* is a rare specimen, and I know of no other
novel that duplicates its purity.

Few texts represent as clearly dissonant or consonant forms
of self-narration as do *A la Recherche* and *Hunger*, or depict as
consistent an attitude of the narrating toward the experiencing self. Having chosen these texts for their typological purity, I will briefly look at a text that mixes the types in interesting ways.
   Michel, the titular figure of André Gide's *Immoralist* is the
self-deceiving narrator par excellence, a self-narrator who

misunderstands himself.[33] As he explains to his assembled friends, he sets out to narrate his past in order to clarify it: "For I have reached a point of my life beyond which I cannot go. Not from weariness, though. But I no longer understand. I need . . . I need to talk, I tell you." [Gide's ellipsis][34] Yet as his increasingly frequent, increasingly bewildered questions indicate, he becomes less and less able to elucidate and evaluate as he proceeds with his account. In midstream, he equivocally calls his revolt against traditional values "this wisdom or this folly," and near the end he still questions whether he is the master of his liberation or its slave: "But had I the power to choose my wishes? to decide my desires?"[35] These open questions of the narrating self pinpoint the contrast between Gide's and both Proust's and Hamsun's narrators: where Marcel illuminates his earlier self with supreme omniscience, and the *Hunger* artist accepts and presents his earlier self with all its incongruities, Michel can neither throw light on his past nor tolerate its dark ambiguities.

His narrative stance wavers accordingly: between an analytic, "Proustean" retrospection on his past self, and an empathic "Hamsunian" fusion with it. The most interesting effects arise when the two stances interfere with each other and become the subject of elaborate explanations. At one point, after a highly analytical passage of self-narration, Michel comments: "I did not have all these thoughts at the time, and here I give a false picture of myself. In reality I did not think at all, I did not analyze myself; a happy fatality guided me."[36] Just as analytic clarity is simultaneously desired and feared, lyric evocation of past feelings never remains intact either:

* Car je suis a tel point de ma vie que je ne peux plus dépasser. Pourtant ce n'est pas lassitude. Mais je ne comprends plus. J'ai besoin . . . J'ai besoin de parler, vous dis-je. [Gide's ellipsis]
* Mais étais-je maître de choisir mon vouloir? de décider de mon désir?
* Toutes ces pensées je ne les avais pas alors, et ma peinture ici me fausse. A vrai dire, je ne pensais point, je ne m'examinais point; une fatalité heureuse me guidait.

I see Malta all white; the approach to Tunis. . . . How
changed I am!
It is hot. It is fine. Everything is splendid. Oh, how I
wish that every sentence here could distill a harvest of delight! . . . I cannot hope to impose on my story now
more order than my life contained. I have been long
enough trying to explain to you how I became who I am.
Oh, if only I could rid my mind of this intolerable logic!
. . . [Gide's ellipses][37]

The explicit longing is for magic fusion of past experience ("a
harvest of delight") and present language ("every sentence").
But instead the self-conscious comment itself destroys the
magic, revealing the discrepancy between life and narration,
between the supposed sensuality of the experiencing self and
the "intolerable logic" of the narrating self. Note that the
evocation of the past—in a desperate effort to preserve its
emotions—is cast in the present tense. This in turn suggests
that Michel associates with the past tense the order and logic
that is necessary to explain "how I became who I am"—an
impulse to narrate from an analytic distance that he alternately
adopts and rejects.

The Immoralist briefly illustrates how directly the narrator's
psychology affects the form of his self-narration, adding a
dimension of meaning entirely lacking in the corresponding
third-person technique. This is not surprising: all formal elements in first-person narration contribute to the characterization of the narrator, and therefore call for more than merely
formal interpretation. But in the case of self-narration the increment of meaning is particularly large. We experience the
child Marcel in the Combray church as the prefiguration of

---

* Je revois Malte toute blanche; l'approche de Tunis . . . Comme je suis
changé!
Il fait chaud. Il fait beau. Tout est splendide. Ah! je voudrais qu'en chaque
phrase, ici, toute une moisson de volupté se distille . . . En vain chercherais-je
à present a imposer à mon récit plus d'ordre qu'il n'y en eut dans ma vie.
Assez longtemps j'ai cherché de vous dire comment je devins qui je suis. Ah!
désembarrasser mon esprit de cette insupportable logique! . . . [Gide's ellip-
ses]

the master psychologist he will become, the nameless protagonist of *Hunger* watching his shoes as a person who will remain caught in his bizarre epiphanies, Michel in Tunis as the subject of a crisis leading to irresolvable conflicts. The dissonance or consonance of self-narration is, in short, a significant autobiographical fact.

The same increment of meaning also attends the monologic techniques in first-person narration, though here interpretation is affected by the *fact* that monologues are reproduced, as much as by their tone and content.

Self-Quoted Monologue

Occasional quotations of past thoughts—on the pattern of "I said to myself: . . ."—are a standard component of traditional first-person narration. At times they take the form of highly rhetorical speeches—of the kind Stendhal uses in third-person context—and render moments of climactic conflict or high pathos. A typical example occurs in Benjamin Constant's *Adolphe*, when the normally highly analytic and distanced narrator quotes verbatim how, on a solitary walk, he lamented his enslavement to his burdensome mistress, Eleonore:

> "She is always accusing me, I said, of being hard, ungrateful, without pity. Ah, had heaven granted me a woman whom social conventions permitted me to acknowledge. . . .
> [a page of monologue]
> How grateful I should be to heaven, and how benevolent towards men!"
> I spoke thus, and my eyes filled with tears, . . .[38]

Note how the quotation marks and the initial inquit phrase clearly fence off the monologue from the narration, with the

---

* "Elle m'accuse sans cesse, disais-je, d'être dur, d'être ingrat, d'être sans pitié. Ah! si le ciel m'eût accordé une femme que les convenances sociales me permissent d'avouer, . . . Combien je serais reconnaissant pour le ciel et bienveillant pour les hommes!"
Je parlais ainsi; mes yeux se mouillaient de larmes, . . .

post-monologic "I spoke thus" introduced for double security. The reason for these precautions is readily apparent: a narrator who quotes his past thoughts runs the risk that the reader will mistake them for his present thoughts (since the basic grammar—present tense, first person—is the same in both cases). This danger is greatest when the past thoughts are detached from their immediate context, and approach a gnomic or essayistic vein. A wise old narrator is therefore especially careful to separate the half-baked mental essays of his youth from his present wisdom by explicit, sometimes ironic, comments.

When set speeches give way to flickering thoughts in more impressionistic first-person novels, the self-quoting technique runs into trouble: it either creates equivocation between past and present thoughts, or it litters the text with unwieldy inquit phrases. For this reason quoted monologue is not the technique most favored in modern autobiographical fiction, except in comic novels like Joyce Cary's *Horse's Mouth*: its pages are dotted with "I thought," "I said," "I said again," "I said to myself," and this bumpy surface adds humorous effects to the saucy content of Gully Jimson's inner discourse.[39]

The device of self-quotation also presents a more substantive problem of credibility. Remembering that a first-person narrator (in contrast to the narrator of third persons who can tune in at will on the silent language of his characters) can reach his past thoughts only by simulation of a perfect memory, long quotation of his past thoughts can quickly appear as a kind of mnemonic overkill, as contrived here as it would be in a real autobiography. It is easier by far to suspend disbelief when a narrator displays total recall in other areas—the description of a locale, the reproduction of a dialogue—than when he quotes "what I said to myself." Self-aware narrators often forestall this objection themselves. Felix Krull, recalling his shock-reaction on first encountering back-stage reality in the actor Müller-Rosé's dressing-room, quotes his thoughts directly, but hedges them carefully: "This then—that's about how my thoughts went at the time—this faded and pimpled individual is the thief of hearts who was just now longingly idolized by the gray masses!" After a couple of monologic pages, he adds: "The above lines suggest the overall gist of the thought-process that my overheated and excited mind followed in Müller-Rosé's dressing room. . . ."[40]

Not surprisingly, Beckett's Molloy finds self-quotation an especially fertile ground for formalistic clowning. The quotation of his inner debate in the forest toward the end of his journey ends as follows:

> But I also said, Yet a little while, at the rate things are going, and I won't be able to move, but will have to stay, where I happen to be unless someone comes and carries me. Oh I did not say it in such limpid language. And when I say I said, etc., all I mean is that I knew confusedly things were so, without knowing exactly what it was all about. And every time I say, I said this, or I said that . . . I am merely complying with the convention that demands you either lie or hold your peace. For what really happened was quite different. And I did not say, Yet a little while, at the rate things are going, etc., but that resembled perhaps what I would have said, if I had been able. In reality I said nothing at all, but I heard a murmur, something gone wrong with the silence. . . .[41]

This self-destruct hits the mark: the convention that pretends "such limpid language" originates in an experiencing self which "in reality . . . said nothing at all," rather than in the reflection of the narrating self. And although Molloy goes on to mention "other figures quite as deceitful as, for example, It seemed to me that, etc.," it is self-quotation which has provided the most successful caper. Molloy's remarks could be placed alongside Musil's, Proust's, or Sarraute's on the subject,[42] except that here the irony addresses itself specifically to

---

* Dies also—so etwa gingen meine Gedanken—, dies verschmierte und aussätzige Individuum ist der Herzensdieb, zu dem soeben die graue Menge sehnsüchtig emporträumte! . . . Obige Zeilen deuten in grossen Zügen den Gedankengang an, den mein Geist, erhitzt und eifrig, in Müller-Rosés Garderobe zurücklegte . . .

the use of this technique by a first-person narrator whose "I said this or I said that" is exposed as a counterfeit of the entire process of mnemonic introspection.

Some novelists, on the other hand, deliberately exploit the ambiguity created by self-quotation in first-person context: by omitting clear signals of quotation, they run together their narrator's past and present thoughts, thereby suggesting that their ideas on a certain subject have remained the same. In *Der Steppenwolf* Hesse imperceptibly merges Harry Haller's past thoughts with the commentary of the narrating self, providing proof that the experiences he records in his "Records" are symptoms of a conflict that remains unresolved to the end. In an early scene, while dressing for his visit to the professor, he introduces an interior monologue explicitly: "Meanwhile I thought: just as now I dress and go out. . . ." Most people, he tells himself, perform such daily routines as dressing mechanically and unquestioningly, while he sees through the absurdity of it all. "Oh, people are right," he concludes, "entirely right to live as they do . . . instead of resisting the dreary mechanism and staring at the void as I do, derailed man that I am." Then abruptly we are no longer with the unwillingly dressing Harry, but are with the recording Harry as he addresses identical thoughts to us, the readers of "these pages," explaining that he is unable to play this mechanical game any longer "now that I have come this far and am standing at the edge of life, where it falls off into bottomless darkness."[43] A merger of past and present thoughts is effected here by the omission of all end-quote signals, melding two present tenses that refer to different moments in time, the "now" of the past locution—"as I now dress"—and the "now" of the present locution—"now that I have come this far." Both these mo-

---

* Zugleich dachte ich: so, wie ich jetzt mich anziehe und ausgehe . . .

* Oh, und sie haben recht, unendlich recht, die Menschen, dass sie so leben, . . . statt sich gegen die betrübende Mechanik zu wehren und verzweifelt ins Leere zu starren, wie ich entgleister Mensch es tue.

* der ich nun einmal so weit gegangen bin und am Rande des Lebens stehe, wo es ins bodenlose Dunkel fällt . . .

ments are so typical of Harry's personality that they become one in the gnomic present tense of the reflections; and this tense, doubly anchored, overarches the temporal gap, and shows Harry duratively locked into his precarious posture.

When signals of quotation are omitted at the beginning as well as at the end of a self-quoted monologue, true indeterminacy can result. Consider this quotation from William Golding's *Free Fall*, where Sammy Mountjoy tells about his incarceration in a dark cell:

> I got my knees up against my chin and put my crossed arms before my face. . . .
> *Eyes that see nothing soon tire of nothing. They invent their own shapes that swim about under the lids. Shut eyes are undefended. How then, what to do?* They opened against my will and once more the darkness lay right on the jellies. My mouth was open and dry.[44] [my emphasis]

The present-tense comments in this passage are framed by retrospective narration of Sammy's physical state and gestures. But the temporal origin of these comments remains indeterminate. Does the narrating Sammy tell us what he thought long ago, while he faced the darkness, or what he is thinking now, while he remembers and records this scene? Even close reading leaves the timing of the reflection undetermined.

These fusions and confusions of past and present thoughts manifest a trend on the part of first-person narrators to close the gap that separates past thoughts from their present narration, and ultimately to abandon retrospection altogether. This trend is compounded when, in addition to effacing the demarcation between his past and present thoughts, a narrator uses the evocative present as a continuous narrative tense: the case of Kafka's "Country Doctor," and other texts approaching the structure of autonomous interior monologues, which I take up in the next chapter. The final section of the present chapter surveys a final technique that remains more clearly within the domain of retrospective narration.

Self-Narrated Monologue

There are sometimes curious moments in autobiographical
novels when the narrator makes statements about past events
that are immediately belied by what happens next, or asks
questions that are clearly answered on the following page of
his text. Take this passage from Iris Murdoch's novel *A Severed Head* where the narrator, locked in embrace with his
mistress Georgie, hears the house door open and thinks his
wife Antonia is about to catch him in the act:

> We stood thus for a second, paralysed. Then I pulled my-
> self roughly out of the embrace.
>   It could only be Antonia. She had changed her mind
> about going to the country, and had decided to come and
> look the furniture over before our interview tomor-
> row.[45]

Seconds later the narrator finds out that the intruder is not his
wife after all. What happens here? The last sentence looks
every bit like a narrative statement; yet it can only be the quotation of a (mistaken) thought of the moment. Despite the absence of quotation signals or the tense of direct discourse it
must signify: "I thought: 'It can only be Antonia. She has
changed her mind. . . .' " Or take this passage from Henry
James' *Aspern Papers*, where the obtuse narrator at long last
realizes that the price he would have to pay for acquiring the
coveted papers of Jeffrey Aspern is marriage to Miss Tita, the
aging spinster who has inherited them:

> He [a gondolier] rowed me away and I sat there pros-
> trate, groaning softly to myself, with my hat pulled over
> my face. What in the name of the preposterous did she
> mean if she did not mean to offer me her hand? That was
> the price—that was the price! And did she think I wanted
> it, poor deluded, infatuated, extravagant lady? . . . Did
> she think I had made love to her, even to get the papers? I
> had not, I had not; I repeated that over to myself for an

hour, for two hours, till I was wearied if not convinced.[46]

The narrator's queries, exclamations, protestations render not
his present, long since confirmed, interpretation of the past
events, but the exact rhetoric of his past wonderment, the
very words in which he "repeated that over" to himself during his gondola ride.

Clearly these passages from Murdoch and James present a
first-person variant of the third technique for rendering consciousness in third-person fiction: the narrated monologue.
The relationship of the narrating to the experiencing self in
these self-narrated monologues corresponds exactly to the relationship of a narrator to his character in a figural third-
person novel: the narrator momentarily identifies with his
past self, giving up his temporally distanced vantage point
and cognitive privilege for his past time-bound bewilder-
ments and vacillations.

The self-narrated monologue has received surprisingly little notice, even from French and German theorists of *style indirect libre* and *erlebte Rede*.[47] One reason is no doubt the relative scarcity of this technique. Even Henry James, addicted as
he was to narrated monologue in his third-person novels,
used it only sporadically in first-person narratives like *The
Aspern Papers*; not only because his first-person narrators are
less introspective than his "central reflectors"—they *are* generally more interested in surrounding events and other characters than in themselves—but also because they like to keep
their distance from the past they recount, and therefore avoid
consonant self-narration and monologic techniques. But even
distant and self-conscious narrators, like the teller of *The Aspern Papers*, occasionally resort to self-narrated monologues,
as a poignantly dramatic device for conveying their past uncertainties and agitations. Some of the weightiest questions
narrator-protagonists ask themselves are cast in this form. It
is the form in which Proust's Marcel tells of his decision to
write his *Recherche*: "But was there still time for me? Was it

not too late?"[48] and it is the form in which Beckett's Moran
asks his seventeen questions which range from "1. Why had I
not borrowed a few shillings from Gaber?" to "17. What
would I do until my death? Was there no means of hastening
this, without falling into a state of sin?"[49]

Under certain circumstances, moreover, the self-narrated
monologue can attain far greater importance in a text: when a
highly self-centered narrator relates an existential crisis that
has remained unresolved. Unable to cast a retrospective light
on past experience, he can only relive his dark confusions,
perhaps in the hope of ridding himself of them. We have already encountered autobiographers of this type: Hamsun's
hungry protagonist, Golding's Sammy Mountjoy, Hesse's
Harry Haller, all narrators who on occasion also employ consonant self-narration, or quoted monologues that melt into
present thoughts. But it is the narrated monologue that offers
these narrators the ideal device for displaying empathy with
their younger selves. Harry Haller employs it frequently, especially during his solitary prowls through the city streets:

> Hesitantly I started on my way home, turned up my coat
> collar, and struck my stick to the wet pavement. No
> matter how long I lingered on my way, I would still find
> myself in my attick all too soon, in my little make-
> believe home. . . . Well, in God's name, I was not going
> to let anything spoil my good evening mood, not the
> rain, nor the gout, nor the araucaria, and though there
> was no chamber orchestra to be had, nor a lonely friend
> with a violon, still that lovely melody sounded inside
> me, and I could perform it for myself after a fashion,
> humming it to the rhythm of my breathing. Reflecting
> thus, I walked on. No, things were not so bad, even
> without the chamber orchestra, and without the friend
> . . . .[50]

* Zögernd trat ich den Heimweg an, schlug den Mantelkragen hoch und
stiess den Stock aufs nasse Pflaster. Mochte ich den Weg noch so langsam
zurücklegen, allzubald würde ich wieder in meiner Mansarde sitzen, in

Note how this passage simultaneously captures inner and outer reality! The concrete images of the return home lead to mental images, which in turn inspire despair, hope, and resignation, while the hesitant promenade proceeds. The continuity is made possible by the sameness of the verbal tense as well as by the omission of all indices of self-quotation in rendering the past thoughts. By barring from the language all elements that draw attention to the verbal gesture of narration itself, the text captures the hyperactive consciousness as a "presence," bridging the distance that separates the experiencing from the narrating self.[51]

In all these respects, the self-narrated monologue corresponds closely to the narrated monologue in third-person fiction. In both its third-person and first-person versions it creates the illusion of a fiction that "tells itself," without the ministrations of a narrator. For this reason the narrated monologue also defines the generic zone where first-person and third-person texts move into closest proximity to each other. This is validated by a unique case history: Kafka's grammatical transformation of *The Castle* in the course of its composition. As the manuscript shows, Kafka began his last novel in first-person form, but after writing about fifty pages decided to shift to the third person. He thereupon proceeded to cross out all the I's in the earlier pages, and to replace them by K.'s (or the appropriate third-person pronouns), effecting this transposition without making any other substantial changes in the manuscript. A narrated monologue passage from *The Castle*—the same passage I quoted earlier to illustrate the narrated monologue in third-person narration[52]— looked as follows when it first flowed from Kafka's pen:

---

meiner kleinen Scheinheimat . . . Nun, in Gottes Namen, ich wollte mir die gute Abendlaune nicht verderben lassen, nicht vom Regen, nicht von der Gicht, nicht von der Araukarie, und wenn kein Kammerorchester zu haben und auch kein einsamer Freund mit einer Violine zu finden war, so klang jene holde Melodie doch in mir innen, und ich konnte sie, leise summend im rhythmischen Atemholen, doch andeutend mir selber vorspielen. Sinnend schritt ich weiter. Nein, es ging auch ohne die Kammermusik und ohne den Freund . . .

At that moment Barnabas stopped. *Where were we? Was this the end of the road? Would Barnabas leave me? He wouldn't succeed.* I clutched Barnabas' arm so firmly that I almost hurt myself. *Or had the incredible happened and we were already in the Castle or at its gates?* [my emphasis][53]

The characteristics of the self-narrated monologue are all in evidence here, including the interrogatives directed to an unknown future. The questions the narrator silently asks have long since been answered as he turns the next corner on that snowy night. A text narrating this scene retrospectively might go something like this: "I didn't know at the time that we were in front of Barnabas' house. When he stopped, I asked myself: 'Where are we? Is this the end of the road? . . .' "—or some such mixture of self-narration and self-quotation, clearly marking the text with the present-past polarity. The self-narrated monologue, by effacing all such marks, makes the experiencing self, with all its vagaries, rule supreme in the text.

The presence of this and many other passages of narrated monologue in the first-person version of *The Castle* suggests the reason that Kafka was able to recast his manuscript into third-person form with relative ease: its focus was fully on the experiencing self, with the narrating self kept out of sight quite as consistently in the first-person text as the conspicuously "absent" narrator of Kafka's third-person novel. In this respect Kafka's *Castle* is the perfect illustration for the "personal" narrative mode defined by Roland Barthes, and the category of "focalized" narration defined by Gérard Genette: third-person texts that one can "rewriter" in first-person form, without the change of person entailing any further alterations.[54] Kafka's manuscript revision is actually a kind of demonstration *ad oculos* of this "rewriter" test (performed in

---

* Da blieb Barnabas stehen. *Wo waren wir? Ging es nicht mehr weiter? Würde Barnabas mich verabschieden? Es würde ihm nicht gelingen.* Ich hielt Barnabas' Arm fest, dass es fast mich selbst schmerzte. *Oder sollte das Unglaubliche geschehen sein, und wir waren schon im Schloss oder vor seinen Toren?* [my emphasis]

reverse), with the narrated monologue passages it contains acting as the optimal pivots for the grammatical switch.

It would be a grave error, however, to take the case of *The Castle* as proof of the unimportance of grammatical person for the structure and meaning of a novel. Kafka would surely not have bothered to make this laborious change in midstream, had he thought that it was of no consequence to his fiction. More or less consciously he must have known that there were advantages to the K. over the I, and the drawbacks of the retrospective techniques for rendering consciousness may have had a share in his decision.[55] Nor is Kafka the only novelist who experimented with the comparative advantages of the two persons in the course of a work in progress. Two famous predecessors come to mind: James considering and almost falling into "the wayside trap" of making Strether "at once hero and historian";[56] and before him Dostoevsky struggling with autobiographical versions of *Crime and Punishment*.[57] These cases are analogous to Kafka's not only because they resolve the dilemma of person analogously, but also because they focus equally on that person's inner life. Could Percy Lubbock be right after all when he suggests that narration in the first-person should "give way to the stronger method . . . as soon as the main weight of attention is claimed for the speaker rather than for the scene?"[58]

We might almost think so when we contemplate the quantity and quality of experiencing minds we know from figural third-person novels, as compared to the few achieved and sustained portrayals of this kind in first-person form. In autobiographical novels the time of intensest reflection is more often the present rather than the past, so that the most memorable minds the genre has produced belong to *narrating* rather than to experiencing selves: Tristram, Marcel, Molloy, Krull, Kafka's ape. Consonant presentation of a past consciousness is dependent on the self-effacement of the narrating voice, and few authors of autobiographical fiction have been willing or able to silence this voice completely. Hamsun is the great exception. But then, in *Hunger* he "deliberately plays on a single string," even if he succeeds in getting "hundreds of tones" out of it.

For writers seeking to present the most complex inner adventures in the most direct possible manner, the consonant techniques in third-person narration offer obvious advantages over the retrospective techniques. Yet a number of the same writers—Dostoevsky and Kafka among them—kept coming back to the first-person medium for further explorations of its potential for immediacy and drama. In their most interesting experiments they tried to cancel the distance between narration and experience altogether by abandoning the realistic conditions and retrospective techniques of fictional autobiography. This gravitation of first-person narration toward the direct presentation of a figural consciousness will concern us in the next chapter, where texts by Dostoevsky and Kafka will again figure prominently. And as we pass from contextual to autonomous presentations of consciousness, our focus also shifts: from techniques in context to the structure of entire texts.

5
From Narration
to Monologue

"In that book the reader finds himself established, from
the first lines, in the thought of the principal personage, and the uninterrupted unrolling of that thought, replacing the usual form of narrative, conveys to us what this personage is doing or what is happening to him."[1] Joyce's
comment to Valery Larbaud about Dujardin's *Les Lauriers
sont coupés*, the novel he, Larbaud, and Dujardin himself regarded as the first interior monologue novel, is a good place
to start a discussion of this fictional form. What could have
led Joyce to describe this form as "*replacing* the usual form
of narrative"—in Larbaud's French quotation "se *substituant
complètement* à la forme usuelle du récit"? The difference from
third-person narration that Joyce draws is clear from the phrases
"from the first lines" and "the uninterrupted unrolling of
that thought": thought-quotation here constitutes an independent form of its own, in contrast to its contextual employment in a novel where a narrator introduces and interrupts the unrolling thoughts.[2] But how does it differ from
first-person narration? Joyce's comment points to that difference too, though more cryptically: with the tense of "what
this personage *is* doing or what *is* happening to him." This
employment of the present tense pinpoints the simultaneity
of language and happening that distinguishes the new form
from "the usual form of narrative" in the first person, where
language always follows happening.

But when word and deed coincide, and the word is unspo-

ken and unwritten to boot, can one still speak of narrative?
Note that Joyce himself does not: he avoids calling the new
form narrative, or its speaker a narrator, though "the principal personage" certainly implies (in French even more clearly
than in English) that he is a character in fiction. His comment
suggests, in other words, that the autonomous interior
monologue is, paradoxically, a non-narrative form of fiction.

This way of looking at the autonomous monologue explains why its relationship with first-person narration is so
complex and so important: as it approaches monologue, narration sheds its narrative characteristics *en route*. (I apologize
in advance for the profusion of spatial imagery I will use in
charting the transitional territory; it will give my description
of this mazy terrain a certain consistency). The several different routes lead up to the monologic form from different sides,
and along these lines of approach one finds intermediate
semi-narrative forms of considerable historical and aesthetic
interest of their own. Approaching the "pure" form—
prototype "Penelope"—in this fashion, one discovers that it
occupies a restricted area that would figure as a mere dot on a
large map of literary genres. Its importance lies not in its size,
but in its location: it is a meeting-place, or, better, a
vanishing-point, for anti-narrative tendencies of all sorts contained within narration itself.

This manner of viewing the relationship of the autonomous
monologue to other first-person forms also helps to account
for the early controversies regarding its origins, as reflected in
Dujardin's disagreement with André Gide, René Lalou, and
others.[3] Dujardin maintained a puristic position, insisting on
the birth *ex nihilo* of the form he created in *Les Lauriers*, at
least so far as fictional antecedents are concerned.[4] However,
when one objectively surveys the pre-*Lauriers* scene, one finds
that, far from having appeared spontaneously, the autonomous monologue has such a profusion of progenitors, such
an overdetermined causality, that its first "pure" incarnation
appears not so much as a creative miracle but as the result of
very high probability. Aside from the quoted interior

monologue in third-person novels—which many regard as its principal antecedent—its sources have been variously identified as confessional literature; narratives based on memory; diary and epistolary novels; digressive narration; the essay; the prose poem; the dramatic monologue; and the stage monologue.[5]

Whether they are valid or not, the variety and wealth of these ancestral lines supports the idea that the autonomous monologue represents a kind of confluence of formal possibilities. But this confluence can be viewed more clearly in synchronic than in diachronic perspective. When one deals with generic problems, a typological approach has an obvious advantage: it permits free choice of the clearest representative texts without attention to precedence or influence. Still, since formal changes happen historically, a typological survey affords glimpses into literary history as well.

Problematic Presentation

The vast majority of first-person novels—including all those discussed in the last chapter—present themselves as written memoirs (like *David Copperfield* or *Felix Krull*), or as spoken discourse subsequently recorded by a listener (i.e., framed, like Joseph Conrad's novels, or *The Immoralist*). In autonomous monologues this realistic motivation of the text's origin is canceled out by the very nature of the genre: it can create the illusion that it renders an unrolling thought only if it effaces the illusion of a causal link between this language and a written text. In the words of one modern theorist: "in the standard interior monologue, the problem of writing is purely and simply bracketed out, obliterated. How could this language arrive at being written, at what moment could writing recover it? These are questions left carefully in the shadows."[6]

This difference between first-person narratives and autonomous monologues appears, at first glance, to provide a reliable criterion for distinguishing between the two forms. Yet there are a number of first-person texts that leave the question

of their ostensible origins deliberately vague, mysterious, indeterminate, or even contradictory. Such ambiguities concerning their narrative presentation bring these works into
close proximity to autonomous monologues, and often make
them subject to border disputes.

Even a text that explicitly asserts its written status can border on the autonomous monologue if its fictional writer con-
tradicts his scribal act. The most notorious instance is Dostoevsky's *Notes from Underground*. Despite its title, an editorial
postscript, and the underground man's own mention of his
writing activity,[7] his stance is emphatically oratorical: he perennially refers to his own "talking" or "speaking," and at one
point even to the breath he has used up in a particularly
exclamatory passage: "I have a right to say so, for I'll go on
living to sixty myself. I'll live till seventy! Till eighty! Wait,
let me catch my breath."[8] The ambiguity between written
and oral language is compounded by a second one, between
self-address and audience-address. Contrasting his notes with
Rousseau's *Confessions*—written for a public, and therefore
full of vainglorious lies—the underground man vouches for
his sincerity, since "I, however, am writing for myself."[9] But
the text belies this affirmation by its continuous posturing before an audience of "gentlemen": phrases like "let me tell
you," "let me explain" introduce almost every sentence. Not
only does he imagine these listeners to be physically present,
he also attributes immediate reactions to them—"I am sure
you are imagining . . ."; "I can feel that you are irri-
tated"[10]—and engages them in imaginary dialogues (especially in chapters 7 and 8).

The ambiguities between writing and speaking, between
audience-address and self-address, are resolved when the underground man himself reveals his audience as a fiction, a
mere prop for his soliloquy: "if I write as though I were addressing readers, that is simply because it is easier for me to
write in that way. It is merely a question of form, only an
empty form. . . ."[11] He gives away, here, the psychological
clue for the contradictory structure of his text: it reflects pre-

cisely the contradictory structure of his psyche; he can find a
road to self-expression only when he takes on the dual roles of
protagonist and antagonist.[12]

The narrative presentation in this story thus consists of at
least three superimposed layers: a written record in its alleged
format; a spoken and audience-directed discourse in its pervasive speech-patterns; a silent self-address in the true meaning
of its verbal gesture. The underground man writes as if he
were thinking, but he thinks as if he were addressing others.
The other-directedness of his thought, far from being an
"empty form," is actually a form filled with significance:
shaping self-communion into a social posture, it suggests that
sincerity is no more available in a discourse addressed to the
self than it is in a discourse addressed to others. Since such
inner splits often attend autonomous monologues, pervading
them with forms of second-person address, *Notes from Underground* creates the impression of monologic presentation *despite* its presentation as a written document.

The underground man is not the only "I" who seems to be
talking to himself as he writes. Beckett's narrators—Molloy,
Moran, Malone—though they often mention working with
pencil and paper, also "sound" more like monologists than
like authors. For their ultimate successor, the Unnamable, the
origin of the text remains undecided, though it is discussed at
some length. His immobile position, "seated, my hands on
my knees," let alone his identity as "a big talking ball," offers
little promise for the scribal act. "How, in such conditions,
can I write, to consider only the manual aspect of that bitter
folly? I don't know." And yet, he asserts as a fact: "It is I who
write, who cannot raise my hand from my knee. It is I who
think, just enough to write, whose head is far."[13] We have
here a last, ironically twisted vestige of the traditional impera-
tive to motivate the connection between head and hand—in a
text that, in most other respects, abandons all semblance of
realistic motivation.

When a first-person text contains no evidence of writing activity or of fictional listeners present on the scene, and yet

adopts a distinct tone of oral colloquy, the narrative presentation itself becomes mysterious, is left—in Butor's phrase—"in the shadows."[14] Take Poe's story "The Tell-Tale Heart," which starts as follows: "True!—nervous—very, very dreadfully nervous I had been and am; but why *will* you say that I am mad?" [Poe's emphasis] Without overture, a listening "you" is addressed, who remains disincarnated to the end: is it a listener mutely present on the fictional scene? is it the reader? or is it an imaginary interlocutor, present only in the speaker's mind? Depending on the way we answer this question, we can interpret the story as a spoken, a written, or a silent discourse. As the teller proceeds with his tale of the old man's murder and its aftermath, no further clues are provided. The generic question cannot be answered, at least not on the basis of the narrative presentation alone. Many texts have analogous narrative presentations: a first person compulsively buttonholes a second person who seems to be simultaneously inside and outside the fictional scene, inside and outside the speaking self.[15]

This indeterminate narrative presentation is epitomized in Camus' novel *La Chute*. At first glance, this text seems to simulate spoken discourse: throughout the six installments its speaker—Jean-Baptiste Clamence by name—addresses an interlocutor whose presence we can discern by implication, by the replies Clamence makes to someone's inaudible questions and comments. It only gradually becomes clear that this ghostly listener is actually a mere sounding-board for the self, or rather—as the concluding paragraph reveals—a double, with an identical past, and therefore with an identical discourse to recite: "I knew all along that you and I were of the same species. Are we not all alike, constantly talking and to no one, forever up against the same questions although we know the answers in advance? So please tell me what happened to you one night. . . ."[16] What we get throughout this

* Je savais bien que nous étions de la même race. Ne sommes-nous pas tous semblables, parlant sans trêve et à personne, confrontés toujours aux mêmes questions bien que nous connaissions d'avance les réponses? Alors, racontez-moi, je vous prie, ce qui vous est arrivé un soir . . .

text, then, is a silent monologue posing as spoken interlocution, a perennial self-address disguised as a confession addressed to the Other. In this fashion, *La Chute* dramatizes the solipsistic process inherent in interior monologue: inner speaker communicating with inner listener. If, referring to Dujardin's classic definition of interior monologue, we ask whether we have here an "unarticulated discourse without a listener expressing a character's most intimate thoughts,"[17] we must answer: yes *and* no. The interiority of the discourse is latent, simultaneously hidden and revealed by the make-believe of the text.

Another text of this general confessional type, Dostoevsky's "A Gentle Creature," is particularly interesting for our purposes: subtitled "A Fantastic Story" it consists in its entirety of the self-address of a man alone in a room with the dead body of his wife. It differs from the works we have considered to this point, in that it overtly poses as a soliloquy spoken in solitude. Dostoevsky evidently felt that this form was so daring that it needed prefatory justification. The result is a revealing document in the history of narrative conventions. The preface begins by explaining the story's subtitle:

> I have given it the subtitle "A Fantastic Story" though I myself regard it as eminently real. But the fantastic is here really and precisely in the very form of the story, which I think it necessary to explain before starting on the story proper. The point is that this is neither a story, nor written notes.[18]

After stressing the psychological realism of his subject, pointing out that certain morbidly depressed people tend to "talk to themselves" at moments of mental stress, he returns again to the problem of presentation. His "fantastic" technique, he says, has a hypothetical analogue in "real life": the notes of an invisible stenographer, who would have recorded everything his protagonist said to himself.[19] Such a record, he admits, "might have been a little rougher, a little less finished than the way it is presented in my story, but the psychological sequence would have remained pretty much the same." In summation, he adds: "It is this suggestion of a stenographer taking everything down in shorthand (after which I should have polished what was noted) that I consider the fantastic element in the story."[20] In this fashion Dostoevsky is underlining the anomaly of a text in the first person that does away with all pretense of written notation or oral communication. The real presented in a "fantastic" (read "unreal") form: there could hardly be a better description for a convention to which the modern reader has become so accustomed that he no longer experiences it as "fantastic."[21]

As this preface also indicates, however, Dostoevsky did not draw the ultimate consequences from his unreal presentation for his story's temporal and linguistic structure. Had he done so, it indeed "might have been a little rougher, a little less finished." And one doubts that "the psychological sequence would have remained pretty much the same": despite its self-conscious annulment of a plausible narrative presentation, "A Gentle Creature" still very largely conforms to the norms of traditional first-person narration. Its speaker tells the story of his marriage from beginning to end, "just as it happened. In the right order."[22] Each consecutive episode fills a titled chapter ("I. Who Was I and Who Was She," "II. A Proposal of Marriage," etc.) and all the circumstances are painstakingly explained, as they need be explained only to strangers, not to the self. Aside from occasional interruptions—"I'm afraid I'm getting a little muddled"—the text draws attention to its present moment of locution only in its first and last paragraph:

> Well, while she is still here everything is all right: I go up and have a look at her every minute. But they will take her away tomorrow and—how can I stay here alone?

> Two o'clock in the morning. Her dear little boots stand by her little bed, as though waiting for her. . . . No, seriously, when they take her away tomorrow, what's to become of me? [Dostoevsky's ellipsis][23]

These symmetric references to the moment of locution surround the forty-page-long retrospective narration with a
frame of self-address without essentially affecting its structure
and language.

Published in 1876, more than a decade before *Les Lauriers*,
"A Gentle Creature" is both typologically and historically
astride autobiographical narration and interior monologue.
And it is entirely in keeping with this position that the story
was one of the texts most frequently mentioned in early controversies concerning the origin and nature of interior
monologue.[24] If one uses the unreal narrative presentation as
the sole criterion, one must agree with André Gide when he
insists that "Dostoevsky's unforgettable Krotkaya" is one of
the "unsurpassable incarnations of the interior monologue
genre."[25] But if one takes into account other criteria that differentiate monologue from narration—a-chronological presentation of past events, focus on the moment of locution, or
non-communicative language patterns—then Dostoevsky's
story must be viewed as one of the "intermediate formulas"
that Dujardin, without precisely defining them, mentions in
this connection.

Chronology and Memory

The combination of monologic presentation and chronologic
narration in "A Gentle Creature" is common to several of the
texts we have considered to this point: "The Tell-Tale
Heart," the second part ("A Propos of the Wet Snow") of
Notes from Underground, *La Chute*. In all these works a lone
speaker recalls his own past, and tells it to himself—in
chronological order. *Autobiographical monologues*, as I will call
texts of this type, create a highly stylized rhetorical effect,
since reciting one's own biography to oneself does not appear
psychologically plausible. Or rather, it appears plausible only
if the speaker pursues a definite aim with this recitation, an
aim of public confession, of self-justification. Despite the absence of listeners, the autobiographical monologue thus re-

tains the meaning of communication, or at least of rehearsal for communication. And this meaning becomes the more paradoxical, the more the muted isolation of the monologist is emphasized. The chronological self-account of the tongue-less missionary in Camus' "Renegade" is, in this respect, a particularly graphic example of the type. Addie's post mortem autobiography in Faulkner's *As I Lay Dying* is an even more spectacular instance, because here a conventional narrative is recited by a ghostly, disincarnated voice.

Note, however, that it is only their adherence to chronology that counteracts the illusion of an unrolling thought process in autobiographical monologues, not their focus on the past *per se*. Most monologues include memories of past experiences, and some—like the monologues in *The Sound and the Fury*—even exclude all else. But in genuine interior monologues the temporal sequence of past events yields to the temporal sequence of present remembrance, and the past is thereby radically dechronologized. Autobiographical monologues share with other autonomous monologues only one characteristic feature: the annulment of a realistic narrative presentation, a feature that is necessary, but not sufficient for creating the illusion of random thought on which the autonomous monologue depends.

Conversely, there are fictional texts that maintain a perfectly conventional narrative presentation but that follow an order determined not by biographical chronology but by associative memory: Ford's *Good Soldier*, Durell's *Justine*, Golding's *Free Fall*. Such a-chronological *memory narratives* approach autonomous monologues along a different route, at right angles to the approach of *autobiographical monologues*. Take Sammy Mountjoy, the narrator of *Free Fall*. He explicitly places himself in a writing situation, and even addresses future readers: "I am poised eighteen inches over the black rivets you are reading"; but at the same time he refuses on principle to let his scribal act chronologize his past, bent as he is on telling his life "in the way it presents itself to me, the only teller."[26] In the course of his narrative he gives some striking formulations to associative memory as a narrative principle: "memory, a sense of shuffle fold and coil, of that day nearer than that because more important, of that event mirroring this, or those three set apart, exceptional and out of the straight line altogether." Or: "[Man] is an incredible bundle of miscellaneous memories and feelings, of fossils and coral growths. I am not a man who was a boy looking at a tree. I am a man who remembers being a boy looking at a tree."[27] Yet, while this mnemonic principle de-chronologizes the sequence which the narrator follows in presenting the episodes from his past, taking some "out of the straight line altogether,"[28] these episodes themselves are narrated quite traditionally, with very little "shuffle fold and coil." Memory narratives, in other words, far more readily disrupt the temporal macro-structure than the temporal micro-structure of a text, revealing the tenacity of the link between realistic narrative presentation and chronological narrative sequence. As long as a narrator writes or speaks, he fashions a language based on communication: he presents, explains, links cause and effect—and thereby inevitably falls back on temporal order. The private associations that determine mnemonic thought-sequences only prevail in first-person forms when the fiction of written or oral communication gives way to the fiction of self-communion, i.e., when narrative chronology and narrative presentation are simultaneously abandoned.

This is precisely what happens in the special variant of the autonomous monologue where the monologist focuses exclusively on past experience. Such *memory monologues*, as I will call them, are typologically an exact cross between autobiographical monologues and memory narratives, combining the monologic presentation of the former with the mnemonic a-chronology of the latter. Their relationship to other retrospective first-person forms can be graphically schematized as follows:

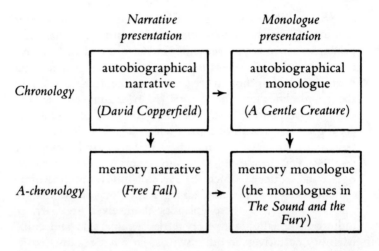

The contrast between conventional narration and memory monologue has been clearly drawn by Claude Simon in a comment on his novel *La Route des Flandres* (1960), one of the finest post-Faulknerian memory monologues: "In contrast to a chronicle where the facts are related in the sequence of their development, this author undertakes less . . . to tell a story than to describe the imprint left by it in a memory and a sensibility."[29] Note that the intent is also essentially mimetic here: "describe"; but the model is not autobiographical communication (telling one's story), it is the self-involvement of memory. And this imitation of a solipsistic process imposes not only a fractured chronology, but also a fragmentary coverage: "I do not fill in the blanks. They remain, like so many fragments," says Simon.[30] The only temporal continuity that memory monologues present is the continuity of the spontaneously remembering mind. Since in this variant of the autonomous monologue the mind is trained exclusively on the past, the remembered events are tied only to each other, and not to a chronologically evolving time-span of silent locution. In their temporal structure, therefore, memory monologues are not only freer than other retrospective fictions but also freer than autonomous monologues, which focus on simultaneous experience.[31] This accounts for their supremely difficult readability: Quentin's monologue is far more disjointed than Molly Bloom's, and *La Route des Flandres* is more tangled than most other monologic *nouveaux romans*.

Some of the structural and textual problems posed by Faulkner's and Simon's texts will be examined in my final chapter. But their position on the generic map of approaches from narration to monologue has become clear: As a retrospective form whose basic tense is the past, the memory monologue is the variant of the autonomous monologue that comes closest to autobiography, while at the same time creating the illusion of the "uninterrupted unrolling" of a thought process.

Before passing on to the aspects of narration that lead to monologues cast in the present tense, a quick backward glance at Proust will be instructive. Critics who have called *A la Recherche* "a soliloquy" or "an immense monologue"[32] have obviously applied these terms only in the most general sense in which they apply to all first-person narratives, and indeed to all written texts: in the sense of a discourse recorded in solitude. In this respect *A la Recherche* differs from other autobiographical novels only quantitatively. A more significant question is whether Proust's novel can be called a memory monologue, or rather—since its written presentation is never in question—a memory narrative: does Marcel present his remembered past in the temporal sequence of its emergence in memory?

As Genette has shown, the composition of the novel remains largely unaffected by the mnemonic processes of its writer-protagonist, with one notable exception: the first part of *Du Côté de chez Swann*, the section entitled "Combray."[33] Here the text shuttles repeatedly between Marcel's moments of remembrance and the remembered moments. But even this section of his novel, as Proust himself insisted, must not be read as "a kind of collection of memories linked according to the fortuitous laws of the association of ideas."[34] Indeed, in its overall structure "Combray" is not a memory narrative, but the narrative of two different moments from Marcel's past—the sleepless nights and the afternoon of the madeleine—in the course of which crucial memories emerge in his mind. The remembered childhood episodes therefore lie at a double retrospective remove from Marcel's text: the time that passed between remembrance and memory, and the time that passed between the moments of remembrance and their recording by Marcel the writer. Had Marcel recorded the Combray scenes at the moments when they impinged on his consciousness—during his sleepless nights or on the day he tasted the madeleine—his text would have conformed to the pattern of memory narrative. Instead, the crucial delay in Marcel's decision to write his work makes "Combray" into a double-layered narrative: the narrative of memory flashbacks that contain the childhood scenes. The episode of Marcel's disillusioning encounter with the Duchesse de Guermantes—which we examined earlier—is therefore a self-narration, set, together with many other remembered scenes, in a larger frame that is itself a self-narration: the mnemonic flashback triggered by the madeleine.

This memory structure, intricate as it is, has nothing to do with the a-chronology of memory narratives, and even less with the intricacies of memory monologues. Proust's macro-structure, like the micro-structure of his dissonant self-narration, maximizes the distance between the narrating and the experiencing selves, so that *A la Recherche* stands in every respect at the pole of first-person narration that is furthest removed from the autonomous monologue.

Discourse and Monologue

When Holden Caulfield (in Salinger's *Catcher in the Rye*) waits in a hotel room for his first "throw" with a prostitute, he gives the following explanation for his protracted virginity:

> The thing is, most of the time when you're coming pretty close to doing it with a girl—a girl that isn't a prostitute or anything, I mean—she keeps telling you to

stop. The trouble with me is, I stop. Most guys don't. I can't help it. . . . Anyway, I keep stopping. The trouble is, I get to feeling sorry for them. I mean most girls are so dumb and all. . . . You take a girl when she really gets passionate, she just hasn't any brains. I don't know. They tell me to stop, so I stop. I always wish I *hadn't*, after I take her home, but I keep doing it anyway.[35]

Taken out of context in this fashion, this passage might easily be taken for an excerpt from an interior monologue text. Its tense is the present, and it renders a speaker's highly subjective reflections. In fact, it is embedded in an autobiographical novel; past narration immediately precedes it: "I was starting to feel pretty sexy and all, but I was a little nervous"; more past narration immediately follows it: "Anyway, while I was putting on a clean shirt, I sort of figured this was my big chance, in a way." Holden's reflections on his difficulty with girls don't pass through his mind at the moment he is waiting in the hotel room, but at a time when he looks back on that nervous moment in the process of narrating it.

Though Holden's comments are uncommonly colloquial for an autobiographer, there is nothing uncommon or untraditional about the fact that he interrupts his narration with commentary, nor that his comments are cast in the present tense. Most retrospective narrators sooner or later tell their opinions as well as their lives, abandoning their past stories in favor of their present thoughts. And when they do, their basic grammar coincides with that of a monologist, no matter how well defined their narrative presentation or how traditional their narrative language. The more digressive a fictional autobiographer, the greater his likeness to a monologist. For this reason it has often been said that Tristram Shandy is an early ancestor of Molly Bloom—despite the fact that he is literature's most self-conscious autobiographer, and she literature's most harebrained monologist.

As the term digression implies, the present-tense discourse of the narrating self appears as a kind of illicit straying from the straight and narrow path of narration into a terrain that does not properly belong to it. Since it is also the terrain where the language of fictional autobiography overlaps most frequently with the language of autonomous monologue, its exploration is essential for the relationship between these two fictional genres.

A starting-point for surveying this generic borderland is provided by Emile Benvéniste's widely accepted distinction between the two linguistic modes of *discours* and *histoire*. Benvéniste defines *discours* as "every utterance assuming a speaker and a hearer, and in the speaker, the intention of influencing the other in some way."[36] The basic tense of *discours* is the present, but it can freely shift to past and future time (using past and future tense); its pronominal base is the first person, but it normally also contains second-person address and third-person references. In contrast to this purely expressive and subjective mode, the complementary *histoire* is a purely narrative and objective mode, characterized by the exclusive use of past tenses and third-person pronouns, and thus by the exclusion of all references to personal speakers or listeners: "No one speaks here; the events seem to narrate themselves."[37] In Benvéniste's system, accordingly, all texts that revolve around the person of the speaker—even when they are cast entirely in the narrative past tense—belong to the mode of *discours*, rather than to the mode of *histoire*.[38]

As Jean Starobinski has noted in an essay on autobiography, this absolute distinction, useful as it is in other respects, fails to account for the wide variations one finds within the autobiographical genre.[39] Even if we grant that the pronoun "I" introduces a discursive element into all statements made in its name, its language can range widely between relatively objective report and relatively subjective expression. Starobinski therefore suggests a modification of Benvéniste's dualistic system that would make it easier to apply to a typology of first-person forms. Noting that pure autobiography combines grammatical features belonging to both *histoire* and *discours* (most clearly in French, where it conjoins the first-person pronoun with the typical tense of narration, the past definite), he prefers to locate autobiography near the center of a sliding scale extended between the poles of third-person *histoire* and first-person *discours*. As autobiography becomes less purely narrative, it gravitates from this relatively objective mid-point to the pole of pure *discours*, which it reaches when the narration of past events gives way completely to the narrator's present thoughts. Significantly, Starobinski calls this limit point of autobiographical texts "monologic writing in its extremest forms," by which he means the articulation (within a written narrative) of the narrator's present thoughts. In this perspective, then, the expression of a narrator's present consciousness lies at one extreme of the autobiographical genre itself, at the point where *histoire* vanishes into pure *discours*, where—as Starobinski says—"the event is none other than the unrolling of the monologue itself, independently of the reported 'facts,' which become immaterial."[40]

This vanishing-point of the autobiographical genre is the precise starting-point for interior monologue as a fictional genre—a generic development that Starobinski does not consider, since he is concerned with real (historical) autobiography, and not with fictional first-person forms. Only fictional characters can be "heard" as they put thoughts into words without speaking them aloud or writing them down; or rather, they can be "overheard," for they address their discourse to no one, least of all to a reader.[41] In this respect the discourse of a monologist no longer conforms to Benvéniste's definition of *discours* as "every utterance assuming a speaker and a hearer," unless we extend this definition to include a hearer who is identical to the speaker.[42] But even as it drops its communicative dimension, interior discourse acquires a new, experiential dimension: it can now render live events that occur simultaneously with the locution. Though interior monologue is still pure *discours*, it no longer unrolls "independently of the reported 'facts,' which become immaterial" (Starobinski); for now, in the course of its unrolling, it "con-

veys to us what that personage is doing and what is happening to him" (Joyce). Events, in other words, re-enter the text,
but they re-enter by way of the present-tense discursive language itself, not (as in autobiography) through the past-tense
narrative language. The divergence between the discourse of
the autobiographer and the discourse of the monologist can
therefore be defined most accurately by the different uses they
make of their common tense.

The present tense, as most standard grammars explain, can
denote three different temporal ranges: the punctual or instant
present, which expresses momentary action (I pick up my
pen); the habitual or iterative present, which expresses repeated action (I always write with a pen); and the timeless or
gnomic present, which expresses generalizations or "eternal
truths" (the pen is mightier than the sword).
The timeless present is a tense that is common to autobiography and interior monologue, and therefore defines a zone of
overlap between the two genres. But since it is the tense of
impersonal statements—statements which exclude first- and
second-person pronouns—the timeless present is more characteristic for the essay or the philosophical treatise than for the
first-person genres. When Tristram, Marcel, and Molloy in-
dulge in extended generalizations about the nature of man,
life, or art, they do in fact become part-time essayists. A work
filled in its entirety by reflections flowing from the pen of a
fictional philosopher would define the exact generic boundary
between the first-person novel and the essay: Valéry attempted something of the sort in some of the *Monsieur Teste*
fragments, as did Gottfried Benn in his *Roman des Phänotyp*.
Similarly, an autonomous monologue could be imagined
whose speaker would be a fictional philosopher, a silent
Zarathustra who kept his improvised wisdom to himself. If
such a text existed—the closest approach to it is probably the
Goethe monologue in Thomas Mann's *Lotte in Weimar*—it
would in turn display the generic proximity between autonomous monologue and essay, an affinity Valéry Larbaud sug-

gested when he placed Dujardin's *Lauriers* in the literary descendance of Montaigne's *Essais*.[43] When we turn from theory to practice, however, the common overlap of first-person narratives and autonomous monologues with the essay is confined to those intermittent moments of timeless present from which both narrators and monologists quickly return to their base: the narrator to his punctual past, the monologist to his punctual present.

In its punctual form the present tense is peculiar to the autonomous monologue. Here is a sample from Dujardin's *Les Lauriers sont coupés*:

> I swing round hastily, seize the windows, push them, slam them to. . . . Nothing! . . . The window's shut. . . . And the curtains? I draw them, there. . . . And night is blotted out. [Dujardin's ellipses][44]

A passage of this kind can occur only in a text that synchronizes verbalization with action or experience, a text like *Les Lauriers* that renders, in Mallarmé's famous phrases, "the daily events so precious to seize" ("le quotidien si précieux à saisir"), "the instant taken at the throat" ("l'instant pris à la gorge").[45] An autobiographical narrator's punctual present, by contrast, is void of all experience, save that of authorship itself. Strictly speaking, a narrator can therefore use the present tense in its punctual meaning solely when he becomes involved in his immediate professional concerns, as Tristram Shandy so frequently does:

> *Chapter 23*
> I have a strong propensity in me to begin this chapter very nonsensically, and I will not balk my fancy. —Accordingly I set off thus: . . .

Tristram here does what he says, writes about what he is writing. In this involuted form of discourse—Michel Foucault has

---

* précipitamment, je me retourne, je saisis les croisées, je les pousse, je les ferme, précipitamment . . . Rien . . . La fenêtre est fermée . . . Et les ridaux? je les tire, voilà . . . La nuit est supprimée. [Dujardin's ellipses]

called it "the discourse linked to the act of writing, simultaneous with its unrolling, and enclosed within it"[46]—the grammar of an autobiographical text momentarily becomes identical to the grammar of an autonomous monologue; but its content refers to the one realm that never enters a monologist's mind at all: his own verbal performance.

The variety of present tense that creates the zone of greatest ambiguity between narration and monologue is the habitual present, the tense in which narrators describe their present moods and circumstances. It is especially frequent in autobiographical novels that stress the polarity between the narrating and the experiencing self, as Beckett's Molloy does quite explicitly when he says: "from time to time I shall recall my present existence, compared to which this [his narrated past] is a nursery tale."[47] These digressive "recalls" punctuate the text, sometimes filling it with long present-tense passages: "But now I do not wander any more, anywhere any more, and indeed I scarcely stir at all, and yet nothing is changed. And the confines of my room, of my bed, of my body, are as remote from me as were those of my region, in the days of my splendour."[48] This passage continues for a page or so, detailing the relationship existing between Molloy and his limbs. Here we observe a present tense which, in difference to the timeless present, refers directly to the narrating "I," so that its grammar is identical to the basic grammar of autonomous monologues. The difference with the punctual present is merely the duration of the state or repetition of the actions described. Every one of these statements contains or implies the adverbs *always, sometimes, never,* or *when* in the sense of *whenever*: "And when I see my hands. . . . And with my feet it's the same, sometimes, when I see them at the foot of my bed. . . . I do not bring them back to me, when they become my feet again. . . ."

With Molloy we always eventually reach an "end of recall" as his "pensum"—the narration of his past—again reclaims him. And this eventual return to his main business is the rule that even a highly digressive narrator will normally follow. There exists a small group of texts, however, cast almost entirely in this iterative-durative present tense: *Malone Dies* and *The Unnamable* (in their first-person sections), the first part of *Notes from Underground*, Sarraute's *Martereau*, several Kafka stories ("The Burrow," "A Little Woman," "A Crossbreed") and Chekhov's significantly entitled "A Boring Story." Closer to self-portraiture than to autobiography, they render abiding, almost inert conditions of the self and its world, in which the present becomes a kind of dead and deadly time, eternal in the worst sense of the word. Here is the sickly young nephew of *Martereau* exploring his relationship to the "normal" members of his family:

> No, there is no way of defending oneself against them, no way of resisting them—they are too overpowering. There would of course be one way for me, a heroic, desperate way, the one used by people who know that they have nothing more to lose. That would be to let myself go completely, to give up everything, release all my brakes, and shout at them that I am no fool. . . .
>
> But I shall never dare. Nobody ever dares to do such a thing. They know that, and can therefore rest easy.[49]

Beginning and ending in durative present, passing through hopeless conditional and negative future, the tenses of this passage shape the stagnancy of its speaker's predicament. Before long, he finds the appropriate imagery for his existence: "turning in circles round himself, a stupid dog that bites its own tail, a ludicrous dervish."[50] The figure of the vicious circle inevitably recurs in texts predominantly cast in the durative present, the tense in which one takes stock of one's

* Non, il n'y a pas moyen de se défendre contre eux, de leur résister—ils sont trop forts. Il y aurait bien un moyen pour moi, héroïque, désespéré, le moyen de ceux qui savent qu'ils n'ont plus rien à perdre. Ce serait de me laisser aller complètement, de tout lâcher, tous les freins, de leur crier que je ne suis pas dupe . . .

Mais je n'oserai jamais. Personne jamais n'ose cela. Ils le savent et sont bien tranquilles.

* tournant sur lui-même, chien stupide qui se mord la queue, derviche grotesque.

circumstances: Kafka's animal of his circular burrow, the Unnamable of his orbital void, Chekhov's professor of his implacable daily round.

The speakers of these durative discourses launch their recitations with deliberation, aiming at sweeping surveys of their status quo. They try, without always succeeding, to repress random thoughts that may disturb their compulsively systematic inventories. What Malone says of himself applies to them all: "Did I say I only say a small proportion of the things that come into my head? I must have. I choose those that seem somehow akin."[51] This tendency to "choose" is what differentiates these discourses from the ostensibly unsifted thoughts of monologists. It builds an order that may be regarded as a kind of synchronic counterpart to the diachronic order of autobiographical narration. Accordingly, when durative discourses are uttered in solitude, they give rise to the same kind of incongruity as autobiographical monologues: the guided tour Kafka's lone animal gives itself through the burrow it built to shelter its solitude is no less paradoxical than the chronological account of Camus' tongueless "Renegade." Both speak a language that is organized for communication, explication, or confession, but that remains immured in the speaker's head. In this respect the durative type of monologue relates to the autonomous monologue in a manner that is analogous to the way autobiographical monologues relate to memory monologues.

A different problem arises when, as sometimes happens within this type of text, the survey of present circumstances leads to exemplification: for then their durative-iterative present begins to modulate to a punctual present. The professor in Chekhov's "Boring Story," for example, as he takes us through his daily routine, starts each new phase of his account in the iterative mode:

> After the lecture I work at home. I read periodicals and
> dissertations, prepare for my next lecture, and some-

times write something. My work is constantly interrupted, for I have to receive visitors.
    The door bell rings.[52]

With this ringing of the doorbell we are no longer securely in
the realm of the "always." And presently, as a relay of visitors enter and depart—an importunate colleague, a student
who has failed his exam, another who requests a dissertation
topic—a series of vignettes passes before our eyes: the visitors' habits of speech are characterized, conversations develop on specific subjects, the professor loses his temper, and
so forth.[53] The implication is that these scenes all stand for a
hundred similar ones, that they reflect the tedium of a life in
which nothing new ever happens. And yet they take on,
willy-nilly, the appearance of singular happenings, the meaning of their present tense shifting imperceptibly from durative
to punctual. But this in turn creates the impression that the
professor speaks to himself *while* he suffers through these
scenes, that language and experience have become syn-
chronized.

    In Chekhov's text these paradigmatic scenes always return
to their iterative base before long, so that the reader again
recognizes that he is listening to a man recording his boring
routine, and not to a monologist thinking while he goes
through live experiences. Something different happens in
Kafka's "Burrow" when the animal—midway through the
story—seems to "forget" the iterative nature of his account,
and begins to tell of a momentous event that radically alters
the circumstances prevailing before its occurrence: the appearance of the hissing sound signaling the approach of a
mortal enemy. Up to this point the animal has described his
habitual subterranean existence in durative-iterative present
tense, stressing especially its blissful silence:

    But the most beautiful thing about my burrow is the
    stillness. Of course, that is deceptive. Suddenly it may be
    interrupted and all is at an end. For the time being, how-

ever, it is still with me. For hours I can stroll through my
passages and hear nothing except sometimes the rustling
of some little creature, which I immediately reduce to silence between my teeth, or the pattering of soil, which
draws my attention to the need for some repair or other;
otherwise all is still. The air of the forest floats in, the
place is both warm and cool.[54]

The event that will destroy this idyllic state has not yet occurred at the time these words are spoken: stillness reigns in
the burrow, the durative stillness that is its *raison d'être*, and
whose disruption would spell the end of "all": "Suddenly it
may be interrupted and all is at an end." Gradually this durative state and the durative tense that describes it modulate to
the iterative mode as the animal recounts his periodic excursions into the outside world: "After such times I make it a
practice . . . to leave it [the burrow] frequently, though only
for short periods of time."[55] There follows an extended description of these trips into the open, the hazards of re-entry,
and the ecstasy of the reunion with the burrow. It is after the
deep sleep that always follows the return that the singulative
catastrophe occurs: "I am awakened as the last sleep dissolves
of itself, my sleep must already be very light, for it is a barely
audible hissing that wakes me."[56]

Now if this hissing eventually subsided, or turned out to be
a passing illusion, this sentence could still be understood as
the description of a recurring experience, which will give way

* Das schönste an meinem Bau ist aber seine Stille. Freilich, sie ist
trügerisch. Plötzlich einmal kann sie unterbrochen werden und alles ist zu
Ende. Vorläufig aber ist sie noch da. Stundenlang kann ich durch meine
Gänge schleichen und höre nichts als manchmal das Rascheln irgend eines
Kleintieres, das ich dann gleich auch zwischen meinen Zähnen zur Ruhe
bringe, oder das Rieseln der Erde, das mir die Notwendigkeit irgend einer
Ausbesserung anzeigt; sonst ist es still. Die Waldluft weht herein, es ist
gleichzeitig warm und kühl.

* Nach solchen Zeiten pflege ich . . . ihn öfters, wenn auch nur für kürzere
Zeit zu verlassen.

* Erst aus dem letzten von selbst sich auflösenden Schlaf werde ich
geweckt, der Schlaf muss nun schon sehr leicht sein, denn ein an sich kaum
hörbares Zischen weckt mich.

again to the habitual peace of the burrow and return the text
to its iterative base. But quite the contrary happens: the hissing sound continues, becomes a terrifying fact of life, and
drags the burrow "into the clamor of the world and its
perils."[57] The static time of the first part of the story now
becomes an evolving time, its durative tense a punctual tense,
as the frenetic animal adopts and rejects various hypotheses
about the origin of the hissing sound. Ultimately the convic-
tion grows that a hostile animal progressively encircles him
and will engage him in a mortal combat. The animal's reflections, and Kafka's story, remain unfinished, suspended in
mid-sentence. The speaker who surveyed his sovereign realm
in durative present tense has been transformed into a monologist who simultaneously experiences bewildering events,
and articulates them in punctual present tense.

Though a number of interpreters of "The Burrow" have
noted the shift in the meaning of its present tense,[58] they have
never fully faced its implication: that it gives this story an illogical temporal structure. But this structure corresponds
exactly to Kafka's paradoxical conception of human time,
which is based on a denial of the distinction between repeti-
tious and singular events. For him, as he once affirmed
aphoristically, "the decisive moment of human development
is everlasting." "The Burrow," by exploiting the ambiguities
of a discourse cast in the present tense, reflects this paradox in
its language as well as its meaning. If the crucial events of life
happen not once, but everlastingly, then the distinction between durative and singulative modes of discourse is effaced:
the durative silence always already contains the hissing sound,
and the destruction it brings lies not in a single future moment, but in a constantly repeated present. The time structure
of Kafka's story is therefore quite as surreal as its protagonist
and his narrative presentation.

It is only when an author breaks the norms of realistic
time-structure in this fashion (whether inadvertently or by
design) that a discourse that initially locks a speaker into a

* in den Lärm der Welt und ihrer Gefahren.

static time frame can "become" a discourse that evolves in time, conveying in the manner of an autonomous monologue "what that personage is doing and what is happening to him." The temporal incongruity of Kafka's "Burrow," in short, lays bare the fine line that normally separates a text cast in durative present tense from an interior monologue text.

Evocation and Synchronization

In the last section, I traced the paths leading from the *narrating* self to the autonomous monologue. The present tense in these texts was always a "true" tense; it referred to a temporal moment that coincided with (or at least included) the moment of its utterance. We have yet to consider the generic approach to the autonomous monologue that springs not from the narrating but from the *experiencing* self. Here again it is the present tense that shapes the connecting link; this time, however, it functions not as a "true" but as a metaphorical tense, working that peculiar grammatical make-believe termed historical, or narrative present. In this tense, as one grammarian puts it, "the speaker, as it were, forgets all about time and recalls what he is recounting as vividly as if it were before his eyes."[59] This "evocative" present—as I prefer to call the narrative present in a first-person context[60]—though it must logically refer to a past experience, momentarily creates an illusory ("as if") coincidence of two time-levels, literally "evoking" the narrated moment at the moment of narration. And this apparent synchronization then makes the language of the text look identical to the "real" synchronization of an autonomous monologue text.

As long as evocative-present passages remain comparatively brief, and as long as they merely report experienced events and sensations, the reader is not in danger of getting caught in the illusion: the deceptive "as-if-ness" of their present tense can be easily recognized, especially when a narrator draws attention himself to the evocative nature of this tense. "If the funeral had been yesterday, I could not recollect it bet-

ter," says David Copperfield before proceeding to narrate his
mother's funeral in the present tense, as though it took place
"before his eyes":

> We stand around the grave. The day seems different to
> me from every other day, and the light not of the same
> colour—of a sadder colour. Now there is a solemn hush,
> which we have brought from home with what is resting
> in the mould, and while we stand bare-headed, I hear the
> voice of the clergyman, sounding remote in the open
> air, . . .[61]

At the conclusion of this episode the narrator further em-
phasizes its presentness (as well as its timelessness) by a telling
spatial metaphor: "Events of a later day have floated from me
to the shore where all forgotten things reappear, but this
stands like a high rock in the ocean." Literally casting the
memorable moment into high relief, this rock image epitomizes the meaning of the evocative present tense.

But when such evocations are less dramatic, and less self-
conscious, when they lengthen to the point of making the
reader forget their retrospective starting-point, and especially
when they begin to intermingle a speaker's past thoughts
with his past experiences, even texts that start out as explicitly
retrospective accounts can suddenly become temporally and
generically ambiguous. Once again, this process can be best
observed in a Kafka text.

"A Country Doctor" starts as a traditional autobiographical story: "I was in great perplexity: I had to start on an urgent
journey; a seriously ill patient was waiting for me in a village
ten miles off."[62] Here a narrator relates a past experience by
using the customary past tense. He tells of his horseless plight
and of the inexplicable emergence of groom and horses from
the pigsty, to his own and his servant Rosa's surprise and de-

---

* Ich war in grosser Verlegenheit: eine dringende Reise stand mir bevor;
ein Schwerkranker wartete auf mich in einem zehn Meilen entfernten
Dorfe; . . .

light. But before long (at the beginning of the second page of
the text), the tense changes to the present in mid-sentence:
" 'Help him,' I said, and the willing girl hurried to hand the
harness to the groom. Yet hardly was she near him, when the
groom *grabs* hold of her and *hits* his face against hers. She
screams, and flees back to me." (I italicize the shift to the
present). For the next five pages, the present tense is used continuously; we hear about the country doctor's unwilling de-
parture from home, about his instantaneous journey to the
house of his patient, about the eventful and contradictory
bedside visit, which ends with the conversation (quoted in direct discourse) between doctor and patient, and the former's
word of honor concerning the distinction of the condemned
boy's wound: " 'It is really so, take the word of honor of a
community doctor with you to the other side.' " In the next
sentence, the text returns to the past tense of the beginning of
the story: "And he took it and was still. But now it was time
to think of my rescue." The doctor's intended return-rescue,
frustrated by the slow motion of the horses ("slowly, like old
men, we traversed the snowy wastes"), continues into infinite time, and the story ends by returning to the present tense,
now no longer narrating events, but describing a wretchedly
stationary and eternally present condition: "Never shall I
reach home at this rate. . . . Naked, exposed to the frost of
this most unhappy of ages, with an earthly carriage, unearthly
horses, I wander about, old man that I am. . . . Betrayed! Betrayed! A false ringing of the night bell once answered—it can
never be made good." In sum, a long present-tense passage

---

   * 'Hilf ihm,' sagte ich, und das willige Mädchen eilte, dem Knecht das
Geschirr des Wagens zu reichen. Doch kaum war es bei ihm, *umfasst* es der
Knecht und *schlägt* sein Gesicht an ihres. Es schreit auf und flüchtet sich zu
mir; . . . [my emphasis]
   * "Es ist wirklich so, nimm das Ehrenwort eines Amtarztes mit hinüber."
Und er nahm's und wurde still. Aber jetzt war es Zeit an meine Rettung zu
denken.
   * langsam, wie alte Männer, zogen wir durch die Schneewüste; . . .
   * Niemals komme ich so nach Hause; . . . Nackt, dem Froste dieses un-
glückseligsten Zeitalters ausgesetzt, mit irdischem Wagen, unirdischen Pfer-
den, treibe ich mich alter Mann umher. . . . Betrogen! Betrogen! Einmal dem
Fehlläuten der Nachtglocke gefolgt—es ist niemals gutzumachen.

framed by two much briefer past-tense passages forms the body of the story; a brief present-tense passage forms the epilogue.

Since the grammatical present at the end of "A Country Doctor" signifies the present moment of narration from which the narrator views his past experiences in retrospect, there can be no doubt that the long present-tense section in the body of the story must be understood as an evocative present. When the grammatical present first sets in, it imperceptibly continues the narration, clearly separating the speaker's thoughts from his report by quoting them explicitly: " 'Yes,' I think blasphemously, 'in cases like this the Gods are helpful.' " But before long the evocative narration becomes increasingly interlaced with what can only be the narrator's past thoughts. Here is the passage where the doctor, having discovered the patient's wound, begins to scrutinize it closely:

> But on a closer inspection there is another complication. *Who can look at this without whistling softly?* Worms, as thick and as long as my little finger, themselves rose-red and blood-spotted as well, are wriggling from their fastness in the interior of the wound towards the light, with small white heads and many little legs. *Poor boy, you are past helping. I have discovered your great wound; this flower in your side is your undoing.* The family is happy, they see me busying myself; the sister tells the mother, the mother the father, the father tells several guests who are coming in, through the moonlight at the open door, walking on tiptoe, keeping their balance with outstretched arms. "Will you save me?" whispers the boy with a sob, quite blinded by the life within his wound. *That is what people are like in my district. Always expecting the impossible from the doctor. They have lost their ancient beliefs; the parson sits at home and unravels his vestments, one after another; but the doctor is supposed to be omnipotent with his merciful surgeon's hand. Well, please yourselves; I have not thrust my services on you; if you misuse me for sacred ends, I let that happen to me*

*too; what better do I want, old country doctor that I am, bereft
of my servant girl!* And so they come, the family and the
village elders, and strip my clothes off me; . . .[63]

I have italicized the sentences I take to be the doctor's self-
quoted monologues. But their quotation remains unsignaled,
and since no change of person or tense sets them off from the
narrative sentences, monologue and narration become fused.
The past thoughts can now be recognized in the narrative
context merely by their emotive, exclamatory syntax: by the
same signs, in other words, that allow us to identify narrated
monologues in a past-tense narration. This analogy is readily
verified by transposing our passage into the past. Its beginning and ending would then read as follows:

> But on closer inspection there was another complication.
> *Who could look at this without whistling softly?* . . .

> *what better did I want, old country doctor that I was, bereft of
> my servant girl!* And so they came, the family and the vil-
> lage elders, and stripped my clothes off me; . . .

It becomes apparent at this point that the symbiosis Kafka
achieves between narrative report and self-quoted monologue
in the central section of "A Country Doctor" is a present-

★ In der Nähe zeigt sich noch eine Erschwerung. *Wer kann das ansehen, ohne
leise zu pfeifen?* Würmer, an Stärke und Länge meinem kleinen Finger gleich,
rosig aus eigenem, und ausserdem blutbespritzt, winden sich, im Innern der
Wunde festgehalten, mit weissen Köpfchen, mit vielen Beinchen ans Licht.
*Armer Junge, dir ist nicht zu helfen. Ich habe deine grosse Wunde aufgefunden; an
dieser Blume in deiner Seite gehst du zugrunde.* Die Familie ist glücklich, sie sieht
mich in Tätigkeit; die Schwester sagt's der Mutter, die Mutter dem Vater,
der Vater einigen Gästen, die auf den Fusspitzen, mit ausgestreckten Armen
balancierend, durch den Mondschein der offenen Tür hereinkommen. "Wirst
du mich retten?" flüstert schluchzend der Junge, ganz geblendet durch das
Leben in seiner Wunde. *So sind die Leute in meiner Gegend. Immer das unmög-
liche vom Arzt verlangen. Den alten Glauben haben sie verloren; der Pfarrer sitzt zu
Hause und zerzupft die Messgewänder, eines nach dem andern; aber der Arzt soll
alles leisten, mit seiner zarten chirurgischen Hand. Nun, wie es beliebt: ich habe mich
nicht angeboten; verbraucht ihr mich zu heiligen Zwecken, lasse ich auch das mit mir
geschehen; was will ich Besseres, alter Landarzt, meines Dienstmädchens beraubt!*
Und sie kommen, die Familie und die Dorfältesten, und entkleiden mich . . .
[my emphasis]

tense analogue to the symbiosis we find when self-narrated monologues are employed in past-tense narration. But Kafka achieves this symbiosis by a contrary method: not by transposing quoted monologue sentences into the narrative tense (the past), but by transposing narrative sentences into the monologue tense (the present). Rather than integrating quoted monologue into narration, he has integrated narration into quoted monologue; or, to put it a different way, instead of narrating the country doctor's monologue, Kafka "monologizes" the country doctor's narration. He thereby arrives at exactly the language peculiar to an autonomous monologue, the genre in which all events are translated into the interior language of a perceiving consciousness.

Generically, what we see here is a monologue in process of emerging out of introspective narration, as the past thoughts of an experiencing self very nearly engulf the events that give rise to them, and to the retrospective narration itself. But this process is arrested the moment the text reverts to its original retrospective frame: the past tense out of which (and into which) the monologic present tense grows forces us to understand it as a stylistic transposition in which events that are known to be past are merely told *as if* they were present.[64]

A text that moves even closer to the autonomous monologue along this line is a story by the Russian Naturalist writer Garshin, entitled "Four Days" (1887). A first reading of this story creates the certain impression that it is an autonomous monologue—until this impression is canceled in its last sentence. It tells of a wounded soldier who lies for four days alone on a battlefield. The soldier seems to verbalize his thoughts and sensations, to describe his gestures and surroundings in a simultaneous, evolving, present tense. The following sample is typical:

> I try to raise myself into a sitting position. It is difficult when both legs are shot through. Several times I almost give it up in despair, but at last, with tears in my eyes from the awful pain, I succeed.

Above me—a scrap of black-blue sky in which a big
star is burning and several smaller ones. Around me
something dark and tall—bushes! I am amongst the
bushes! They have missed me! I feel how the very roots
of my hair move. . . .[65]

and so on for about thirteen pages. But then comes the surprise ending: not a surprise turn of the story's plot, but of its
form. The soldier, finally rescued by his company, loses consciousness, only to awaken in a hospital, as a doctor leans
over him. Then the text ends with the sentence: "I am able to
talk, and tell him all that I have written here."[66] If we view
the story in retrospect from this conclusion, it now no longer
appears as an autonomous monologue, but as a retrospective
narrative cast entirely in an evocative present tense. In sum: a
make-believe interior monologue, which gives away its
sleight of hand only when its last sentence closes a sentence-
thin frame of retrospection—which was never opened.[67]

With Garshin's story we have again reached a typological
limit case, not unlike the case of Dostoevsky's "Gentle Creature" (which was published the same year), but diametrically
opposed to it: whereas Dostoevsky uses a traditional language
and temporal structure, but frames it in a monologic presentation, Garshin uses a monologic language and temporal structure, but frames it in a traditional narrative presentation. Not
surprisingly, then, "Four Days" has likewise been a popular
candidate for the position of "first interior monologue."[68]

No matter how diverse the first-person texts we have considered to this point, all have had one point in common: the
narrator has stood at the live center of his narration, whether
his introspective focus was on his present or on his past self.
In a well-known obverse type, the "I-as-witness" type, the
narrator focuses on others, or acts as memorialist for a collective experience, and as long as it is cast in the past tense this
type of first-person narration remains far removed from an interior monologue text. But as soon as the focus shifts from

completed past to ongoing present, the synchronization of language and reported events is a ground common to this reportive type of text and interior monologue texts.

The sections given over to Darl, the most loquacious of the Bundren brothers in Faulkner's *As I Lay Dying*, are among the most consistent examples of this type.[69] Darl tells what he sees, hears, does, and says in the episodes of the funeral journey, but never what he thinks or feels. This is one reason that, contrary to the other members of the family, he remains such an enigmatic figure; it is also why his ultimate lapse into insanity carries such great shock-value. The section in which he tells of the river crossing is typical; this is how it starts:

> Before us the thick dark current runs. It talks up to us in a murmur become ceaseless and myriad, the yellow surface dimpled monstrously into fading swirls travelling along the surface for an instant, silent, impermanent and profoundly significant. . . .[70]

This present is descriptive, detailing a natural scene in poetic style, as in a landscape poem. Before long figures appear in the landscape, including the self.

> Cash and I sit in the wagon; Jewel sits the horse at the off rear wheel. . . . He sits erect, poised, looking quietly and steadily and quickly this way and that, his face calm, a little pale, alert. Cash's face is also gravely composed; . . .[71]

This still picture, minutely and objectively rendered, now gives way to equally minute reproduction of dialogue, intermingled with exact descriptions of gestures, looks, and inflections. There follows another description of the river, with the family and animals immobile, poised for the crossing. Now, as the action begins to develop, Darl's style begins to sound like that of a radio-reporter giving a blow-by-blow account of the action developing in front of his eyes:

> Jewel shouts at the horse; again he appears to lift it bodily

between his knees. He is just above the top of the ford
and the horse has a purchase of some sort for it surges
forward, shining wetly half out of water, crashing on in a
succession of lunges. It moves unbelievably fast; . . .[72]

Note the impassiveness of the report: no exclamations, generalizations, or questions—the entire emotive rhetoric of
inner discourse is missing, as though the reflective and affec-
tive components of the mind had been bracketed, leaving
only its aptitude for instant perception.

Darl's total removal of affect makes one hesitate to call this
text an interior monologue. Should his language even be understood as simultaneous with the events he describes? Is it
not rather a retrospective narration in evocative present tense?
Translated into the past, it yields, at any rate, a straightfor-
ward report of events. And there is even a clue in the river-
crossing scene that tips the balance in favor of this evocative-
present interpretation: the single italicized paragraph in this
section, which is cast in the past tense.[73] Coming as it does at
the climax of the episode—when the floating log surges up in
the river and very nearly causes disaster—it seems as though
Faulkner had deliberately reversed the customary tense pattern: the past tense appears at the unforgettable moment in an
episode narrated in the present tense throughout.[74]

Faulkner's generally inconsistent narrative patterns make it
impossible to answer with certainty the questions raised by
this text. When one finds similar experiments in the tech-
nique-oriented New Novelists in France, one is assured that
they purposefully exploit the ambiguities of present-tense
narration.[75] The best-known case is Robbe-Grillet's novel *La
Jalousie*, which has been interpreted alternately as an extreme
example of objective, dehumanized narration, and as the obsessive interior monologue of a jealous husband. This novel
carries Faulkner's removal of affect from a present-tense text
one step further: it removes the first-person pronoun as well.
The speaker of *La Jalousie* is literally conspicuous only for his
absence, a narrator "en creux," as Robbe-Grillet himself
called him. That the voice which generates the text must be-

long to *somebody* (other than merely a neutral narrator) becomes clear only by extrapolation: the changing angles of vision and spatial distances, the obsessive repetitions of language and scene, insistently prompt the reader to postulate a human eye (and "I") behind the voice—not just a camera eye.[76] But since the jealous "I" remains behind the scene, his monologue remains unhinged, and Robbe-Grillet's text presents itself as a third-person narration.

Genuine interior monologue lies to the other side of Darl's synchronous report, and some of Darl's relatives in *As I Lay Dying* show the closeness of this relationship. The discourse of his father and siblings, by merely adding the subjective ingredients missing from Darl's discourse, clearly create the illusion of mental self-address. Anse thinks:

> Durn that road. And it fixing to rain, too. I can stand here and same as see it with second-sight, a-shutting down behind them like a wall, shutting down betwixt them and my given promise. I do the best I can, much as I can get my mind on anything, but durn them boys.

And Vardaman:

> The trees look like chickens when they ruffle out into the cool dust on the hot days. If I jump off the porch I will be where the fish was, and it all cut up into not-fish now. I can hear the bed and her face and them and I can feel the floor shake when he walks on it that came and did it. That came and did it when she was all right but he came and did it.[77]

These speeches too describe scenes and happenings, but one would never be tempted to understand them as evocative past narratives. Transposing their tenses yields nothing but self-narrated monologues. Anse's and Vardaman's language is charged with all the elements linguists associate with the emotive-expressive function of language, the function that focuses on the speaker and on his attitude toward his subject: exclamations, interjections, repetitions, hesitations, elisions—not to mention the dialect idioms and the fantastic visions.

The contrast between Darl's language and the language of Vardaman or Anse points up the relationship between the reporter and the interior monologist: both share the concurrence of language and experience, but their language gestures are poles apart. The reporter acts as a neutral medium verbalizing events for others, not present on the scene. The monologist reacts as a subjective psyche communicating with itself about events it perceives and therefore needs not verbalize. Simple reportive language therefore threatens the credibility of interior-monologue fiction, and the best craftsmen of the genre tend to avoid it. In "Penelope," as we will see, the language is so thoroughly emotive that it is hard to find a single declarative sentence in the entire text.

Diary and Continuity

"One step beyond the 'personal diary' and the 'interior monologue' appears," says Larbaud, as he traces the ancestry of Dujardin's novel.[78] Richard Ellmann concurs when he sees the diary at the end of Joyce's *Portrait of the Artist* as an important stepping-stone in Joyce's evolution: "Having gone so far, Joyce in *Ulysses* boldly eliminated the journal, and let thoughts hop, step, jump, and glide without the self-consciousness of a journal to account for their agitation."[79]

There are many reasons why the fictional diary is a close relative—and an important ancestor—of the autonomous monologue. For one thing, the two forms share the fiction of privacy: diarists ostensibly write, as monologists speak, only for themselves. Neither has any use for overt exposition: the fiction of privacy collapses the moment either one of them explains his existential circumstances to himself in the manner of an autobiographer addressing future readers (or an oral narrator a listener). For the same reason, a diarist's past history normally emerges in the order it presents itself to his memory: fragmented and allusive, rather than continuous and explicit. Diary novels that focus extensively on the past (like Rilke's *Malte Laurids Brigge*) may therefore more closely resemble memory monologues than retrospective memory narratives written in one sitting.

But the diary is also traditionally the first-person form that lends itself most naturally to a focus on the *present* moment: since a diarist's moment of narration progresses in time, he has to tell his inner and outer condition anew every time he picks up his pen for a new installment, as a monologist is continuously verbalizing his changing condition in his mind. Note, however, that in another respect the diarist has not progressed beyond the autobiographer: he is still in the same position—sitting at his desk, pen in hand. He can therefore never record instant happenings at the instant they happen, at least not without breaking the mimetic norms of his genre. When Richardson says in his prefaces that his epistolary form achieves "*instantaneous* descriptions and reflections," "immediate impression of every circumstance," or "writing to the minute," these words can hardly be taken literally.[80] Logically, there is always an interval between each episode and its recording. The nearest Clarissa comes to true immediacy is when she describes in the present tense what happens in the time zone that surrounds her epistolary activity: "All is in a hurry below-stairs. Betty is in and out like a spy. Something is working, I know not what. I am really a good deal disordered in body as well as in mind. Indeed I am quite heartsick."[81] Despite the employment of the present tense Clarissa here covers a time-span that extends beyond the writing moment. Even when she refers to her own writing activity she refers it to the immediate past: "You will not wonder to see this narrative so dismally scrawled. It is owing to different pens and ink, all bad, and written by snatches of time; my hand trembling too with fatigue and grief."[82] It is interesting to note, however, that contemporary parodies of Richardson approach "writing to the minute" more literally, overstepping a boundary the original merely skirts. William Shenstone in his *Letters* comes quite as close as Beckett's Malone to

writing at length about his sole contemporary activity: "So I
sat down and wrote thus far: scrattle, scrattle, goes the
pen—why, how now? says I—what's the matter with the
pen? . . ."[83] And in Fielding's *Shamela*, a character writes
while he is doing something else: "Mrs. Jervis and I are just in
bed, and the door unlocked; if my master should come—
Ods-bobs! I hear him just coming in at the door. You see I
write in the present tense, as Parson William says. Well, he is
in bed between us. . . ."[84] This "present tense" actually resembles the less successful passages of *Les Lauriers sont coupés*
and other action-oriented autonomous monologue texts
somewhat more than poor Pamela's most nervous letters.

A more serious—though sometimes inadvertently comic
—attempt to synchronize narration and experience is found in
fictional diaries with closely spaced entries, where the diarist
shuttles back and forth at breakneck speed between the great
outdoors, the drawing room, or the bed, and his writing
desk. This rhythm becomes existentially meaningful in
diaries that record the progression toward an imminent death.
An interesting example is Victor Hugo's novel *Le dernier
Jour d'un condamné*, a work to which Dostoevsky alludes ad-
miringly in the previously discussed preface to "A Gentle
Creature." One must agree with him when he calls Hugo's
narrative form "an even greater improbability" than his own
hypothetical stenographer, since it assumes "that a man sen-
tenced to death is able (and has the time) to keep a diary not
only on his last day, but during his last hour and, literally, his
last minute."[85] It is more improbable, we might add, precisely on account of its adherence to the realistic norms of the
fictional diary: presented by an editor as a "bundle of yellow
pages," it contains no fewer than forty-nine entries, including
a "missing" one (XLVII, "My Story") which, according to
this same editor, the poor man perhaps did not have time to
write.[86] Quantitatively then, this diary is entirely beyond belief. Yet the writing situation itself is at every point painstakingly justified. The condemned man, having promised to

continue "this journal of my sufferings—up to the moment when it will be *physically* impossible for me to continue it,"[87] (Hugo's italics), disbelief sets in only when we find him reporting how he felt—as he mounted the scaffold! But that too is explained: he begged to have his hands untied at the last to write the ultimate entry of his "necessarily unfinished story."

The Hugo text is instructive not so much for the psychological insights it offers (subtle views of human nature were hardly Hugo's strong point) as for the limits to which it stretches the diary form: a "record of the mind in agony," its close spacing approaches continuity, leaving only a short step from here to interior-monologue texts. This step is very nearly taken in Poe's story *A Manuscript Found in a Bottle*. Its writing situation is no less problematical than that of Hugo's condemned man: this diarist finds himself on a ghostly vessel traveling through a chasm of ice, "whirling dizzily in immense concentric circles." Yet he intrepidly continues to write undated diary entries, spaced at shorter and shorter intervals, until—

> But little time will be left me to ponder upon my destiny! The circles rapidly grow small—we are plunging madly within the grasp of the whirlpool—and amid a roaring, and bellowing, and thundering of ocean and tempest, the ship is quivering—oh God! and——going down!

This is how his last entry ends. In difference from Hugo, Poe is here trying for true simultaneity between writing and death. Note the present progressive "going down!" with the neat exclamation mark pointing up the incongruity of this calligraphy *in extremis*.

In sharpest contrast to these melodramatic Romantic strains, a gently humorous interlude in a German novel from the Poetic Realist period shows that diary-writing can be realistically sychronized with life only when life slows to a crawl. Wilhelm Raabe's *Chronicle of Sperling Street* (1857) is on the whole a blandly traditional diary novel. But at one point its principal diarist invites a whimsical friend—by profession a caricaturist—to leave his mark in the manuscript. This results in some revealing horseplay with the diary form, especially when the caricaturist decides to record everything he sees and hears within an hour's time, dating his running record by the minute. Things get a little tense when a fly enters through the window:

> Look, a fly! What a find for a writer of chronicles! She buzzes against the sunny window pane, . . . gives up, circles around me. Hold it! Now she sits down on my knee . . . , she takes her head between her front legs, scratches herself behind her ears, and—you little . . . ! Off she goes, leaving a trace on my knee and—in the Chronicle of Sperling Street.[88]

This fly underscores the adjacency of diary and monologue form: a diarist who managed to close the gaps between his entries (wrote as fast as he thought), would produce an autonomous monologue in written form. But only in a *gemütlich* Biedermeier household can life move so slowly that it can be recorded by hand. Out in the world at large writing interferes with living, and living with writing. A continuous diary that adheres to the formal mimeticism of the genre is doomed to remain an empty form. A different form is needed to synchronize language and experience, a form whose reality model is faster and freer than a written, or even an oral record. Michel Butor relates the diary and the monologue form both generically and historically when he says: "it is natural that one should have tried . . . to attain a narration that is absolutely contemporary with what it narrates; only since one obviously can't at the same time write and fight battles, eat, make love, one has had to come up with a convention: interior monologue."[89]

---

* Wahrhaftig, da ist ja eine Fliege! Welch ein Fund für einen Chronikenschreiber! Summend stösst sie gegen die sonnebeschienenen Scheiben, . . . sie lässt ab und umfliegt mich. Halt! jetzt setzt sie sich auf mein Knie . . . ; sie nimmt den Kopf zwischen beide Vorderbeine, kratzt sich hinter den Ohren und—kleiner . . . ! Dahin geht sie, eine Spur hinterlassend auf meinem Knie und—in der Chronik der Sperlinggasse.

With the development of the various direct techniques for narrating consciousness in first- and third-person forms, the diary novel, formerly the favorite "short-cut to the heart" (Ian Watt), has largely lost its appeal for modern writers who focus on the inner life. Largely, but not entirely: Sartre's *Nausea* is the classic case of new wine in an old bottle. But the wine is so fermented that it keeps breaking the bottle.

In its external structure, Sartre's novel maintains the diary fiction from start to finish, complete with editorial apparatus, dated entries, and frequent references to the activity of diary writing. Some of the time he maintains the logic of the form in individual entries as well: adventures away from Roquentin's desk are narrated in the past tense after his return (the first attacks of nausea, as well as the negative epiphany to which they eventually lead in the Public Garden). But a great many other action scenes (in the library, on the boulevard, in the café) are cast in the present tense, and their relationship to the writing moment is not always clear. Is he recounting scenes just past in the evocative present? Or is he observing these scenes, notebook in hand, while they unfold before his eyes? At times the former seems more likely, at others the latter. But there is at least one long entry where neither interpretation fits, where one must conclude that Sartre has broken the laws of his chosen form, and slid—perhaps inadvertently—into the terrain of the autonomous interior monologue.

In the early pages of this entry Roquentin is at his desk, observing himself exist here and now, and his record is a convincingly simultaneous one:

> I exist. It's sweet, so sweet, so slow. And light: you'd think it floated all by itself. It stirs. It brushes by me, melts and vanishes. Gently, gently. There is bubbling water in my mouth. I swallow, it slides down my throat, caresses me—and now it comes up again into my mouth.[90]

---

* J'existe. C'est doux, si doux, si lent. Et léger: on dirait que ça tient en l'air tout seul. Ça remue. Ce sont des effleurements partout qui fondent et

This minute introspection continues for some pages, becoming increasingly involuted as thought itself becomes the subject of his thought, increasingly associative as he tries to break rational thought patterns. The simultaneity of language and experience is complete, but it does not yet contradict the narrative presentation of the diarist.

This happens only when Roquentin leaves his desk:

> Half past five strikes. I get up, my cold shirt sticks to my flesh. I go out. . . .
> I buy a newspaper along the way. Sensational news. Little Lucienne's body has been found! Smell of ink, the paper crumples between my fingers.[91]

The sexual-existential phantasmagoria that now follows is closely intertwined with his physical movements through the city streets:

> The house springs up, it exists; in front of me along the wall I am passing, along the wall I exist, in front of the wall, one step, the wall exists in front of me, one, two, behind me a finger scratching at my pants, scratches, scratches, and pulls at the little finger soiled with mud, mud on my finger. . . .[92]

and so on for two further pages. This veritable cataract of hallucinatory consciousness subsides only when Roquentin, having entered a café, hears the record with the jazz song. The entry ends there, without returning to pen and paper; the causal relationship between the experience and its recording is

---

s'évanouissent. Tout doux, tout doux. Il y a de l'eau mousseuse dans ma bouche. Je l'avale, elle glisse dans ma gorge, elle me caresse—et la voilà qui renaît dans ma bouche. . . .

  * C'est la demie de cinq heures qui sonne. Je me lève, ma chemise froide se colle à ma chair. Je sors . . .

J'achète un journal en passant. Sensationnel. Le corps de la petite Lucienne a été retrouvé! Odeur d'encre, le papier se froisse entre mes doigts.

  * La maison jaillit, elle existe; devant moi le long du mur, je passe, le long du long mur j'existe, devant le mur, un pas, le mur existe devant moi, une deux, derrière moi, un doigt qui gratte dans ma culotte gratte, gratte et tire le doigt de la petite maculé de boue, la boue sur mon doigt . . .

left suspended. Pointedly contrasting in both form and content, the next entry reads in its entirety:

TUESDAY
Nothing. Existed.[93]

Sartre has made Roquentin do the impossible here: write and run through the streets of Bouville simultaneously. Most readers will applaud the existential experience caught in the raw and fail to notice the sleight of hand by which it is caught: deliberately or not, Sartre has broken the logic of his diary form right in the middle of a diary entry.

This incongruent sequence from *Nausea* is a final instance of a pattern encountered repeatedly in the texts examined in this chapter: the tendency to break away from the norms of first-person narration in the midst of a text that begins or ends by adhering to these norms. When the form of a text imitates written memoirs, oral reports, or diary entries, any action conveyed simultaneously is illogical. But if a text never adheres to formal mimeticism in the first place, it can shape a different logic of its own, in which the same simultaneity of language and action helps to create and to sustain the illusion of a mental quotation.

This illusion depends on the confluence of the various anti-narrative tendencies described in this chapter: unreal presentation, a–chronological remembrance of things past, coincidence between verbalization and perception or experience, expression in emotive language, continuous evolvement of the discourse in present time. Sustained when all these tendencies reinforce each other, the illusion of silent self-communion is easily dispelled when narrative patterns return: when, for example, explicit exposition, or chronological recitation create the impression of a discourse aimed at communication; or when monologic language lapses into simple statement, which could be interpreted as evocative narration or synchronous report.

On our spatial model of approaches from narration to

monologue, then, the traffic also moves in the reverse direction. The autonomous monologue is a form that can easily backslide into the zone that separates it from autobiographical narration. The two-way traffic can be observed historically as well as typologically, which explains why there are as many offspring of the interior monologue on our map as there are ancestors. The works of Beckett, Sarraute, and Robbe-Grillet, in particular, return the interior monologue to the ambiguous semi-narrative terrain—a development that has led one critic to speak of "the avatars of the interior monologue in the *nouveau roman*."[94] Because of this two-way movement, the analysis of autonomous interior monologues in the next chapter will dovetail with the preceding discussion at many points. But the perspective will be altered by the focus on single-minded texts.

6 ∮ The Autonomous Monologue

"Penelope" as Paradigm

Within the limited corpus of autonomous interior monologues the "Penelope" section of *Ulysses* may be regarded as a *locus classicus*, the most famous and the most perfectly executed specimen of its species. Given its position within the broader context of Joyce's novel, however, the question must be raised whether it is at all legitimate to consider "Penelope" as an example of an autonomous fictional form. Would it even be comprehensible to a reader unfamiliar with the preceding sections of the novel? A difficult question to answer empirically, since it would be very nearly impossible to find an experimental subject untainted by at least a hearsay acquaintance with Joyce's work. This much seems certain: Joyce's task of making the "plot" of an interior monologue text comprehensible to the reader despite the strict implicitness of reference demanded by the logic of the form was greatly eased by placing it at the end of his novel rather than at its beginning. The fact, moreover, that we know so much of what Molly knows before we hear her silent voice enhances our enjoyment of it by myriad cross-references to the rest of the novel. Even more important, the fact that we know much that Molly does *not* know (for example, the entire truth about Bloom's erotic experiences on Bloomsday) injects an element of dramatic irony into our reading experience that would be lost if "Penelope" were read as a separate novella.

Nonetheless, more than any of the other chapters of *Ulys-*

ses, and more than ordinary narrative units within other novels, "Penelope" stands apart from its context, as a self-generated, self-supported, and self-enclosed fictional text. Joyce himself stressed its extra-mural status when he commented on the ending of *Ulysses*: "It [the "Ithaca" chapter] is in reality the end as 'Penelope' has no beginning, middle or end."[1] The spherical image he used to describe "Penelope" in a well-known letter to Frank Budgen further underlines its self-enclosure: "It begins and ends with the female *Yes*. It turns like the huge earthball slowly surely and evenly round and round spinning."[2] Joyce's two self-exegetical schemas add yet another element that sets "Penelope" apart: in contrast to the numbered hours that clock all the other episodes, the "Time" marked for the ultimate episode is infinity (∞) in one schema, "Hour none" in the other.[3] But surely the most important sign of "Penelope" 's formal independence is its form itself: the only moment of the novel where a figural voice totally obliterates the authorial narrative voice throughout an entire chapter.[4] No matter how closely the content of Molly's mind may duplicate, supplement, and inform the fictional world of *Ulysses* as a whole, the single-minded and single-voiced form of "Penelope" justifies its consideration as an independent text, a model for that singular narrative genre entirely constituted by a fictional character's thoughts.

One of the most striking structural peculiarities of an autonomous monologue, classically illustrated by "Penelope," is the stricture it imposes on the manipulation of the time dimension. Before we discuss this point, a brief glance at the over-all temporal sequence of Molly's thoughts will dispel a critical commonplace. Critics have tended to take Joyce's mythical image of the spinning earth-ball (in the letter cited above) so literally that they have overstressed the eternal return of the same in "Penelope," while neglecting its sequential unrolling in time.[5] Yet the circularity of Molly's arguments (including the identity of its first and last words) is decisively counteracted by elements that underline its temporal sequence. Prime among these is the fact that her monologue contains a central happening: the inception of her menses (769)[6]; on this account alone it seems to me impossible to maintain that "breaking into ["Penelope"] at any point does not upset the order or sequence."[7] This event is more than incidental; it alters the direction of Molly's thoughts, clearly dividing them into a before and after: whereas her thoughts of Boylan and others concerning the immediate and distant past dominate before, Boylan almost disappears and all memories diminish after. They are replaced by thoughts of the future, largely in the form of scenarios for seducing Stephen and for re-seducing Bloom. Molly, in other words, enters a "new moon" in the course of her monologue—a decidedly temporal event, no matter how eternal its mythological overtones.[8] It is an event, moreover, that strongly ties Molly to biological time, the time of a biological organism on its way from birth to death. If we can talk of the circular shape of Molly's monologue at all, then only in the modified sense of the coils of a spiral whose direction (upward or downward?) is left ambiguous, but whose linear advance along the coordinate of time is never left in doubt.

This advance, even if we disregard the evolution of Molly's thoughts, is built into the very technique Joyce chose to express them: for a continuous interior monologue is based on an absolute correspondence between time and text, narrated time and time of narration.[9] The single mark for the passage of time here is the sequence of words on the page. Whereas in ordinary narration time is a flexible medium that can be, at will, speeded up (by summary), retarded (by description or digression), advanced (by anticipation), or reversed (by retrospect), an autonomous monologue—in the absence of a manipulating narrator—advances time solely by the articulation of thoughts, and advances it evenly along a one-way path until words come to a halt on the page. Note, however, that this chronographic progress is associated only with the successive moments of verbalization itself, and not with their content: it remains unaffected by the a-chronological montage of events that prevails in a monologist's mind, notoriously in Molly's helter-skelter references to different moments of the past and the future.[10]

This even-paced unrolling of time in an autonomous monologue is analogous to the temporal structure of a dramatic scene (or the uninterrupted rendition of dialogue in a narrative scene). The dramaturgic concept of unity of time, in the strictest neo-classical sense of identifying time of action with time of performance, could be applied here, except that the terms of the identity would have to be modified. For if monologue time flows evenly, there is no telling how fast it flows—unless the monologist explicitly clocks himself. Molly's sense of time being what it is ("I never know the time," 747), the exact length of her insomnia cannot be known.[11] But since it starts sometime after two and ends sometime before daybreak (four o'clock on a June day at Dublin's latitude?) Molly probably thinks faster than most readers read her thoughts, and certainly faster than anyone can recite them. The time of "Penelope" would thus correspond to the common view that thoughts move faster than speech.

The relentless continuity of Molly's text, reinforced as it is by the omission of punctuation, makes its division into eight paragraphs (or "sentences," as Joyce called them) stand out the more distinctly: even these brief interruptions in the print inevitably convey moments of silence, time passing without words. These instant pauses appear like a drawing of mental breath before a new phase of mental discourse; or, to use the analogy with drama again, a curtain quickly drawn closed and reopened between the acts of a play in which absolute unity of time prevails. The very fact that paragraphing calls for an interpretation of this kind in "Penelope" shows that paginal blanks, regardless of their size, tend to carry much more than routine significance in interior monologue texts: they convey not only passage of time, but interruption of thought. For this reason lapse into sleep is the most convincing ending for a text of this sort, just as waking out of sleep is its most logical beginning. Molly's monologue, of course, ends in this optimal fashion, but its beginning does not coincide with her awakening. Instead, "Penelope" begins in the only alternate way available to an autonomous monologue, namely *in medias res*, or, better, *in mediam mentem*, casting the reader without warning into the privacy of a mind talking to itself about its own immediate business: "Yes because he never did a thing like that before as ask to get his breakfast in bed with a couple of eggs since the *City Arms* hotel when he used to. . . ."(738) This beginning is obviously meant to give the impression of being "no beginning" (" 'Penelope' has no beginning, middle or end"), not even a syntactical beginning. Both "Yes" and "because" (not to mention "he") refer to a clause antecedent to the text's inception, which the reader can only gradually reconstruct from clues that will eventually appear in the text. Not until one reaches the words at the very bottom of the first page ("yes he came somewhere") does it become entirely clear that the thought immediately antecedent to "Yes because" must have concerned Molly's suspicion of her husband's infidelity. But beyond this specific syntactic riddle, this beginning leaves unexplained whose voice speaks, where, when, and how.

The inception of "Penelope" points up the special limitations imposed on a fictional text if it is to create for the reader the illusion that it records a mind involved in self-address. Since it would be implausible for Molly to expound to herself facts she already knows, all exposition (in the usual sense of conveying information about past happenings and present situations) is barred from the text. The facts of Molly's life pass through her consciousness only implicitly, incidentally, by allusive indirection. And all that remains understood in her thoughts can be understood by the reader only by means of a cumulative process of orientation that gradually closes the cognitive gap.

Yet Joyce could not have exposed Molly's inner life without exposition if he had not placed her in a highly pregnant moment, a crisis situation that brings into mental play the key conditions of her life (and of life). Though Molly's may be an

ordinary mind, Bloomsday is not—for Molly any more than
for Bloom or Stephen—an entirely ordinary day. Its extraordinary events (the afternoon tryst, Bloom's tardy return) are
necessary to awaken in her the thoughts that keep her awake,
and thus to make what is implicit at least partially explicit.
Though she does not tell herself the story of her day, nor the
story of her life, both stories transpire through her agitated
thoughts, or better, in spite of them.

Doubtless the most artful stratagem Joyce employed, however, is to set Molly's mind into its turbulent motion while
setting her body into a state of nearly absolute tranquility.
This obviates a major difficulty inherent in the autonomous
monologue form: to present through self-address the physical
activities the self performs within the time-span of the
monologue. Molly, to be sure, does once rise from her bed
(769-772), but her gestures during this brief interlude are so
obvious and so elemental that they can be gathered without
being directly recorded. As Dujardin's *Les Lauriers* and
Schnitzler's *Fräulein Else* show, when monologists become
much more enterprising they begin to sound much less convincing; forced to describe the actions they perform while
they perform them, they tend to sound like gymnastics
teachers vocally demonstrating an exercise.

But Joyce not only places the monologizing mind in a body
at rest; he also places that body in calm surroundings.[12] The
sensations that impinge on Molly's consciousness are few and
far between: the whistling trains (754, 762, 763), the chiming
bells (772, 781), a lamp (763), a creaking press (771), the sleeping Bloom (771). Only minimally deflected by perceptions of
the external world, her monologue is "interior" not only in
the technical sense of remaining unvoiced, but also in the
more literal sense: it is directed to and by the world within.
The perfect adherence to unity of place thus creates the condition for a monologue in which the mind is its own place:
self-centered and therefore self-generative to a degree that can
hardly be surpassed.

The classic unity (and unities) in the over-all structure of "Penelope" are both matched and mirrored by its linguistic texture. Without intending a complete linguistic-stylistic description of the text,[13] I will focus on three features of its language that spring directly from the autonomous monologue form, and at the same time contrast sharply with the language of retrospective narration: 1) the predominance of exclamatory syntax; 2) the avoidance of narrative and reportive tenses; and 3) the non-referential implicitness of the pronoun system. Note that my approach to Molly's language is different from the approach I took to Bloom's language in the chapter on quoted monologue: there the emphasis was on the contrast between monologue and dialogue, here it is on the contrast between autonomous monologue and narration.

The following excerpt from "Penelope" (769) will serve as the starting-point. I have divided it into thirty numbered segments, each of which corresponds to a "sentence" in the generally accepted sense of a syntactic unit of meaning, or (as one linguist defines it[14]) "a word or set of words followed by a pause and revealing an intelligible purpose":

1. I bet the cat itself is better off than us
2. have we too much blood up in us or what
3. O patience above its pouring out of me like the sea
4. anyhow he didnt make me pregnant as big as he is
5. I dont want to ruin the clean sheets
6. the clean linen I wore brought it on too
7. damn it damn it
8. and they always want to see a stain on the bed to know youre a virgin for them
9. all thats troubling them
10. theyre such fools too
11. you could be a widow and divorced 40 times over
12. a daub of red ink would do or blackberry juice
13. no thats too purply
14. O Jamesy let me up out of this

15. pooh
16. sweets of sin
17. whoever suggested that business for women what between clothes and cooking and children
18. this damned old bed too jingling like the dickens
19. I suppose they could hear us away over the other side of the park till I suggested to put the quilt on the floor with the pillow under my bottom
20. I wonder is it nicer in the day
21. I think it is
22. easy
23. I think Ill cut all this hair off me there scalding me
24. I might look like a young girl
25. wouldnt he get the great suckin the next time he turned up my clothes on me
26. Id give anything to see his face
27. wheres the chamber gone
28. easy
29. Ive a holy horror of its breaking under me after that old commode
30. I wonder was I too heavy sitting on his knee

The most immediately apparent aspect of this language is its agitated, emotional tone. Leaving aside for the moment the several interrogatory sentences (2, 17, 20, 25, 27, 30), almost every sentence would, in normal punctuation, deserve—and some would require—a final exclamation mark: most obviously the seven sentences that are, or contain, interjections (3, 7, 14, 15, 16, 22, 28). But since the essence of exclamations is that "they emphasize to the listener some mood, attitude, or desire of the speaker,"[15] almost all the other sentences could be classed as exclamations as well. The passage abounds in emphatically expressive forms: wishes (5, 26), fears (29), disparaging generalizations (9, 10). A highly subjective tone pervades even those sentences that come closest to statements of fact. They are either marked by introductory verbs of conjecture: "I bet" (1), "I suppose" (19), "I think"

(21, 23); or by patent overstatement: "divorced 40 times over" (11); or by omission of the copula (18); or by emphatic adverbs and conjunctions: "and" (8), "anyhow" (4), the thrice-uttered "too" (6, 10, 18). No sentence, in short, takes the form of a simple statement; all contain emotive, expressive signals, whether they concern past events or present happenings.

If we remember that interior monologue is, by definition, a discourse addressed to no one, a gratuitous verbal agitation without communicative aim, then this predominance of exclamatory syntax appears perfectly in keeping with the nature of monologue. As the form of discourse that requires no reply, to which there *is* no reply, exclamation is the self-sufficient, self-involved language gesture par excellence.[16] Since interrogation, by contrast, is uttered in the expectation of a reply, and thus dialogic by nature, it at first seems surprising that this passage contains so many questions. But Molly's questions are of a kind fitting easily into a monologic milieu: they are themselves essentially exclamatory. This is most obvious where they are rhetorical, either implying their own answer ("wouldnt he get the great suckin the next time he turned up my clothes on me," 25) or uttered without the expectation of an answer ("whoever suggested that business for women," 17, "have we too much blood up in us or what," 2). The latter type is particularly characteristic for Molly: existential questions abound in her monologue, questions pleading against the absurd order of the universe, especially its division into pleasure-seeking males and long-suffering females: "whats the idea making us like that with a big hole in the middle of us" (742); "clothes we have to wear whoever invented them" (755); "why cant you kiss a man without going and marrying him first" (740); "where would they all of them be if they hadn't all a mother to look after them" (778); and many more. But also when Molly asks herself genuinely interrogatory questions, she asks them in an exclamatory fashion, usually by introducing them with the phrase "I wonder": "I wonder is it nicer in the day" (20), "I wonder was I too heavy sitting on his knee" (30). A kind of pathetic anxiety or insecurity comes to the fore in this form of query, especially when the unknown is the impression she made on Boylan (cf. "I wonder was he satisfied with me"; "I wonder is he awake thinking of me or dreaming am I in it," 741). In this sense self-interrogation seems the natural complement to exclamation in the turbulent syntax of language-for-oneself, counterpointing attitudes toward the known with attitudes toward the unknown.

But even as exclamation and interrogation stamp Molly's discourse with subjectivity, these sentence forms also orient it away from a neutral report of the present moment, and away from the narration of past events. Since language-for-oneself is by definition the form of language in which speaker and listener coincide, the technique that imitates it in fiction can remain convincing only if it excludes all factual statements, all explicit report on present and past happenings. The various tenses in Molly's monologue further determine its anti-narrative, anti-reportorial orientation.

I have intentionally chosen my sample passage from the section of Molly's monologue where she begins her most ambitious physical activity of the night—the excursion to the "chamber"—in order to show how Joyce manages to convey Molly's bodily gestures without a single direct statement of the I-am-doing-this-now type. If her activity becomes clear to an attentive reader, it is not because she explicitly reports what she does, but because what she does is implicitly reflected in her thoughts, roughly as follows: "O patience above its pouring out of me. . . . I dont want to ruin the clean sheets" (she decides to get a sanitary napkin); "O Jamesy let me up out of this" (she strains to raise her body); "this damned old bed too jingling" (she moves her body out of bed); "I think Ill cut all this hair off me" (she lifts her night-gown); "wheres the chamber gone" (she decides on the interim stop, and reaches for the needed object); "easy Ive a holy horror of its breaking under me" (she lowers herself onto it). Her subsequent performance—"O Lord how noisy" (770), its conclusion—"Id better not make an all night sitting on this affair" (771), the activity with "those napkins"—"I hope theyll have something better for us in the other world . . . thats all right for tonight" (772), and finally the return to bed—"easy piano O I like my bed" (772), are all rendered by exclamatory indirection as well. In sum, we search in vain through "Penelope" for a first-person pronoun coupled with an action verb in present tense—precisely the combination that creates the most jarring effect in less well-executed interior monologues (like *Les Lauriers sont coupés*), because it introduces a reportorial dimension of language into a nonreportorial language situation.

The first-person, present-tense combination in Molly's monologue occurs exclusively with verbs of internal rather than external activity. She supposes, thinks, wishes, hopes, and remembers many times over on every page, so that the punctual present of her inner discourse continuously refers to and feeds on the very activity she literally performs at every moment of her monologue.[17] It is in this present moment of mental activity that all Molly's other verbal tenses and moods are anchored. And she uses them all: past, future, indicative, conditional, and quite prominently the present of generalization. This constant oscillation between memories and projects, the real and the potential, the specific and the general, is one of the most distinctive marks of freely associative monologic language. Our sample passage contains it in motley display, especially toward its end, when we get in rapid succession past (19), present (20-21), future (23), conditional (24-26), and again present (27-29) and past (30). Note how the punctual present of the mental verbs in turn subordinates the past ("I suppose they could hear us"), the generalizing present ("I wonder is it nicer in the day I think it is"), the future ("I think Ill cut all this hair") and the reversion to the past ("I wonder was I too heavy").

There are moments in Molly's monologue when she adheres more extensively to one or another of these tenses and

moods. Since she is not much of a planner,[18] her looks into
the future verge on the imaginary, whether she uses the conditional or the indicative: thus "supposing he stayed with us"
introduces the wish dream of the *ménage à trois* with Stephen
(779-780), whereas her dreams of glory as a poet's muse (776)
and the alternate scenarios for seducing Bloom (780) are cast
in future tense. Her fantasies—"the cracked things come into
my head sometimes" (779)—cluster in the last third of
"Penelope," whereas memories are denser in the first two-
thirds.

In the earlier sections the recalls are so extensive that the
past tense actually predominates over the present, with the
past sentences at times in straight narrative form, unsubordi-
nated by thinking verbs. Yet even where a consecutive sequence of events takes shape in her mind, the narrative idiom
rarely prevails without being interrupted by opinionated
comments. The following samples from the courtship scene
alternate typically:

> he was shaking like a jelly all over *they want to do every-
> thing too quick take all the pleasure out of it* . . . then he
> wrote me that letter with all those words in it *how could
> he have the face to any woman after* . . . dont understand you
> I said and wasnt it natural *so it is of course* . . . then writing
> a letter every morning sometimes twice a day *I liked the
> way he made love then* . . . then I wrote the night he kissed
> my heart at Dolphins barn *I couldnt describe it simply it
> makes you feel like nothing on earth* . . . (746-747)

I have italicized the sentences that regularly turn a reflective
gaze back on each narrative sentence—generalizing, questioning, evaluating; and this discursive language retards, and
eventually displaces, the narrative language, as the concern
for the present moment again prevails. In this fashion even
the moments of Molly's monologue when she comes closest
to narrating her life to herself—see also the recall of the Mulvey affair (759-761) and the love-scene on Howth Head (782-
783)—never gain sufficient momentum to yield more than
briefly suggestive vignettes.

Molly's memories occur to her in thoroughly random order, her mind gliding ceaselessly up and down the thread of time, with the same past tense now referring to the events of the previous afternoon, now reaching back to her nymphet days in Gibraltar, now again lingering on numberless intervening incidents. This a-chronological time montage—as Robert Humphrey calls this technique[19]—provides the data for a fairly detailed Molly biography; but her monologue itself is autobiographical only in spite of itself.

A further, and perhaps the most telling, symptom for the non-narrative and non-communicative nature of Molly's language is the profusion and referential instability of its pronouns.[20] This initially bewildering system puts the reader into a situation akin to that of a person eavesdropping on a conversation in progress between close friends, about people and events unknown to him but so familiar to them that they need not name the people or objects to which they refer. In this sense Molly's pronominal implicitness combines both traits of language-for-oneself discussed earlier in connection with Bloom's monologic idiom: grammatical abbreviation and lexical opaqueness—traits in other respects far less prominent in Molly's than in Bloom's language. But even as Joyce creates this impression of cryptic privacy he plants just enough signposts to guard against total incomprehensibility.

The only pronoun that has an invariant referent in "Penelope" is the first person singular. Since "I" is by definition "the person who is uttering the present instance of discourse containing *I*,"[21] and since an autonomous monologue is by definition the utterance of a single speaker, this fixity of the first person is endemic to the genre. So, of course, is its frequency. In the sample passage more than half the sentences contain a self-reference, and several contain more than one. This egocentricity is typical of Molly's entire monologue.

All her other pronouns confront the reader with more or less unknown quantities, mostly without immediate antecedent, identifiable only from the broader context. Third-person pronouns—particularly in the masculine gender—display the

most obvious referential instability, and may contain significant equivocation as well. Molly presumably always knows
the who-is-who of her pronouns, but the reader is sometimes
left guessing as to which *he* is on her mind at any moment.
The *he* who "didnt make me pregnant as big as he is" (4) is
clearly Boylan (who must also be the owner of the knee in
30)—even though his name has not been mentioned for three
pages. But the *he* whose face she wants to see "the next time
he turned up my clothes" (25-26) could be either Bloom or
Boylan. And watch the rapid shuttling of the he-reference
(between Bloom and Stephen) in the following passage:

> he [Stephen] could do his writing and studies at the table
> in there for all the scribbling he [Bloom] does at it and if
> he [Stephen] wants to read in bed in the morning like me
> as hes [Bloom] making the breakfast for 1 he can make it
> for 2. . . . (779)

On the larger scale of her monologue, a slower relay of
he-men can be observed as the Bloom-Boylan alternation
gives way to the Bloom-Stephen one, an evolution that coincides with the decreasing past and mounting future and conditional tenses. But the "he" of the exact mid-pages of
"Penelope" (759-762) is the explicitly introduced "Mulvey
was the first," who will return only pronominally to fuse
with Bloom at the very end: "and how he kissed me under the
Moorish wall and I thought well as well him as another and
then I asked him with my eyes to ask again yes and then he
asked me would I yes" (783). As Richard Ellmann has remarked, this is the point when "her reference to all the men
she has known as 'he' has a sudden relevance";[22] for here the
undifferentiated reference at the point of sleep underlines the
contingency of the erotic partner. But this ultimate indiffer-
ence is counterpointed by an overarching constancy, Bloom
being the referent for the first "he" she uses in her monologue, as well as for the last.

In his play with the male pronoun, then, Joyce makes symbolic and amusing use of a realistic feature of speech-for-

oneself. Other pronominal games attain their effect more by pointing to Molly's fixed ideas than to her fickle feelings. Their key lies in the discovery not of her past, but of her private logic and its system of notation. The neuter pronoun refers with comic constancy to her favorite unmentionable, most densely on the first pages:

> anyway love its not or hed be off his feed thinking of her so either it was one of those night women if it was down there he was really and the hotel story he made up a pack of lies to hide it planning it . . . or else if its not that its some little bitch or other . . . and then the usual kissing my bottom was to hide it not that I care two straws who he does it with. . . . (738-739)

The plural pronouns are equally specific in their generality: they express Molly's sexual polarization of the world. "We," whenever it does not signify the self and a specific partner (as in 19), signifies the genus women, as in "I bet the cat itself is better off than us have we too much blood up in us or what" (1-2).[23] The pronominal enemy of this female kinship group is *they*, the genus men: "they always want to see a stain on the bed . . . all thats troubling them . . . theyre such fools too" (8-10). This meaning attends the third person plural in the clichés Molly coins: "they havent half the character a woman has" (761), "1 woman is not enough for them" (739), "arent they thick never understand what you say" (757), "grey matter they have it all in their tail if you ask me" (758), etc. But when Molly's kinship with other women turns to venom, *they* turns into a feminine pronoun: "lot of sparrowfarts . . . talking about politics they know as much about as my backside . . . my bust that they havent . . . make them burst with envy," etc. (762-763). Our passage also shows Molly's feminine perspective on the second person pronoun in the impersonal sense of *one*: "to know youre a virgin for them" (8) or "you could be a widow" (11).[24]

"You" as the pronoun of address, finally, is used very sparingly by Molly, and in this she differs from most other

monologists. If we leave aside an occasional rhetorical phrase
("if you ask me," 758; "I tell you," 751), imagined interlocutors are almost entirely absent. I find only three exceptions: one is the "O Jamesy let me up out of this" (14) in our
passage—with Molly perhaps calling on her creator-author in
a spirit of Romantic irony;[25] "give us room even to let a fart
God" (763) is her only address to another higher power; and
"O move over your big carcass" (778) her only address to a
fellow human being. Molly also occasionally uses the second
person for self-address, but only in brief admonishments:
"better lower this lamp" (781), "better go easy" (763), "O
Lord what a row youre making" (770), "now wouldnt that
afflict you" (769). The extended inner debates that feature
second- and even third-person self-references in some of her
fellow monologists would be out of character with the
single-minded monologist who spins her yarn here.

Variations of the Form

Among the works (or separate sections within works) presented as autonomous monologues, "Penelope" is the only
text that has attained universal celebrity. But there are a
number of others that conform to the same essential norms. I
have selected six texts of this kind for comparative analysis,
with a view to establishing the range of possibilities, as well as
the limitations inherent in this form: Dujardin's *Les Lauriers
sont coupés*, Schnitzler's *Leutnant Gustl* and *Fräulein Else*, Larbaud's "Amants heureux amants," Simone de Beauvoir's
"Monologue," and "The Seventh Chapter" (the Goethe
monologue) from Thomas Mann's novel *Lotte in Weimar*.

Schnitzler's *Leutnant Gustl* (1901), though less well-publi-
cized than Dujardin's work, shares with it the historical precedence to *Ulysses*. It also displays many (perhaps not entirely
coincidental) parallels to *Les Lauriers*.[26] Both render the
thoughts of *hommes moyens sensuels*, typical representatives of
their cultures—respectively Parisian and Viennese—during
typical episodes: Dujardin's Daniel Prince endures a frustrat-
ingly indecisive evening as would-be lover of a venal demi-

mondaine; Schnitzler's Gustl spends a night contemplating suicide in response to an insult from an aggressive civilian. Both monologists roam about a good deal, perceive the changing scene, and engage in conversations with other characters. Schnitzler repeated this basic scheme in his much later monologue novella *Fräulein Else* (1924), but with a psychologically more complex protagonist, a more dramatic plot, and a tragic ending. The titular heroine is a young girl whose neurotic-erotic turmoil, intensified by an indecent proposal, leads to a psychotic crisis in the course of which she disrobes in public and ultimately commits suicide. A kind of case study in psychopathology, this text relates far more complicated and dramatic happenings than other autonomous monologues.

Most post-Joycean autonomous monologues simplify the outer scene. Larbaud's "Amants, heureux amants" (1921)—probably written under the direct impact of "Penelope" and dedicated "To James Joyce my friend and the only begetter of the form I have adopted in this piece of writing"[27]—voices the consciousness of a young dilettante (Franca) during three solo scenes that interrupt his amorous trifling with a pair of girls. Beauvoir's much later "Monologue" (1967) is spoken by a far more cantankerous woman than Molly, but in similarly static nocturnal isolation, except when she harangues her estranged husband on the telephone toward the end.

In contrast to all these monologists, who belong to Northrop Frye's low-mimetic, or even to his ironic, mode, Thomas Mann in his Goethe monologue ventured to present a high-mimetic mind—even one that verges, at least for Germans, on the mythical. It depicts the sexagenarian Goethe waking from an erotic dream, and thinking about his life and works as he moves from bed to washstand to barber chair to working table. The monologue is interrupted by conversations with several intimates, one of which (with his son) ends the chapter. Only here does he learn of the visit to Weimar of Charlotte Buff—the woman on whom he had modeled Werther's Lotte forty years earlier. The event that gives the novel its title is thus not known to Goethe at the time of his monologue, which depicts an extraordinary mind on an entirely ordinary day.

These monologues diverge from the perfectly "classic" form of "Penelope" in various ways, some already evident from the summary descriptions. The most obvious is the more or less dramatic action built into the six texts. Whereas in "Penelope" the crucial events that set Molly's mind in motion precede the monologue itself, in *Les Lauriers, Leutnant Gustl*, and *Fräulein Else* the thought-provoking events fall *within* the time-span of the monologue, so that their occurrence, as well as their effect, is rendered through the articulation of the experiencing mind. Though Mann's, Larbaud's, and Beauvoir's monologues come closer to "Penelope" in this respect, none of them has quite as quiet a setting as Joyce's text.

This basic difference is reflected in three narrative dimensions which are largely absent from "Penelope": the changing external scene, the monologists' own physical motion, and their verbal exchanges with other characters.

When a monologue adheres to unity of place, the description of peripheral surroundings enters only peripherally, if it enters at all. But when the monologist moves around a good deal, the need arises to describe, or at least to identify, the space he traverses or enters. Since explicitly narratorial descriptions are barred, space can be rendered only as pure perception, which most naturally takes the form of nominal (verbless) phrases.[28] Here is a typical example from the café scene in *Les Lauriers*:

> Illuminated, red, golden, the café; flashing mirrors; a
> waiter with white apron; pillars hung with hats and
> overcoats. . . . Illuminated, golden, red, with the mir-
> rors, this flashing; what? the café; the café where I am.[29]

---

* Illuminé, rouge, doré, le café; les glaces étincelantes; un garçon au tablier blanc; les colonnes chargées de chapeaux et de pardessus. . . . Illuminé, doré, rouge, avec les glaces, cet étincellement; quoi? le café; le café où je suis.

This purely perceptive meaning is lost the moment verbs enter, the moment even a copula links nouns and adjectives, as in this balcony scene from the same work:

> Here, the cool night, black; the night cooler, darker yet; behind me the room, hotter, more humid, with the limpid candlelight; it *is* cool outside, inside warmer, softer; it *is* cool outside, almost cold; these dark spaces *are* sad in the end; . . . [my emphasis][30]

Here pure perception has become descriptive statement, creating the impression that Daniel is self-consciously practicing his poeticizing faculty. He does so frequently, as does his Symbolist descendent, Larbaud's Franca.

Even more characteristic for interior monologue than these static descriptions of surroundings is the so-called *description ambulatoire*, which renders the passing scene during displacements.[31] These kinetic perceptions appear in the following street scene from *Les Lauriers*:

> old houses, limewashed walls; on the pavement, children, urchins, sitting on the ground, taciturn; and the Rue du Rocher, and here, the boulevards; lights here, noises; traffic here; the rows of gas lamps right and left; and diagonally, at the left, a carriage under the trees; a group of workmen; the horn of the tramway. . . .[32]

A little farther on in this passage, when Daniel hears an organ grinder perform, a miniature musical score alternates with the printed words in the lines of the text, suggesting that Daniel silently hums what he hears. The same device is more elabo-

---

* Ici, la nuit fraîche, noire; la nuit plus fraîche, plus noire; derrière, la chambre plus chaude, plus moite, avec les bougies limpides; le dehors *est* frais, l'intérieur *est* plus tiède, plus doux; le dehors *est* frais, presque froid; ces noirs à la fin *sont* tristes; . . . [my emphasis]

* de vieilles maisons, des murs en chaux; sur le trottoir, des enfants, des gamins, assis par terre, taciturnes; et la rue du Rocher, et ainsi, les boulevards; là, des clartés, des bruits; là, des mouvements; les rangées de gaz, à droite, à gauche; et, obliquement, à gauche, une voiture parmi les arbres; un groupe d'ouvriers; la corne du tramway . . .

rately and perhaps less effectively used by Schnitzler in the mad scene of *Fräulein Else*: entire excerpts from a Schumann piano piece interrupt the printed text here, detailed in all their notational complexity.[33] Even if Else identifies the music she hears as a piece from her own repertoire—"Schumann? Yes, Carnival. I once studied that myself!"—it is difficult to accept this score simply as a quotation of her consciousness; it appears more like an authorial collage that draws attention to the behind-the-scenes "production" of the text we are reading.

With this one exception, the visual and auditory impressions recorded by the monologists in these texts do not interfere with the basic convention of the genre. Graver problems arise when they record their own bodily movements. Here is Daniel telling himself what he is doing in the café: "I sit down"; "I lean against the back of the bench"; "I am wiping my fingers on my napkin"; "I get up, I put on my overcoat, . . . I leave."[34] And here, even more grotesquely, is Else reaching for the lethal dose of sedatives: "I raise my hand, I move my fingers, I stretch my arm, I open my eyes wide. I see, I see. There stands my glass."[35] It is the statement-quality of first-person pronouns combined with present action verbs that mars the mimesis of self-address. The jarring effect disappears as soon as declarative statements are replaced by questions, nominal sentences, pre-active intentions or post-active comments: "What? I'm out on the street already? How did that happen?" (Gustl's exit from the theater); "a white shirt, . . . the cuff-links, the collar, . . . my vest, my watch in the pocket." (Daniel dressing); "I'll go watch them sleep" (Franca approaching the two girls); "Oh! I banged too hard, I cracked my skull" (Murielle hitting her head against the wall). Most frequent and most effective is the conveying of actions by imperatives or admonishments: "Well, in we go," "Up you get" (*Leutnant Gustl*); "Let's turn the pillow around" ("Amants"), "Down with this dress," (*Fräulein Else*). The pervasiveness of emotive syntax is graphically apparent in the riot of ellipses, dashes, question and exclamation marks on a typical monologic page.[36] Even Dujardin often uses expressive syntax instead of clumsy statement, most comically and effectively in the passage in which Daniel prepares himself for the hoped-for intimacy with Lea ("better take my precautions while I am alone"), and which may well be the first—and only pre-Joycean—urination scene in literature: "let's open the door; careful! no noise; on tip-toes . . . what luck! the light is on; the door is ajar, by chance; let's go . . . and see you don't get any of it on you . . . there! and by no means an unnecessary precaution"; [Dujardin's ellipses].[37] The norms of good taste here force Dujardin to use the kind of indirection he so often forgoes in less risqué situations.

In sum: the autonomous monologue can accommodate behavior ranging from perfect immobility to perpetual mobility, from Molly's prone reverie to Daniel's or Else's ambulatory actions and reactions.[38] These kinetic variations may correspond to variations in mental focus that range from the most absolute introspection to the "extrospection" of the monologist who renders the surrounding scene. When the latter dominates over the former, an interior-monologue text borders on a synchronous report, with the monologist producing a verbal film of sights and happenings. And these opposite directions within the genre affect the language as well as the structure of individual texts.[39]

Yet another variation of the form is its conjunction with dialogues. Dujardin, Schnitzler, and Mann all allow their monologists to socialize, while still strictly excluding a narrator from the scene. The effect is rather different from that of those scenes in third-person novels where sub-conversations counterpoint conversations (Stephen and Mr. Deasy):[40] in the autonomous monologue, the impression is created that the spoken words enter the unrolling consciousness as they are

---

* ouvrons la porte; attention! sans bruit; sur la pointe des pieds . . . quelle chance! il y a de la lumière; justement la porte est entrebâillee; allons . . . gare aussi à ne pas me salir . . . ouf! la précaution n'était pas inutile; [Dujardin's ellipses]

uttered by the self or another, momentarily effacing and replacing silent thoughts. It is obviously the common dramatic
structure that allows dialogue to enter the monologic frame
without disturbing the basic logic of its presentation.[41]

In practice, the problem of identifying the speaking voices
in such dialogues presents a certain difficulty, at least for authors who don't share Faulkner's aloofness from the reader's
struggle with orientation. *Les Lauriers* and *Leutnant Gustl* are
still marred by clumsy pseudo-narrative inquit phrases ("I
say"; "says she"; "is that him talking to me?"),[42] whereas
Fräulein Else achieves a coherent meshing of heard, spoken,
and silent discourse by simple typographic signals. In the
scene where Else tries to borrow money from the lecherous
Herr von Dorsday, her own spoken words are in quotation
marks, her interlocutors italicized:

> *"How much did you say, Else?"*—Hasn't he heard me say
> it, why does he torture me? "Thirty thousand, Herr von
> Dorsday. Really a ridiculously small amount." Why did
> I say that? How stupid. But he smiles. Stupid girl, he
> thinks. . . .—*"Not quite so ridiculous, dear child,"*—Why
> does he say 'dear child'? Is that a good sign or not?—*as
> you imagine. Even thirty thousand gulden have to be earned.*
> . . ." What's this? Is he taking my hand? What's gotten
> into him?—*"Haven't you known about it for a long time,
> Else."* If only he'd let go of my hand! Now, thank God,
> he lets go of it. Not so close, not so close.—*"You
> wouldn't be a woman, Else, if you hadn't noticed it. Je vous
> désire."* He could have said that in German just as well,
> the Herr Vicomte.—*"Need I say more?"*—"You have al-
> ready said too much, Herr Dorsday." And I am still
> standing here. What for?[43]

* *"Wieviel sagten Sie, Else?"*—Aber er hat es ja gehört, warum quält er
mich denn? "Dreissigtausend, Herr von Dorsday. Eigentlich eine lächerliche
Summe." Warum habe ich das gesagt? Wie dumm. Aber er lächelt. Dummes
Mädel, denkt er. . . .—*"Nicht ganz so lächerlich, liebes Kind,"*—Warum sagt er
'liebes Kind'? Ist das gut oder schlecht?—*wie Sie sich das vorstellen. Auch dreissigtausend Gulden wollen verdient sein. . . ."* Was ist das? Er fasst nach meiner
Hand? Was fällt ihm denn ein?—*"Wissen Sie es denn nicht schon lange, Else."* Er

In scenes of this kind Schnitzler creates an effect of near-simultaneity between words and thoughts, even as the tension builds between outer appearance and inner reality, and between conflicting impulses in the self. The effect is similar to that of dramatic scenes interrupted by "asides," but with a reversal of emphasis: here the dominant scene is internal, and dialogue intrudes on thought, rather than thought on dialogue.

A very different effect is achieved by Mann in his Goethe chapter, where he alternates six dialogues and six monologues without intertwining them. This scenic intermittence gives the entire text a far more dramatic countenance: since it is not subsumed under the medium of thought, dialogue is given equal status with monologue, if not equal complexity or interest. This effect is also reinforced by the rhetorical, even pontificating, tonality of Goethe's self-address, whose silent idiolect differs little from his spoken language. Mann obviously aims at showing a Goethe who has attained supremely sublimated control in both spheres, so that his thoughts remain largely unaffected by the intruding conversations.

A final, more monodramatic variation is introduced by Beauvoir when she has her shrewish Murielle monologize into the telephone in a self-defeating effort to communicate with the outside world. Her husband's responses are not and need not be recorded, since they never reach her consciousness ("I know your answers by heart I've heard them a hundred times"[44]). Here the monologizing habit carries over into would-be dialogue, becoming the cause, as well as the result, of the impossibility to communicate.

These texts also display variations in their manner of handling the unity of time, when they maintain this unity at all.

---

soll meine Hand loslassen! Nun, Gott sei Dank, er lässt sie los. Nicht so nah, nicht so nah.—"*Sie müssten keine Frau sein, Else, wenn Sie es nicht gemerkt hätten. Je vous désire.*" Er hätte es auch deutsch sagen können, der Herr Vicomte.—"*Muss ich noch mehr sagen?*"—"Sie haben schon zu viel gesagt, Herr Dorsday." Und ich stehe noch da. Warum denn? [Schnitzler's emphasis]

There is a remarkable consistency in the length of both their narrated time and their time of narration: all six texts render only a few hours of clock time (in no case more than a day or a night),[45] and none extends over fewer than thirty or more than sixty average-size pages.[46] Yet the narrated time is not always evenly covered by the text. This unevenness is most apparent in *Leutnant Gustl*, who is a compulsive time-watcher. In the early section he thinks at the rate of nine pages an hour, in a later section he speeds through three hours in only six pages. These irregularities, if deliberate, would indicate that Gustl's verbalizations are not continuous, hence that the ellipsis marks strewn through the text are literal indicators of time passing between thoughts.

Some texts also contain paginal blanks that indicate more extended lapses of time and of inner speech: though time cannot be compressed without a narrator, it can be silently elided or syncopated. Murielle has an inarticulate crying-spell during the single break in her monologue, indicated by the *ex post facto* "That crying did me good";[47] Gustl, during a similar paginal space, naps for three hours on a park bench.[48] An interesting counterpoint to these instances is the textual lacuna in Goethe's monologue: as indicated by the (untranslatable) line from a Goethe poem that precedes it—"Schöpft des Dichters reine Hand"[49]—this halt in the silent thoughts is motivated not by consciousness falling off to a subverbal plane, but by its heightening to the hyperverbal plane of poetic creation. This seems to be Mann's way of saying that, as the poet puts pen to paper, a language reigns in the mind different from the language of interior monologue, a language that stops even the pen of a novelist who has irreverently exposed the everyday workings of a genius-mind.

All these interruptions of the monologue, even when—as in the last instance—the manipulating hand of the author is tacitly in evidence, relate to the psychology of the monologizing mind. The two pauses in the text of Larbaud's "Amants" are more arbitrary; here the mind of the protagonist presumably continues to function normally during the time elided by the textual blanks: during his displacement to a new locale, and during the hours he spends in the company of the two girls. By tuning in and out of Francia's mind in this fashion "Amants" in effect consists of three discontinuous mental "entries," a structure that moves the monologic genre back in the direction of the traditional diary form (Clarissa running back to her room to write down whatever has just occurred).

But even more disturbing than this intermittent break in the unity of time are purely typographic breaks that occur when unity of time is maintained. This is the case in *Les Lauriers*: its nine numbered chapters do not correspond to temporal discontinuities, but merely mark the most important spatial stations of Daniel's round.[50] This vestige of traditional narratorial subdivisions was abandoned by all later practitioners, who seem to have realized that vacancies in the printed text of an autonomous monologue, unlike those in a text mediated by a narrator, inevitably carry the suggestion of vacancies in the verbal flow of the monologizing mind.

By the same token, sleep and other states of suspended consciousness also offer the most natural boundaries for autonomous monologues. Several texts do in fact begin as their speakers awaken, or close as they drift off into sleep: Mann's Goethe and Larbaud's Francia wake from morning slumber, and Gustl from somnolent presence at a concert; Molly and Else submerge respectively in sleep and death. Curiously none of these texts uses the border of sleep at both ends of the text, perhaps because their authors sensed that an unremitting inner voice enduring over an entire waking day would become unendurable for the reader.

The effectiveness of a matinal beginning is enhanced by the opportunity it offers for locating the speaker in the time, space, and circumstance of his life, since it is the moment when the consciousness, momentarily disoriented, most naturally reminds itself of all it has left behind during its somnolent absence. Goethe's first person explicitly "emerges" out of its dream world—"it [the dream] fades into nothingness, and I emerge"—to orient itself first in its spatial setting—"Where

do you come to? Jena? Berka? Tennstädt? No, this is the
Weimar bed cover. . . ."—later in its temporal moment—
"What is the clock? Did I awake into the night? No. . . ."—,
still later to take stock of the immediate duties awaiting him
that day—"How one forgets down below! Now the daytime
ghosts arrive again, the whole lot of them."[51]

Indirect self-presentations of this kind appear far more ar-
tificial when the beginning of a monologue does not coincide
with the moment of awakening. In order for such *in mediam
mentem* beginnings to appear realistic, they must create the
impression of cutting into a continuing mental process at an
absolutely random moment, by avoiding all semblances of
exposition. Such abrupt beginnings, though attempted by
Schnitzler and Beauvoir, are rarely convincing—at least when
they are contrived by lesser masters than Joyce.

In this connection it is interesting to observe how *Les
Lauriers*—the first full-fledged autonomous monologue
novel—introduced itself. Like Goethe, Daniel also explicitly
emerges—"je surgis"—into self-awareness. But since he does
so in broad daylight on a Paris street, his emergence takes on
the quality of a highly self-conscious "prelude"[52] that, in
hindsight, seems curiously appropriate to the launching of a
new genre:

> An evening of setting sun, distant air, deep skies; and
> confused crowds; noises, shadows, multitudes; spaces
> stretched out endlessly, a vague evening. . . .
> For under the chaos of appearances, amid the durations
> and the locations, in the illusion of things self-begotten
> and self-conceived, one among others, one like the
> others, distinct from others, similar to others, one the
> same and one more, from the infinity of possible exist-
> ences, I emerge; . . . [Dujardin's ellipsis]

*Dass . . . [es] in nichts zerfliesst und ich emportauche . . . Wo kommst
Du zu dir? Jena? Berka? Tennstädt? Nein, das ist die Weimarer Steppdecke
. . . Was ist die Uhr? Erwacht ich in die Nacht? Nein, . . . Wie man vergisst
dort unten! Nun kommt der Tag-Spuck wieder herauf, das ganze Zeug,. . .
* Un soir de soleil couchant, d'air lointain, de cieux profonds; et des foules

At first the impression is created that we find ourselves in a third-person novel, in which a narrator introduces a character by picking him at random out of "confused crowds." But once we have found out that this character bears the name of the first-person pronoun, we are forced to read this beginning as a self-presentation of sorts: as the self-dramatized entrance of the monologizing "I" into a text (and into literature). No sooner has he made his appearance than this speaker locates himself within the immensity of time and space—"amid the durations and the locations"—in his own specific time and space, the *hic et nunc* of interior monologue: "it is the today; it is the here; the hour that strikes; and, around me, life; the time, the place, an April evening, Paris, . . ." Note how the use of definite articles ("l'aujourd'hui," "l'ici") reinforces the impression that this text has a demonstrative intent: it has been aptly called "a kind of manifesto for interior monologue."[53]

If the introductory moment of an autonomous monologue appears most natural when it is least introductory, its concluding moment appears most natural when it is least conclusive. Unless a monologue puts its speaker to sleep, the most logical ending is the projection of a figurative *et cetera*, suggesting that the *perpetuum mobile* of consciousness continues beyond the last printed word. In practice, writers rarely resist the urge to conclude more forcefully; either the discourse rises to a frenzied pitch (Murielle's furious prayer, Gustl's bloodthirsty threat); or it levels off to a provisional appeasement (Daniel's resignation over his amorous defeat, Franca's idle musings about future encounters with the girls).

---

confuses; des bruits, des ombres, des multitudes; des espaces infiniment étendus; un vague soir . . .

Car sous le chaos des apparences, parmi les durées et les sites, dans l'illusion des choses qui s'engendrent et qui s'enfantent, un parmi les autres, un comme les autres, distinct des autres, semblable aux autres, un le même et un de plus, de l'infini des possibles existences, je surgis, . . . [Dujardin's ellipsis]

★ c'est l'aujourd'hui; c'est l'ici; l'heure qui sonne; et, autour de moi, la vie; l'heure, le lieu, un soir d'avril, Paris, . . .

Still, in all cases, the future is implicitly open, even as it is
explicitly invoked in the final sentences.

The language of autonomous monologue by no means is
limited to a specific tenor,[54] but can accommodate a wide
range of thought-idioms. Goethe's elevated rhetoric and Molly's vulgar colloquialness are, in this respect, poles apart, and
the distance between them is graded by the precious elegance
of Larbaud's Franca, the pseudo-lyric effusion of Dujardin's
Daniel, the upper-middle-class clichés of Schnitzler's Else, the
colorful dialect of his Gustl, and the gross Gallic jargon of
Beauvoir's Murielle. Each adds a special tonality to a genre
that depends more on the shaping of a consistent mental
idiolect than on such stylistic criteria as the "direct sentences
reduced to a syntactical minimum" in Dujardin's famous
definition.[55] Mann's Goethe monologue, with its long
hypotactic sentences, is no less persuasive a mimesis of interior discourse than Molly's or Daniel Prince's, if we grant that
fiction can render the minds of singular historical figures as
validly as those of contemporary social types. But even when
the tenor of a monologue becomes highly formal, it maintains
some qualities of oral discourse. When Mann has Goethe in-
dulge his well-known leaning to sententiousness, he gives it
clever monologic twists: "Man cannot tarry long in consciousness; he must from time to time flee back into unconsciousness, for there he has his living root. A maxim."[56]
Note how the final genre identification ("A maxim") anchors
the adage in the thought-process, maintaining an impression
of spontaneity, even as it casts a mildly ironic light on its professional producer.

Despite these wide divergences in tenor, a number of syntactical patterns recur, conforming on the whole to those in
"Penelope." In all these texts the proliferation of pronouns
shapes set patterns characteristic of the monologist's prevail-

---

* Im Bewusstsein kann der Mensch nicht lange verharren; er muss sich
zuweilen wieder ins Unbewusste flüchten, denn darin lebt seine Wurzel.
Maxime.

ing concerns, and poses puzzles for the reader. Larbaud's Franca has almost as many feminine references as Molly has masculine ones, beginning with the cryptic "Elles dorment encore," and ending with a nameless "Celle à qui je pense." Goethe refers to his women more elaborately ("the little woman," "the clever darling," "the little one") but no less cryptically—at least for a reader unacquainted with the details of Goethe's love life. He also plays a more weighty referential game when he fuses Schiller and Christ in a capitalized "He," culminating in the apodictic statement: "Yes, He had much in common with Him." ("Ja, Er hatte viel von Ihm.")[57]

The most significant variant in pronominal patterns among the different monologues concerns their use of the second person singular. Far more frequently than Molly, other monologists address their inner discourse to one or more mind-haunting interlocutors, living or dead, human or divine. Goethe's favorite mental partner—formally addressed as "Sie . . . mein Bester"—is Schiller (long dead in 1816); he also apostrophizes various forces of nature, not to mention his bath sponge. Daniel periodically talks to Lea in anticipation of their rendezvous, in contrast to his later tongue-tied performance in her presence. Else compulsively works up scenarios for speeches to Dorsday, both before and after the actual encounter. And Gustl addresses furious diatribes to his prospective dueling partner, ending his monologue with the announcement: "I'll make chopped beef out of you!"

All these make-believe communications underscore the pervasive loneliness of the monologist, whose only true interlocutor remains the "Imprisoned Self" (Erika Höhnisch's apt title phrase). In the grammar of interior monologue the speaker often doubles as listener, and is literally addressed as one. Mann's and Schnitzler's monologues feature second-person self-address most prominently, using it to characterize their protagonists' self-images: Goethe is self-reverent to the point of pomposity, so that the familiar "Du" almost appears *too* familiar. At times this personal "Du" fuses with the recipient of Goethean wisdom, to whom so many of his poems and maxims are addressed—some of which are quoted verbatim in the text. Leutnant Gustl, in radical contrast, addresses himself like an invalid child, with alternate pity and gentle chiding. In *Fräulein Else* the pervasive self-address reaches a fitting climax in the narcissistic mirror-scene that precedes the public self-exposure:

> Am I really as beautiful as I look in the mirror? Oh, won't you come closer, beautiful lady. I want to kiss your blood-red lips. I want to press your breasts to my breasts. What a pity that there is this glass between us, this cold glass. How well we would get on together. Don't you agree? We would need no one else.[58]

Here the schizoid split between ego and alter ego that always suggestively attends direct self-address is objectified and literally mirrored.

Another recurrent feature is the rapid swerving of tenses, as the monologist in turn remembers his past, formulates general ideas, apprehends his future, projects conditional scenarios, and views his present situation. Different monologues differ in the importance they give each of these temporal dimensions. The gnomic present plays a much larger role in some monologues than in others, ranging from Goethe's reflective language through Gustl's or Murielle's clichés to Daniel's purely ad hoc language. But it is the varied weighting of past time and tense that yields the most significant variations. As we might expect, the most active monologists (Daniel, Gustl, Else) reminisce least,[59] the most quiescent (Molly, Murielle, Franca, Goethe) reminisce most. But no matter how large a portion of the text is filled with memories, the past is always anchored in the present moment of locution, and thus commented and exclaimed upon rather than plainly narrated. At

---

* Bin ich wirklich so schön wie im Spiegel? Ach, kommen Sie doch näher, schönes Fräulein. Ich will Ihre blutroten Lippen küssen. Ich will Ihre Brüste an meine Brüste pressen. Wie schade, dass das Glas zwischen uns ist, das kalte Glas. Wie gut würden wir uns miteinander vertragen. Nicht wahr? Wir brauchten gar niemanden andern.

the limit, when present experience gives way altogether to associative remembrance, we get the special, and specially fascinating, sub-genre I call "memory monologue," which merits separate discussion.

Memory Monologue

The memory monologue, as I defined it in the last chapter,[60] is a variant of the autonomous monologue in which the mind is trained full-time on the past. In contrast to other autonomous monologues, in memory monologues the present moment of locution is a moment emptied of all contemporary, simultaneous experience: the monologist exists merely as a disembodied medium, a pure memory without clear location in time and space. The monologic presentation itself is reduced to zero here, to a kind of vanishing point of the mnemonic process. The monologues of *The Sound and the Fury* conform closely to this type, as do several novels of Claude Simon, Faulkner's closest relative among the French New Novelists. Critics who simply call these texts interior monologues, without qualification, miss the peculiarity of their structure as widely as do those who simply call them first-person narratives. The fact that the two terms are alternately applied in discussion of *The Sound and the Fury* suggests that neither fits comfortably, and that an in-between generic position needs to be labeled and defined. The model of the memory monologue will help to clarify the common structure of the Faulkner and Simon texts, as well as their differences.

The three speakers of Faulkner's monologues never allude to the time or place in which they verbalize their memories. Only the moment *post quem* of their locution can be determined with any degree of certainty: since they refer to the events of the days that entitle their respective sections in the past tense, their monologues must postdate these titular days. The moment *ante quem*, on the other hand, can only be inferred from circumstantial evidence. This evidence points, in every case, to the moment just before sleep (in Quentin's case just before death) on the last day they carry in their memory: Benjy would then monologize on April 7, 1928, Quentin on June 2, 1910,[61] and Jason on April 6, 1928. That these dates stand at the heads of the three sections provides a broad hint, supported by various data provided in the other sections: Jason confirms that Quentin committed suicide as planned; Benjy carries none of the events of Easter Sunday (April 8) in his memory; and Jason still ignores those developments of his niece Quentin's affair with the showman that take place on the Easter weekend (April 7 and 8).

The moment of locution is equally indeterminate in the two novels by Claude Simon that adhere closely to the structure of memory monologues: *La Route des Flandres* (1960) and *Histoire* (1967). We learn nothing about the circumstances in which Georges, the protagonist of *La Route des Flandres*, monologizes, except that they must postdate the latest experience he entwines into his mnemonic strand: the night he spends after the war with Corinne, the woman who has been the object of his erotic fantasies during his years as a war prisoner.[62] In *Histoire* the nameless memorialist remains equally unsituated. The most recent moment he recounts is the day on which he finds a collection of family postcards in a chest he has decided to sell. But in Simon's novels the moments of locution remain even more indeterminate than in *The Sound and the Fury*: since his novels consist of single memory monologues, they provide no comparative context from which the moment *ante quem* could be gathered. The remembering mind exists in an absolute temporal void, with the moment of remembrance located in an indefinite (and perhaps eternally repetitive) present.

A recurrent pattern in all these texts is that the most recent remembered episode plays a privileged role in the mnemonic discourse. It acts as a kind of triggering device that releases into the mind a shower of memories from the more distant past. These memories, which may range from earliest childhood (or even prenatal family history) to the critical moments of adult life, arrive helter-skelter, in time-montage fashion. The generating episode itself, by contrast, is usually remembered in the temporal sequence of its occurrence, in the fashion of an autobiographical narrative.

The three Compson brothers articulate the events of their last days (the dated days of their locution) in strictly chronological order: Benjy from the moment he watches the golfers "Through the fence, between the curling flower spaces" to the moment when Luster undresses him for sleep; Quentin from the moment "When the shadow of the sash appeared on the curtains" as he wakes to the moment when he dresses for death; Jason from the breakfast conversation with his mother to the nocturnal inspection of his money-box. But in the case of Benjy and Quentin this sequential replay of "actual scenes" is persistently interrupted by "remembered scenes" that belong to earlier time frames.[63]

The episodes that generate the mnemonic process in Simon's novels also develop chronologically, though they are threaded more discreetly into the tissue of earlier memories. In *La Route des Flandres* the scenes of the single night with Corinne are eclipsed for hundreds of pages by the obsessively repeated reminiscences of combat, defeat, and imprisonment. Just the same, these love-scenes shape a single consecutive strand that leads to Corinne's eventual exit from the bed, the room, and presumably from Georges' life.[64] Similarly, the day on which the monologist of *Histoire* finds and reads the family correspondence is chronologically intact, though its progress is constantly impeded by the remembered and imagined episodes from his own and his parents' lives.

In an important sense, the chronological structure of the generating episode in memory monologues corresponds to the live present of autonomous monologues like "Penelope." It shapes the principal time-plane to which the temporal chaos of earlier memories relates and periodically returns. But at the same time it introduces additional ambiguities into memory monologues. Since its tense does not distinguish the generating episode from earlier memories, the reader must watch carefully for other signposts. Faulkner is more accommodating than Simon in this respect, since his changes of type-face (once one has figured out his system) provide at least *some* guidance. But both writers like to cut without warning from the principal time-plane to earlier ones, sometimes in midsentence, thereby aggravating all the other difficulties of following a monologic time-montage. Since memory-monologues also adhere to all the other features of language-for-oneself—the absence of explicit exposition, the beginning *in medias res*, non-referential language, abbreviated syntax, idiosyncratic vocabulary—it is small wonder that texts of this type are notoriously "unreadable."[65]

Another problem is even more vexing, though on theoretical rather than on practical grounds: the question as to whether the stream of memories springs up in the monologist's mind at the (indeterminate) moment of locution, or in the course of the generating episode itself.

This ambiguity is present from start to finish in Benjy's monologue. As has often been remarked, Benjy's language suggests that he has no sense of time or of causality. The fact that the distant past of his childhood and the immediate past of his thirty-third birthday are cast in the same tense therefore corresponds to the synchronism of his arrested mental world. Nor is there any other linguistic distinction in Benjy's text between remembered and actual scenes. Both are related in simple reportorial language, without discursive commentary, interpretation, or expression of emotion.

> We went along the fence and came to the garden fence, where our shadows were. My shadow was higher than Luster's on the fence. We came to the broken place and went through it.
> "Wait a minute." Luster said. "You snagged on that nail again. Cant you never crawl through here without snagging on that nail."
> *Caddy uncaught me and we crawled through. Uncle Maury said to not let anybody see us, so we better stoop over, Caddy*

said. Stoop over, Benjy. Like this, see. We stooped over and crossed the garden, where the flowers rasped and rattled against us. [Faulkner's emphasis][66]

When does the childhood memory of crawling through the fence with Caddy occur in Benjy's mind: at the moment he crawls through with Luster, or at the moment he *remembers* crawling through with Luster (that is, at the moment he "speaks" his monologue)? Nothing in the language of the text permits us to answer this question; both interpretations seem equally valid. Faulkner himself (in letters to his publisher) referred to the scene-shifts in the Benjy section as "thought transferences,"[67] a phrase that suggests that he attributed these associations to the moment when Benjy remembers his last day after it draws to a close. On this basis, we would be justified in calling the Benjy section as a whole a memory-monologue. For the chronologic unrolling of his last day would then serve merely as a mental context (or pretext) for the jumbled memories.

The same question as to the moment of remembrance arises again in Quentin's monologue. But here the relationship between the account of the last day and the memories of earlier days is far more varied, and the text cannot be reduced to a consistent pattern, not even to a consistently equivocal one.

Quentin mostly uses a sober reportorial language for the events of the last day—a language more complex but no more emotional than Benjy's. He uses a far more emotive language for memories (whenever they do not merely reproduce remembered dialogues). This emotive language, however, is not limited to memories, but also comes to the fore whenever he comments on the events of his last day. Such comments always very rapidly lead to remembered scenes, forcing one to interpret the memory as "thought transferrence," occurring at the moment of locution:

I climbed the gate into a woodlot and crossed it and came to another wall and followed that one, my shadow behind me now. There were vines and creepers where at

home would be honeysuckle. Coming and coming especially in the dusk when it rained, getting honeysuckle all
mixed up in it as though it were not enough without
that, not unbearable enough. *What did you let him for kiss*
kiss
   I didn't let him I made him watching me getting mad. . . .
[Faulkner's emphasis][68]

The word "honeysuckle" is the hinge between narration and
evocation. But note that it is not a sensation that triggers the
memory of home (there is no honeysuckle on the scene), it is
the *word* used in the comparative description ("There were
vines and creepers where at home would be honeysuckle").
The next sentence—significantly not yet printed in the italics
that usually signal memories in the Quentin text—relives an
emotion that flows directly out of the narrative process
("Coming and coming . . .") and leads directly to the recall
of the verbal exchange with Caddy ("What did you let him
for . . ."). Here, then, the chronological monologue, as it is
eclipsed by a-chronological memories, is transformed into a
memory-monologue.

There are other moments, however, when Quentin's consciousness seems to generate memories simultaneously with
the action he performs on his last day. This is especially true
in the last pages of the section: here memories repeatedly
grow out of present-tense passages that quote Quentin's tortured thoughts as the moment of suicide approaches:

I returned up the corridor, waking the lost feet in whispering battalions in the silence, into the gasoline, the
watch telling its furious lie on the dark table. Then the
curtains breathing out of the dark upon my face, leaving
the breathing upon my face. A quarter hour yet. And
then I'll not be. The peacefullest words. Peacefullest
words. *Non fui. Sum. Fui. Non sum.* Somewhere I heard
bells once. Mississippi or Massachusetts. I was. I am not.
Massachusetts or Mississippi. Shreve has a bottle in his
trunk. *Aren't you even going to open it* Mr. and Mrs. Jason

Richmond Compson announce the *Three times. Days.
Aren't you even going to open it* marriage of their daughter
Candace . . . [Faulkner's emphasis][69]

The first two sentences report Quentin's return from bath-
room to bedroom. With the words "a quarter hour yet. And
then I'll not be" a quotation of Quentin's past thoughts begins: he is clocking his suicide, thinking ahead to a moment
which must already lie in his past before he begins his
monologue. An uninterrupted stream of associations now
connects this self-quotation to fragmented memories of the
more distant past: bells in Mississippi, the arrival of Caddy's
wedding announcement, and a welter of further reminiscences that continue for over two pages; until the "quarter
hour" has run its course, and he reports in punctual past
tense: "The three quarters began." Here, then, the text seems
to conform to the structure of a chronological monologue
that directly quotes past thoughts and memories, rather than
to the structure of a memory monologue.

Even more often than the two patterns just discussed, one
finds that neither clearly prevails, and that the memories
could spring with equal plausibility from the unsituated remembering mind or from the mind involved in its last day's
experience. It is not possible to decide, for example, whether
the longest uninterrupted memory sequence of all—the failed
suicide pact with Caddy and the fight with Dalton Ames[70]—
is meant to be understood as the content of Quentin's consciousness while he is fighting Gerald Bland, or as a retrospective screening-out of the recent fight as he remembers this
event at day's (and life's) end. In short, the same ambiguity
that seems to be endemic to memory-monologues, and that
corresponds to the confusions arising within all retrospective
first-person forms whenever past thoughts are not explicitly
fenced off from the narrative discourse.[71]

Jason's monologue has, in this and other respects, a simpler
structure, and one even hesitates to classify it as a memory-
monologue at all. Since it works its way relentlessly through
the events of April 6, with very few halts and detours, it

comes closer to a simple autobiographical monologue. Only one longer passage flashes back to the distant past: to baby Quentin's arrival, the father's funeral, Caddy's attempts to see her daughter.[72] But these memories are invariably anchored in the present moment of locution. Recalling Uncle Maury's words to his mother at the funeral—"Now, now. Don't you worry at all. You have me to depend on, always"—Jason immediately adds: "And we have. Always." Only then does he return to one of the incidents of his last day, the arrival of Uncle Maury's letter: "The fourth letter was from him."[73] The intervening present-tense comment clearly relates the early memory to the discursive moment, dispelling all temporal ambiguity.

Jason also always explicitly separates the thoughts on his past day from his present comments. The former are usually introduced by the phrase "I was thinking," the latter by the phrase "Like I say." Past thoughts are purely empirical reactions to the events of the moment, present "sayings" are rationalizing adages:

> Like I say you cant do anything with a woman like that, if she's got it in her. If it's in her blood, you cant do anything with her. The only thing you can do is to get rid of her, let her go on and live with her own sort.[74]

This discursive saying-language continually interrupts Jason's chronological account. It is the ground level, the alpha and omega of his retrospection. In this respect also Jason's monologue moves away from his two brothers' memory-monologues; and by the same token it moves closer to autonomous monologues cast in the present tense. His argumentative, opinionated, cliché-ridden language in fact displays a surprising resemblance to Murielle's, to Leutnant Gustl's, even to Molly's monologic idioms. And because Jason, unlike Benjy and Quentin, speaks (and lives) in the present, his discourse also opens to the future. The final sentence of his monologue matches Molly's erotic future—"Yes I will"—with his financial future: "I just want an even chance to get my money back. And once I've done that. . . ."

Though Jason's discourse conforms to some of the criteria of a memory-monologue—the indeterminate monologic situation, the focus on the past—it lacks the essential a-chronological structure of the genre. Jason is not the type of character who can take full advantage of the genre in which he speaks. Only a character heavily burdened with his entire past can be expected to dechronologize a discourse dealing with a specific past experience; the full deployment of the monologic genre's mnemonic variant thus depends on a mind that creates (and is created by) a "swarming and vigorous disorder of memory."[75]

Epilogue: The Relation to Drama and Lyric

The fact that narrative elements are reduced to zero in the autonomous monologue affiliates it closely with the two non-narrative genres. It is interesting to remember in this connection that the first "pure" texts of this type appear in the Symbolist and immediately post-Symbolist period, at a time when borderlines between the traditional genres are more freely crossed and more deliberately effaced than in earlier periods: when poetry meets prose (in the prose poem and the lyric novel), drama meets poetry (in dramatic monologue and poetic drama), and fiction meets drama (in early epic theater and the scenic novel). And it is precisely where the lyric and the dramatic genres converge that they also verge on the autonomous monologue.

The dramatic quality of autonomous monologues is literally dramatized in the theatrical performances that they occasionally receive: "Penelope" has been "acted" by Siobhan McKenna and Bea Manley, Schnitzler's *Fräulein Else* by several Austrian actresses. Not a word needs to be added or subtracted to obtain a "playable" script (though length is of course a problem in practice). It goes without saying that such recitations go counter to the very convention on which fictional monologues are based: their silence.[76] If they are nonetheless successful on the stage, it is probably less because their performance corresponds to our reading experience, and more because it comes to meet a reverse convention, which corresponds to any seasoned playgoer's expectations: the convention of stage monologue. The two conventions are poles apart: stage monologue presents speech as though it were thought; fictional monologue presents thought as though it were speech; the first turns *up* the sound level (the silence) we associate with thought, the second turns *off* the sound level we associate with speech. These poles are brought together when internal fiction is staged as external drama, proving once again that extremes can be made to touch.

Since stage soliloquy had been the only instance within the traditional genres where a fictional mind was displayed without authorial mediation, it was an obvious model for the autonomous monologue. This is surely one reason why Dujardin dedicated his *Lauriers* "to the supreme novelist of souls, Racine." In *Le Monologue intérieur* he views Racine as the past master in the technique of presenting the subconscious by means of stage dialogue and monologue, making his characters speak "things . . . that in reality would never have risen to their mouths." And he shows full awareness of the common ground between stage monologue and fictional monologue when he adds: "The prime object of interior monologue is, while remaining within the conditions and the frame of the novel, to do away with the intervention . . . of the author, and to permit the character to express himself directly, as the traditional monologue does in the theater."[77]

What Dujardin leaves unmentioned is that an occasional soliloquy or aside in a play corresponds more closely to a quoted monologue in a third-person novel than to an interior monologue presented as an independent text. The closest dramatic analogue to the autonomous monologue would be a play-length soliloquy or monodrama: a genre that exists mostly in the mind of theorists, only occasionally on paper, very rarely on the stage. Mallarmé's vision of ideal theater as "état d'âme" or "spectacle de Soi" is essentially monodramatic, and similar conceptions can be found in later Symbolist, Surrealist, and Expressionist theorists. In practice, the single player—even in plays that call themselves monodrama—is supported by one or several alter egos, or by incarnations of remembered or imagined figures (as in Strindberg's *To Damascus*, Max Frisch's *Biographie*, or Evreinov's *Theater of the Soul*). Beckett is probably the playwright who comes closest to realizing monodrama in the theater, but even the single open mouth in *Not I* addresses a silent listener on stage, and Krapp carries on something of a dialogue with his last tape. But even if pure monologue is generally felt to be unworkable in texts that aim at stage performance, it is still a limit-point toward which drama can and does evolve whenever dramatists find internal happenings more gripping than interpersonal ones. At this monologic limit, the dramatic genre meets the narrative genre at *its* monologic limit. A pure monodrama written for stage performance would differ from an interior monologue written to be read only with regard to its author's intention.

Dramatic monologue, as the order of noun and modifier indicates, is not a form of drama; in approaching it we cross the line between drama and lyric, a line hazier in theory than in practice.[78] The term dramatic monologue usually refers to a poem whose speaker is a character invented by the poet, not the poet himself: Wordsworth's Margaret, as compared to the "I" of *The Prelude*; Goethe's Sorcerer's Apprentice, as compared to the "I" of *Die Trilogie der Leidenschaft*; Yeats' Crazy Jane, as compared to the "I" of *Sailing to Byzantium*. This presence of a fictive speaker relates the dramatic monologue not only to soliloquy in drama, but also to fictional narrative in the first person—a relationship that has been largely disregarded in discussions of the dramatic monologue, perhaps because of the "dramatic" emphasis of the English term.[79] Viewed from this vantage point, all dramatic monologues are first-person narratives in verse form. The basic structural variants of the genre tally exactly with the basic variants of prose fiction in the first person: speakers of dramatic monologues can address silent listeners, or speak to themselves; they can narrate the lives of others, or their own; they can recount a past experience, or focus on a present predicament. A dramatic monologue in which a lone speaker articulates a contemporary experience is the analogue within the lyric genre of the autonomous monologue in prose fiction.

To display the proximity in structure between interior and dramatic monologues, I quote from a letter dated 1922, in which a highly esoteric literary work is described by its author: "It is a reverie, with all the discontinuities, repetitions, and surprises of a reverie. But it is a reverie which has as its subject, and as it object as well, *conscious consciousness*. Imagine someone waking up in the middle of the night, and reliving, reciting to herself her entire life. . . . Her sensuality, memories, emotions, body feelings, depth of remembrance, lights or anterior skies revisited, etc. This thread which has neither a beginning nor an end, but only knots,—I have made a monologue out of it, after subjecting it to formal conditions as strict as its *content* was free." A newly discovered Joyce letter explaining "Penelope?" The date would fit, as would most of the content (though the style would give one pause). The letter is, in fact, Paul Valéry's, and its subject is his poem *La jeune Parque* (1917).[80] It would be difficult to imagine two texts with more different surfaces than Valéry's highly wrought, meticulously alexandrined mythological poem about a narcissistic, virginal Fate and the rambling, earthy monologue of Joyce's highly sexed Dublin housewife. Yet, if we leave aside these surface elements of diction and fiction, and focus—as Valéry does in his letter—on the underlying structure and intent, the two texts move into close proximity:

★ C'est une rêverie qui peut avoir toutes les ruptures, les reprises, et les surprises d'une rêverie. Mais c'est une rêverie dont le personnage en même temps que l'objet est la *conscience consciente*. Figurez-vous que l'on s'éveille au milieu de la nuit, et que toute la vie se revive et se parle à soi-même . . . Sensualité, souvenirs, émotions, sentiment de son corps, profondeur de la mémoire et lumières ou cieux antérieurs revus, etc. Cette trame qui n'a ni commencement ni fin, mais des noeuds,—j'en ai fait un monologue auquel j'avais imposé, avant de l'entreprendre, des conditions de forme aussi sévères que je laissais au *fond* de liberté.

both consist in their entirety of the direct quotation of a figural mind spinning its mental filament ("this thread which has neither a beginning nor an end"); in both night-thoughts are verbalized as they rise to consciousness, moment by moment, interrupted only by sleep (Molly's ultimate fade-out is matched by the *jeune Parque*'s momentary one, from which she reawakens to the rising sun); and in both the apparently random thoughts persistently return to obsessive themes and images—the nodules or knots (*des nœuds*) of the weaving consciousness.

That these obsessive themes themselves are similar is perhaps less surprising: each woman embodies her creator's conception of the eternally feminine (the *jeune Parque* even calls herself "lasse femme absolue"); each is preoccupied with the eternal masculine, and with maternity, menstruation, and other corollaries; each faces a characteristically feminine conflict, and ultimately embraces her roles in a final Yes—of sorts. Here are selections that illustrate both analogy and contrast:

Chers fantômes naissants dont la soif m'est unie,
Désirs! Visages clairs! . . . Et vous, beaux fruits d'amour,
Les dieux m'ont-ils formé ce maternel contour
Et ces bords sinueux, ces plis et ces calices,
Pour que la vie embrasse un autel de délices,
Où mêlant l'âme étrange aux éternels retours,
La semance, le lait, le sang coulent toujours?
Non! L'horreur m'illumine, exécrable harmonie!
Chaque baiser présage une neuve agonie. . . .
                                        [Valéry's ellipses][81]

whats the idea making us like that with a big hole in the middle of us like a Stallion driving it up into you because thats all they want out of you with that determined vicious look in his eye I had to halfshut my eyes . . . the last time I let him finish it in me nice invention they made for women for him to get all the pleasure but if someone gave them a touch of it themselves theyd know what I

went through with Milly nobody would believe cutting
her teeth too[82]

Valéry's well-known loathing for the novel as a genre is
perhaps relevant in this connection; the anti-realist intent of
his high-poetic diction is no less evident than the realist intent
of Joyce's low-mimetic colloquy. Like many other dramatic
monologues, Valéry's is "dramatic" in a very special sense: it
reverts to the language of the great dramatic tradition, and
thus to the language of stage monologue. But even as this poetic diction counteracts realism, it also loses the essential intent of interior monologue in fiction: to present a mind in un-
hampered motion, speaking without intent or purpose, as it
never was meant to speak in the strait jacket of regular versification, much less in the rhymed alexandrine.

Other contrasts between the quoted texts are equally obvious: the abstract, euphemistic nouns that abound in the poem,
reflecting the abstracted universe the *jeune Parque* inhabits, as
Molly's vulgar concretions reflect her palpable world; or the
absence of "real" characters in the *jeune Parque*'s mind (a serpent being her sole past acquaintance) as compared to the
motley array of embodied males in Molly's life.

I have purposely picked extreme examples of verse and
prose monologues to make my point. Other poets, particularly in Valéry's and Joyce's own generation, modulate the
dramatic monologue toward a more relaxed, more casual
idiom, which sometimes resembles Joyce's language more
than Valéry's. Conversely, writers like Dujardin and Larbaud
cast their monologues into a more elevated idiom, on occasion verging on free verse.[83] But even when a dramatic
monologist speaks in more prosaic tones and in freer verse, he
still takes on the stance of a poetic speaker, like Eliot's Pru-
frock in his "Song." When, on the other hand, an interior
monologue is lyric in tone, we attribute this tone to the character's romantic mood, or to his Symbolist upbringing,
rather than to his aesthetic intent as speaker of poetry. In the
end, the distinction between the dramatic and the fictional

monologues comes down to the distinction between verse and prose; the sharper the line one draws between the two realms of literary language, the sharper the line one must draw between verse and prose monologue.

This brings us to the question of the relationship between autonomous monologue and prose poem. If we agree with Northrop Frye that "The lyric poet normally pretends to be talking to himself,"[84] the common denominator between the lyric poem and the interior monologue springs into focus: they have in common what Frye calls their "radical of presentation." When lyric language becomes freed from the bonds of versification in the prose poem, the lyric speaker begins to speak in the manner of the interior monologist. Not all prose poems are self-centered—no more than all verse poems—and even fewer center on the self in the present moment. But those that do could be mistaken for autonomous monologues: brief ones, to be sure, since brevity is of the essence in the prose poem.

There are interesting historical links between the development of prose poetry and the genesis of interior monologue.[85] In retrospect, a sentence in the preface to Baudelaire's *Le Spleen de Paris* (1869) acts as a kind of prophetic signpost: "Which one of us, in his moments of ambition, has not dreamed of the miracle of a poetic prose, musical, without rhythm and without rhyme, supple enough and rugged enough to adapt itself to the lyrical impulses of the soul, the undulations of revery, the jibes of conscience?"[86] Baudelaire's *Spleen* volume itself is not the stream of consciousness that this preface seems to promise, but a collection of separate prose poems (one of the earliest). Their form and content vary widely, from anecdotes in the third person to second-person invocations. Certain pieces that are cast in first person

---

* Quel est celui de nous qui n'a pas, dans ses jours d'ambition, rêvé le miracle d'une prose poétique, musicale, sans rhythme et sans rime, assez souple et assez heurtée pour s'adapter aux mouvements lyriques de l'âme, aux ondulations de la rêverie, aux soubresauts de la conscience?

and present tense, however, can be read as language that corresponds directly to "the lyrical impulses of the soul, the undulations of revery, the jibes of conscience." Take "Artist's Confiteor" ("Le Confiteor de l'Artiste"): it expresses the speaker's rising delight before a seascape on an autumn evening: "What bliss to plunge the eyes into the immensity of the sky and sea"; he reaches an ecstatic climax, then sinks into deepest depression: "My nerves are strung to such a pitch that they can no longer give out anything but shrill and painful vibrations."[87] The progressive recording of these feelings at the moment they are experienced is very close to an autonomous monologue: this prose poem could easily be imagined within the larger context of a work like Larbaud's "Amants" or Dujardin's *Lauriers*. And yet there is a decisive reason why we do not experience it as fiction: nothing differentiates its speaker from its author, nothing signals a fictional character behind the voice. And since we look for a person behind every written text, we attribute this voice to the person whose name appears on the title page, Charles Baudelaire. Since he has not donned a mask, we must assume that he is speaking in his own name.[88]

Solely the identification of the speaker as a fictional character distinguishes an interior-monologue text from a prose poem of this type. In the majority of cases, generic confusion is ruled out: most autonomous monologues present themselves as fictions by title (e.g., *Leutnant Gustl*), or subtitle (*Novelle, récit*, etc.). Or they introduce the character's name within the text, locate the speaker in a distinctive setting and situation, give him a mate, and shape a minimal plot. No one will mistake the speaker of Camus' "Renégat" (tongueless, tortured, and converted by the African natives he came to convert) for the author who created him. But the assigning of a genre becomes more difficult in those instances where au-

---

* Grand délice que celui de noyer son regard dans l'immensité du ciel et de la mer!

* Mes nerfs trop tendus ne donnent plus que des vibrations criardes et douloureuses.

tonomous monologues contain no signals of fictionality. Certain brief Kafka texts are ambiguous in this way, especially those published from his untitled notebooks. In the page-long sketch "Heimkehr," we hear a person monologizing at the moment he enters his parental home (a farmhouse) after a long absence: "I have returned, I have crossed the threshold and I look around. It is my father's old farmstead. . . ."[89] A typical Kafka figure, he remains arrested on the threshold, assailed by silent questions—to the end of the text. If we did not happen to know that Kafka's father was a business man, there would be little justification in viewing this prodigal son of a farmer as a fictional figure, or in assigning this text to the corpus of Kafka's "stories."

We can see now that the dramatic monologue and the prose poem are both relatives of the autonomous monologue, but that they belong to different sides of its family: the interior monologue shares its fictive speaker with the dramatic monologue, its expressive prose language with the prose poem. These relations are not merely academic. There is at least one major novelist who has dwelt at (and on) this generic crossing-point at length: Virginia Woolf, while writing *The Waves*. In this novel she explores and exploits the confluence of drama, lyric poetry, and narrative fiction principally by fashioning monologic texts of an unusual type. Woolf's diary entries concerning the work in progress repeatedly indicate her own awareness of the crossbreed she was hatching. From the start—years before she created her characters and their strange language—she conceived of her future book as "a new kind of play . . . prose yet poetry; a novel and a play." The descriptive term she soon came to prefer for the work was "play-poem" (also spelled "playpoem"). But more than three years passed before its final structure jelled in her mind. "*The Waves* is I think resolving itself . . . into a series of dramatic soliloquies."[90]

---

* Ich bin zurückgekehrt, ich habe den Flur durchschritten und blicke mich um. Es ist meines Vaters alter Hof. . . .

It is immediately apparent that the speeches of the six characters in *The Waves* have more in common with dramatic
monologues (or the soliloquies of drama) and with prose
poems than with the silent monologues of modern narrative
fiction. For one thing, they are all cast in a uniform idiom,
which varies neither laterally (from one character to another),
nor temporally (from childhood to maturity), thereby dispelling all sense of psychological verisimilitude. Nor can these
speeches be understood as the spontaneous unrolling of
thoughts at a random moment: Woolf makes her characters
speak to themselves formally, deliberately, and highly self-
consciously, each in turn taking up the stance of a poetic
speaker. References to the act of locution abound: "Now let
me try . . . before we go to tea, to fix the moment in one
effort of supreme endeavour"; "What am I? I ask. This? No I
am that. Especially now, when I have left a room, and people
talking"; "But I am too nervous to end my sentence properly.
I speak quickly, as I pace up and down, to conceal my agitation."[91]

There is, moreover, one grammatical feature that raises the
prose of these soliloquies to prose poetry even when they deal
with the most prosaic matters. When the speakers describe
their own gestures, as they often do, they replace the progressive present customary in spoken English by the tense reserved for English poetry—for which George T. Wright has
suggested the name "lyric present."[92] Jinny, for example,
says "I move, I dance," "I bind my hair with a white ribbon,"
"I glance, I peep, I powder," "I fill my glass again. I drink,"
"I stoop. I pick a blue flower," just as Shelley, in the verses
Wright uses as paradigms, says "I fall upon the thorns of life! I
bleed!", or "I die! I faint! I fail!" It is mainly because of these
verb forms that Jinny's gestures are not understood as occurring simultaneously with her locution, but in the temporally
anomalous, "timeless" dimension associated with gestures in
a poem. This is also why the jarring effect that we previously
noted when a monologist directly records his own gestures
does not arise in *The Waves*, for this effect is disturbing only

when autonomous monologues attempt to create the illusion that the reader is overhearing a "real" mind thinking its thoughts. Woolf's soliloquies, from start to finish, convey the idea that they are subject to poetic license, and that they must *not* be understood as realistic reproductions of the characters' mental idiom. This poetic license also applies to the self-conscious perception verbs that so frequently recur and stamp the speeches with an anti-realist intent from their inception: " 'I see a ring' said Bernard. . . . 'I see a slab of pale yellow,' said Susan. . . . 'I hear a sound,' said Rhoda. . . ."

For all these reasons, then, the "dramatic soliloquies" of *The Waves* cannot be understood as realistic reproductions of figural thought or speech, but must be understood as poetry fashioned by a single creative mind. Beyond that, the many redundancies between the soliloquies and the nine italicized interludes suggest that the same mind is responsible for the entire text contained between the book's covers. A number of recent critics have suggested that this mind is in fact incarnated within the book in the person of Bernard.[93] The most important intrinsic evidence for this interpretation is the last section of the novel, where Bernard recapitulates all the preceding sections in a soliloquy that takes the precise form of an autobiographical monologue. Further support is provided by several of Woolf's diary entries, above all the one where she notes: "I am not trying to tell a story. Yet perhaps it might be done in that way. A mind thinking. . . . Autobiography it might be called."[94] If this interpretation is correct, *The Waves* as a whole would have to be understood as a single autonomous monologue produced, in chronological order, by Bernard's creative memory. The speeches of the six figures (including Bernard's own) then appear as interior monologues Bernard invents to articulate his memories, embedding them in his own all-pervasive autobiographical monologue.

Woolf's play-poem-novel is a unique experiment. It works variations on the interior monologue form that do not belong to the main stream of the fictional genre. That is also why it could be accommodated in this study only *in extremis*.

Notes

Notes

Introduction—pages 3-17

1. *Tristram Shandy*, pp. 75-76 (Book I, chap. 23).
2. E.T.A. Hoffmann, *Meister Floh*, p. 806.
3. *Remembrance of Things Past*, I, trans. Moncrieff, p. 64.
4. Truman Capote, *In Cold Blood*, pp. 243-244.
5. E. M. Forster, *Aspects of the Novel* (New York, 1927/1954), p. 45.
6. "Versuch über das Theater," *Gesammelte Werke* (Frankfurt, 1960), X, p. 29.
7. José Ortega y Gasset, "Notes on the Novel," in *The Dehumanization of Art and Other Writings on Art and Culture* (Garden City, N.Y., 1956), p. 95.
8. "The Art of Fiction," in *The Future of the Novel*, ed. Leon Edel (New York, 1956), pp. 5 and 14.
9. "Preface to *The Portrait of a Lady*," in *The Art of the Novel*, ed. Richard P. Blackmur (New York, 1962), p. 45.
10. *Op. cit.*, pp. 48 and 51.
11. *Op. cit.*, p. 57.
12. Trans. Marilynn J. Rose (Bloomington, Indiana, 1973). Originally published as *Die Logik der Dichtung* (Stuttgart, 1957; 2nd revised edition, 1968).
13. *The Logic of Literature*, p. 83.
14. It is important to realize, however, that Hamburger excludes from her category of epic (narrative) fiction all forms of first-person narration. Only narration in the third person creates a mimetic reality, whereas first-person narrative forms have a structure that imitates non-fictional (mainly autobiographical) texts.
15. See Erich Kahler, *The Inward Turn of Narrative*, trans. Richard and Clara Winston (Princeton, N.J., 1973). See also Richard Brinkmann, *Wirklichkeit und Illusion* (Tübingen, 1957) for a theory of Realism as progressive "subjectivization" of reality.

16. "Die Kunst des Romans," *Gesammelte Werke* (Frankfurt, 1960), X, pp. 356-357.

17. "Modern Fiction," in *The Common Reader* (New York, 1948), pp. 212-213.

18. *Versuch über den Roman* (1774; rpt. Stuttgart, 1965), pp. 264-265.

19. *Sämtliche Werke*, ed. Arthur Hübscher (Wiesbaden, 1947), VI/2, pp. 468-469.

20. See especially Georg Lukács, "Erzählen oder Beschreiben? Zur Diskussion über Naturalismus und Formalismus" (1936), in *Begriffsbestimmung des literarischen Realismus*, ed. Richard Brinkmann (Darmstadt, 1969); Erich Auerbach, *Mimesis: The Representation of Reality in Western Literature* (Garden City, N.Y., 1957), pp. 551-553; Wolfgang Kayser, *Entstehung und Krise des modernen Romans* (Stuttgart, 1954); Leon Edel, *The Modern Psychological Novel* (New York, 1955); David Daiches, *The Novel and the Modern World* (Chicago, 1960), pp. 1-11.

21. *The Dehumanization of Art*, p. 33.

22. The following are some of the most frequently quoted studies in this vein: Frederick J. Hoffman, *Freudianism and the Literary Mind* (Baton Rouge, La., 1945); Lawrence E. Bowling, "What is Stream of Consciousness Technique?", *PMLA* 65 (1950), 333-345; Robert Humphrey, *Stream of Consciousness in the Modern Novel* (Berkeley, 1954); Melvin Friedman, *Stream of Consciousness: A Study in Literary Method* (New Haven, 1955); Leon Edel, *The Modern Psychological Novel* (New York, 1955); Shiv K. Kumar, *Bergson and the Stream of Consciousness Novel* (New York, 1963). The same imprecise approach to the technique problem also pervades the recent book by Erwin R. Steinberg, *The Stream of Consciousness and Beyond in Ulysses* (Pittsburgh, 1973).

23. Edel establishes a rough equivalence between stream of consciousness and interior monologue, and also uses the terms alternately to refer to techniques and to types of novels. See, for example: pp. 11, 18, 24, 56.

24. Humphrey distinguishes four techniques: direct interior monologue, indirect interior monologue, description by an omniscient author, and soliloquy (pp. 23-41).

25. "Modes of Interior Monologue: A Formal Definition," *Modern Language Quarterly* 28 (1967), 229-239. Bickerton establishes the following equivalences with Humphrey's categories:

soliloquy: direct speech
omniscient description: indirect speech
indirect interior monologue: free indirect speech
direct interior monologue: free direct speech

(The last of these categories is Bickerton's term for direct speech that is not explicitly introduced or quoted.)

Seymour Chatman has recently proposed a similar, if more refined, fourfold correspondence to the modes of speech quotation; see "The Structure of Narrative Transmission" in *Style and Structure in Literature*, ed. Roger Fowler (Oxford, 1975), pp. 213-257, esp. pp. 248-257.

26. Gérard Genette, *Figures III* (Paris, 1972), pp. 191-193.

27. These terms are used by Bickerton (p. 254) and Bowling (p. 343). Humphrey's "description by an omniscient author" and Scholes and Kellogg's "narrative analysis" have similar disadvantages (See *The Nature of Narrative* [New York, 1966], p. 193.)

28. Humphrey, p. 33. Humphrey must be given credit, however, for acknowledging the existence of this "conventional" technique in stream of consciousness novels. Other critics have categorically denied that novels of this type include such "omniscient" passages. See Bowling, pp. 343-344, Friedman, pp. 5-6, Bickerton, p. 235.

29. See, for example, Bickerton's analysis of a passage from *Middlemarch*, pp. 235-236.

30. See Edouard Dujardin, *Le Monologue intérieur* (Paris, 1931), pp. 7 and 65-73. Also W. J. Lillyman, "The Interior Monologue in James Joyce and Otto Ludwig," *Comparative*

Literature 23 (1971), 45-54, esp. pp. 49-50; Bickerton, "Modes of Interior Monologue," pp. 233-235; and Humphrey, pp. 36-38.

31. Dujardin himself sums up the distinction like this: "The essential innovation of the interior monologue consisted in its object, which was to evoke the uninterrupted flux of thoughts that traverse the mind of the character, at the moment they arise, without explaining their logical linkage, while giving the impression of haphazardness. . . . The difference is not that the traditional monologue expresses less intimate thoughts than the interior monologue, but that it coordinates them by showing their logical linkage." (*Le Monologue intérieur*, p. 68.)

32. I have previously argued in favor of this grammatical criterion (and against the interior monologue – soliloquy distinction) in "Narrated Monologue: Definition of a Fictional Style," *Comparative Literature* 18 (1966), 97-112, p. 109. See also Scholes and Kellogg, who introduce their admirable discussion of direct thought-quotations from Homer to Joyce by clearly distinguishing interior monologue from stream of consciousness and identifying it with "unspoken soliloquy" (p. 177). W. J. Lillyman tries to refute these arguments on the grounds that the true (Joycean) interior monologue "lacks all signs of a narrator's presence, all signs of a narrator's control" (p. 47). But the only "signs" of this kind that he is able to find in pre-Joycean monologues are external to the actual though-quotation, and concern rather the manner in which the monologue is tied into the context: whether or not it is explicitly introduced (p. 49). In this respect Joyce did of course introduce an innovative pattern that needs to be discussed.

33. Scholes and Kellogg, p. 193.

34. See "Narrated Monologue: Definition of a Fictional Style."

35. I have resisted replacing the familiar terms "first-person" and "third-person" by the corresponding Genettean terms "homodiegetic" and "heterodiegetic." Genette is en-

tirely correct in pointing out that the traditional terms are inexact because "all narrative is, by definition, virtually in the first person." (*Figures III*, p. 252.) But the unfamiliarity of Genette's terms is a heavy price to pay for the small gain in precision. Caution in using the approximate older terms seemed to me preferable for the purposes of this study.

36. Genette, for example, does not take differences of person (voice) sufficiently into account in his discussion of focalization (point of view) in *Figures III*, pp. 203-211. See the critique by Shlomith Rimmon: "A Comprehensive Theory of Narrative: Genette's *Figures III* and the Structuralist Study of Fiction," *PTL* 1 (1976), 33-62, pp. 58-59.

37. David Goldknopf, *The Life of the Novel* (Chicago, 1972), pp. 38-39.

38. This distinction has been disregarded in the studies (referred to above) by Dujardin, Bowling, Humphrey, Friedman, Edel, Bickerton, Scholes and Kellogg, Lillyman. It also remains unmentioned by Valéry Larbaud in his preface to *Les Lauriers sont coupés*. Only Genette views the distinction correctly and suggests that texts of the *Les Lauriers* type "which one has rather unfortunately baptized the 'monologue intérieur' should more properly be called *discours immédiat*" (*Figures III*, p. 193).

39. Cited in English by Richard Ellmann, *James Joyce* (New York, 1959), p. 534. Ellmann translates Joyce's comment from its French quotation by Valéry Larbaud in the preface to the 1925 edition of *Les Lauriers sont coupés*, which reads as follows: "Dans *Les Lauriers sont coupés*, me dit Joyce, le lecteur se trouve installé, dès les premières lignes, dans la pensée du personnage principal, et c'est le déroulement ininterrompu de cette pensée qui, se substituant complètement à la forme usuelle du recit, nous apprend ce que fait ce personnage et ce qui lui arrive."

40. It is therefore highly misleading to take Joyce's description of *Les Lauriers* as his "definition of interior monologue" generally, as W. J. Lillyman does in his article "The Interior Monologue," p. 50.

41. According to Ellmann, "Penelope" was completed in October, 1921, and the comment to Larbaud was made in November, 1921. (*James Joyce*, pp. 533-534.)

42. There is no evidence Joyce himself used the term interior monologue. But in the "Linati Schema," he shows his awareness of the difference between "Penelope" and sections like "Proteus" by calling the "Technic" of the former "Monologue," that of the latter "Soliloquy." See Richard Ellmann, *Ulysses on the Liffey* (New York, 1972), Appendix.

Some critics have applied the term interior monologue exclusively to interior-monologue novels, notably Michel Butor in "L'usage des pronoms personnels dans le roman" (*Répertoire II* [Paris, 1964], pp. 61-72), and Erika Höhnisch, *Das gefangene Ich: Studien zum inneren Monolog im französischen Roman* (Heidelberg, 1967).

1   Psycho-narration—pages 21-57

1. *Vanity Fair*, p. 50 (chap. 4).

2. The distinction between "contextual" and "intrinsic" knowledge of characters is drawn in W. J. Harvey, *Character and the Novel* (Ithaca, N.Y., 1965), p. 32. Though Harvey acknowledges the importance of both kinds of characterization in fiction, his book deals solely with "contextual" knowledge.

3. *The Rise of the Novel* (Berkeley, 1967), pp. 268-280.

4. *Tom Jones*, p. 527 (Book XI, chap. 8) and p. 158 (Book IV, chap. 14).

5. *Tom Jones*, p. 270 (Book VII, chap. 2).

6. *Vanity Fair*, p. 360 (chap. 31).

7. *Le Père Goriot*, p. 891.

8. Henry James hints at this seesawing relationship when he argues—in the preface to *The Princess Casamassima*—for protagonists with rich and subtle minds, but concedes that Tom Jones can get away with his mindlessness because "his author—*he* handsomely possessed of a mind—has such an amplitude of reflection for him and round him that we see

him through the mellow air of Fielding's fine old moralism, fine old humour and fine old style. . ." (*The Art of the Novel* [New York, 1962], p. 68).

9. Wayne C. Booth, *The Rhetoric of Fiction* (Chicago, 1961), p. 164.

10. The terms "dissonant" and "consonant" I apply to these two types of psycho-narration are my own. But the typological contrast they define corresponds to the two typical narrative situations Franz Stanzel defines for third-person narration, which he names "authorial" and "figural" (in German *auktorial* and *personal*; see *Narrative Situations in the Novel: Tom Jones, Moby Dick, The Ambassadors, Ulysses*, trans. J. P. Pusack [Bloomington, Indiana, 1971], pp. 23-25, 27-29, and chaps. 2 and 4). I will use both pairs of terms in conjunction throughout this study, with the term "dissonant" applying specifically to the relationship between the narrator and the protagonist in an authorial narrative situation, the term "consonant" to the narrator-protagonist relationship in a figural narrative situation.

Both the authorial-figural and the dissonant-consonant pairs correspond approximately to a whole series of polarities proposed by other critics: *vision par derrière - vision avec* (Pouillon, Todorov), telling—showing (Booth), non-focalized—focalized (Genette) etc. For a recent correlation of French, German and American approaches to the problem of narrative perspective, see Françoise Van Rossum-Guyon, "Point de vue ou perspective narrative: Théories et concepts critiques," *Poétique* I (1970), 476-497.

11. *Der Tod in Venedig*, pp. 493-494.

12. Sartre's well-known polemic against Mauriac centers on this point. Though we may readily agree with him that Mauriac explains the inner life of his characters in an irritatingly patronizing manner, Sartre throws out the baby with the bath-water when he bans all psycho-narration from the novel: "the introduction of absolute truth or of God's standpoint constitutes a double error in technique" (François Mauriac and Freedom," in *Literary and Philosophical Essays*,

trans. Annette Michelson [London, 1955], p. 15). For Booth's
disagreement with Sartre, see *The Rhetoric of Fiction*, pp.
50-53. Booth's own views are most explicitly stated in the
chapter "The Uses of Reliable Commentary."

13. *The Ironic German: A Study of Thomas Mann* (Boston,
1958), p. 99.

14. Cf. William M. Schutte's *Introduction to Twentieth Century Interpretations of A Portrait of the Artist as a Young Man*
(Englewood Cliffs, N.J., 1968), p. 12. Schutte counts nineteen such phases or "presents," and explains: "As the action
moves from present to present . . . the style subtly modulates
to reflect the inevitable changes in the quality of Stephen's apprehension of the world about him." See also in the same
volume, F. Parvin Sharpless, "Irony in Joyce's Portrait: The
Stasis of Pity," p. 97.

15. *A Portrait of the Artist*, pp. 175-176.

16. For this reason Wayne Booth's "Problem of Distance
in *A Portrait of the Artist*" (*The Rhetoric of Fiction*, pp. 323-336)
seems to me more his problem than that of Joyce's text. When
he charges Joyce with "confusion of distance," all he is really
saying is that Stephen is a complex literary creation who gives
rise to contradictory interpretations. This is equally true of
Don Quixote, Hamlet, Alceste, Faust, Anna Karenina, and
Kafka's K.

17. Cf. Robert Scholes' different, though not necessarily
contradictory, view that the text preceding the stanzas of the
villanelle is "an elaborate explication" of the poem by the author ("Stephen Dedalus, Poet or Aesthete," *PMLA* 89 [1964],
484-489).

18. *A Portrait of the Artist*, p. 217.

19. "Sprachmengung als Stilmittel und als Ausdruck der
Klangphantasie," in *Stilstudien* II (1922, rpt. Munich, 1961),
pp. 84-124, esp. p. 98.

20. As Derek Bickerton has shown, there are very few direct thought-quotations in the *Portrait* ("James Joyce and the
Development of Interior Monologue," *Essays in Criticism* 18
[1968], 32-46, pp. 40-41). The villanelle must, however, be
added to the three other instances he mentions.

21. See above, p. 12.

22. *Emma*, p. 923 (chap. 31).

23. Cf. Eberhard Lämmert's similar classification of modes of time-condensation in *Bauformen des Erzählens* (Stuttgart, 1955), pp. 83-84.

24. *Madame Bovary*, pp. 423, 438.

25. *Op. cit.*, pp. 438, 521.

26. *Op. cit.*, p. 361.

27. Cf. Sartre's awareness of the unsuitability of summary psycho-narration for novels using a figural narrative situation: "Indeed, if without mediation we plunge the reader into a consciousness, if we refuse him all means of surveying the whole, then the time of this consciousness must be imposed upon him without abridgment. If I pack six months into a single page, the reader jumps out of the book." (*What is Literature?*, trans. Bernard Frechtman. New York, 1949, p. 228, n. 2.) See also the correspondence between temporal structure and narrative situation in Lämmert, p. 87 and Franz Stanzel, *Narrative Situations in the Novel* (Bloomington, Indiana, 1971), pp. 103-105.

28. *The Portrait of a Lady*, chap. 42.

29. Preface to *L'Ere du soupçon* (Paris, 1956), p. iii.

30. Derek Bickerton's definition of "omniscient description" (his term for psycho-narration) as "inner speech rendered in indirect speech" seems to me erroneous, implying as it does that psycho-narration can generally be transposed into a direct quotation of inner speech ("Modes of Interior Monologue: A Formal Definition," *Modern Language Quarterly* 28 [1967], 229-239, p. 238). The durative summary from *Middlemarch* he uses to illustrate this mode (p. 235) cannot possibly be transposed in this manner. For this reason it is also highly misleading to classify "omniscient description" as a "mode of interior monologue."

31. *A la recherche du temps perdu* I, pp. 268-269; English based on *Remembrance of Things Past* I, trans. Moncrieff, p. 206.

32. See below, pp. 79-81.

33. This story is reprinted in *Prosa, Dramen, Späte Briefe*

(Hamburg, 1957), pp. 162-199. The translation by Wilkins and Kaiser is contained in *Five Women*.

34. *Tagebücher, Aphorismen, Essays und Reden* (Hamburg, 1955), p. 131.

35. "Die Vollendung der Liebe," pp. 173-174; English based on "The Perfecting of a Love," trans. Wilkins/Kaiser, pp. 139-140.

36. *Tagebücher*, p. 775.

37. *Prosa*, p. 72. Musil's rationale for avoiding monologic techniques is most clearly expressed in his early novel *Young Törless* (from which the above quotation is taken). For further discussion of this problem and of "The Perfecting of a Love" see my article "Psyche and Space in Musil's 'Die Vollendung der Liebe,' " *Germanic Review* 49 (1974), 154-168.

38. *Mrs. Dalloway*, p. 182.

39. *To the Lighthouse*, p. 275.

40. *Le Planétarium*, pp. 11, 74-75, 166; English: *The Planetarium*, trans. Jolas, pp. 14, 88, 192.

41. Preface to *L'Ere du soupçon*, p. iii.

42. Ortega y Gasset, *The Dehumanization of Art*, p. 33.

43. See the Preface to *What Maisie Knew*, in *The Art of the Novel*, pp. 144-146.

44. *What Maisie Knew*, p. 33.

45. Occasionally James will make a half-hearted attempt to color his psycho-narration with child-language, as when he mentions Maisie's "tucked-in and kissed-for-good-night feeling" for Miss Wix (p. 36). But these phrases always stand in sentences of typically complex Jamesian syntax.

46. *Op. cit.*, p. 165.

47. *Crime and Punishment*, p. 63.

48. *Buddenbrooks*, p. 658.

49. *Törless*, p. 116.

50. *Women in Love*, p. 443.

51. *Op. cit.*, pp. 9, 98, 65-68. In Lawrence such electric images, and imagistic psycho-narrations generally, are by no means limited to erotic scenes. Cf. the passage from *Aaron's Rod*, where the narrator theorizes about his method for ren-

dering the protagonist's consciousness: "his thoughts and ideas, were dark and invisible, as electric vibrations are invisible. . . . If I, as a word-user, must translate his deep conscious vibrations into finite words, that is my own business." (London, 1954, p. 160.) The passage is more fully quoted by Scholes and Kellogg to illustrate an author's "dissatisfaction with words as conveyors of feelings" (*The Nature of Narrative* [New York, 1966], pp. 198-199).

52. See below, pp. 72-74, 132-134.

53. " 'Voir' as a Modern Novelistic Device," *Philological Quarterly* 23 (1944), 354-374.

54. *Der Tod in Venedig*, p. 447.

55. Another text that displays similar imagery is Stephen's obscene vision of hell in *A Portrait of the Artist*. Its extended introduction works an interesting variation on mental optics: "He desired with all his will not to hear or see. He desired till his frame shook under the strain of his desire and until the senses of his soul closed. They closed for an instant and then opened. He saw.

A field of stiff weeds and thistles. . ." (p. 137).

56. In a recent dissertation Nils Ekfelt has used statistical methods to show how closely the stylistics of dream narration conform to the general stylistic norms in the work of Mann and Schnitzler. ("The Narration of Dreams in the Prose Works of Thomas Mann and Arthur Schnitzler: A Stylistic Study," Ph.D. Diss. Indiana, 1973.)

57. See *Crime and Punishment*, pp. 115-116 and 270-272.

58. See K.'s dream in *Das Schloss*, pp. 382-383, and Joseph K.'s dream in "Ein Traum," in *Erzählungen und kleine Prosa* (New York, 1946), pp. 164-166.

59. *Tod in Venedig*, p. 516.

60. *Op. cit.*, p. 515.

61. *Remembrance of Things Past*, I, p. 29. In this dream of Swann's about Odette, the narrator also introduces in mid-dream a remarkable quasi-Freudian analysis, translating the dream's manifest meaning into its latent meaning.

62. Interesting effects are obtained in certain instances

where introductory dream-signals are omitted, especially
when time and space within the dream are contiguous to the
"real" time and space of the dreaming character. See, for
example, Raskolnikov's fever fantasy about a violent scene
taking place outside his door (*Crime and Punishment*, pp. 115-
116). The structure of this and other "narrated dreams" has
been analyzed by R. J. Lethcoe, "Narrated Speech and Consciousness," Ph.D. Diss. Wisconsin, 1969, pp. 257-265.

63. For an analysis of the title concept, see my study *The
Sleepwalkers: Elucidations of Hermann Broch's Trilogy* (The
Hague, 1966), pp. 137-167.

64. The clearest theoretical statement of these aims is contained in a text entitled "Bemerkungen zu den 'Tierkreiser-
zählungen,' " in *Die unbekannte Grösse* (Zurich, 1961), pp.
187-193.

65. *Die Schlafwandler*, p. 376.

66. *Op. cit.*, p. 404.

67. *Op. cit.*, pp. 461, 498, 568.

68. *Op. cit.*, pp. 588-589.

69. Frederick J. Hoffman, *Freudianism and the Literary Mind*
(Baton Rouge, La., 1945/1967), p. 128; Melvin Friedman,
Stream of Consciousness: A Study in Literary Method (New Haven, 1955), p. 5; Erwin R. Steinberg, *The Stream of Consciousness and Beyond in* Ulysses (Pittsburgh, 1973), pp. 251-252.

70. *The Modern Psychological Novel* (New York, 1955), p.
55 (Edel's emphasis).

2   Quoted monologue—pages 58-98

1. For the use of monologue in earlier fictional forms (epic
and romance), see the excellent presentation in Scholes and
Kellogg, *The Nature of Narrative*, pp. 177-190, and 284-289.

2. Wieland, *Agathon*, p. 398 (Book I, chap. 10).

3. G. Gougenheim ("Du discours intérieur au monologue
intérieur," *Le Français moderne* 14-15 [1946-1947], 242-248)
documents this fact in 17th and 18th century French writers.
His distinction between "discours" and "monologue," based

exclusively on inquit formulas, is too sharp, however, since many later authors use "he said" when they mean "he thought" (see note 13, below).

4. In a novella entitled "Who is the Betrayer?" Goethe even makes a habitual monologist into a comic hero. The slim psychological motivation that sets the plot in motion is a young man's excessive introversion which inhibits communication with others, and thereby heightens the need for (and the volume of) solitary discourse; he finally gets to marry the right girl only because his eavesdropping friends overhear his private thoughts.

5. *Little Dorrit*, p. 422 (Book II, chap. 1).

6. *Le Rouge et le noir*, p. 37 (Book I, chap. 7).

7. *Op. cit.*, p. 299 (Book II, chap. 44).

8. *Crime and Punishment*, p. 4.

9. *Op. cit.*, p. 5.

10. Genette, *Figures III* (Paris, 1972), pp. 196-197.

11. *Les Faux-monnayeurs*, pp. 933-934.

12. *Op. cit.*, p. 1150.

13. Jane Austen for example, who habitually uses "said she" in the first sentences of monologues, at times simply omits this inquit formula (*Emma*, pp. 844, 923); "thought she" appears when thoughts are quoted during conversational scenes (*Emma*, p. 970). But also some modern writers continue to use saying verbs, notably Faulkner—who even establishes their equivalence with thinking verbs when "he [Hightower] says it, thinks it" (*Light in August*, p. 305).

14. *Les Misérables*, I, p. 277; English based on *Les Misérables*, trans. Wilbour, pp. 189-190.

15. *Crime and Punishment*, p. 90 (Part 2, chap. 1).

16. *Ulysses*, pp. 56-57.

17. See Breon Mitchell, *James Joyce and the German Novel 1922-1933* (Athens, Ohio, 1976), esp. pp. 112, and 136-137.

18. *Berlin Alexanderplatz*, p. 11.

19. "Intimité," pp. 103, 104.

20. *Op. cit.*, p. 136.

21. Some of Joyce's disciples further increased the cohesion

between interior monologue and the surrounding narrative context by using the same (present) tense for both. Valéry Larbaud, one of Joyce's earliest and closest imitators, does this in his story "Mon plus secret Conseil."

22. *Mrs. Dalloway*, p. 72.

23. *Light in August*, p. 133.

24. Though the lyric interludes present an authorial voice of sorts too, it is one that moves—not only typographically—on a different level from the rest of the text. See below, pp. 263-265, for a more detailed discussion of *The Waves*.

25. "Le Renégat," pp. 45 and 72.

26. *Le Rouge et le noir*, p. 85 (Book I, chap. 13.)

27. *Vanity Fair*, pp. 499-500 (chap. 41).

28. *Der Tod in Venedig*, p. 521.

29. In Proust's *Un Amour de Swann*, where quoted monologue is also used sparingly, its capacity to carry dramatic irony is artfully exploited in the final sentence: "And with that old, intermittent fortuity, which reappeared in him now that he was no longer unhappy, and lowered, at the same time, the average level of his morality, he cried out in his heart: 'To think that I have wasted years of my life, that I have longed for death, that the greatest love that I have ever known has been for a woman who did not please me, who was not my style!' " (*Remembrance of Things Past* I, trans. Moncrieff, p. 292).

30. *The Death of Ivan Ilych*, p. 148.

31. *Loc. cit.*

32. *Loc. cit.*

33. *Op. cit.*, pp. 150-151. The analysis that follows is based entirely on the Aylmer Maude translation, despite significant deviations from the Russian. According to Jurij Striedter (whom I wish to thank for this information) the pattern of repetition between monologue and narration, though present in the original, is less marked than in this translation.

34. The following is a list of the *Ulysses* sections in which monologues consistently alternate with third-person narra-

tion (with S indicating that the monologues are Stephen's, B
that they are Bloom's): Telemachus (S), Nestor (S), Proteus
(S), Calypso (B), Lotus Eaters (B), Hades (B), Lestrygonians
(B), Scylla and Charybdis (S), Nausicaa, second part (B).

35. *Ulysses*, p. 49.

36. The echo in Stephen's mind is a line from Mallarmé's
poem "L'Après-midi d'un faune": "Inerte, tout brûle dans
l'heure fauve"; (cf. William York Tindall, *A Reader's Guide to
James Joyce* [New York, 1959], p. 149).

37. *Ulysses*, pp. 49 and 44.

38. *Op. cit.*, p. 101.

39. Erwin Steinberg seems to have disregarded this
dovetailing of narration and monologue in presenting his
statistics on the quantity of "omniscient author's sentences"
in "Proteus" and "Lestrygonians" (*The Stream of Consciousness and Beyond in* Ulysses [Pittsburgh, 1973], pp. 92-96).
Since he does not state his criteria for distinguishing these sentences from those he attributes to the characters' "stream of
consciousness," his counts look more precise than they are.

40. The haziness of the dividing line between narration and
monologue has been noted in passing by several critics,
among them H. A. Kelly ("Consciousness in the Monologues of *Ulysses*," *Modern Language Quarterly* 24 [1963],
3-12, p. 5) and S. L. Goldberg (*The Classical Temper: A Study
of James Joyce's* Ulysses [London, 1961], pp. 276 and 279).
Steinberg's stylistic comparison of "Proteus" and "Lestrygonians" goes into somewhat greater detail: he points out several instances where "omniscient author's sentences" are "infected" by Stephen's or Bloom's "idioms" (pp. 100, 102,
112); and he concludes that in these two sections "Joyce tried
to make his omniscient author's sentences less obtrusive by
flavoring them with the characteristics of the stream of consciousness of the characters with which he was dealing at the
time" (p. 121). But this problem has never been rigorously
studied for *Ulysses* as a whole.

41. *Berlin Alexanderplatz*, p. 356. I omit translation of this
quotation, since I cite it for its use of (untranslatable) dialect.

The contamination of the narrator's language by the popular jargon of his characters was a deliberate tactic on Döblin's part; cf. the essay "Der Bau des epischen Kunstwerks," where he speaks of the compulsive force ("Zwangscharakter") that the linguistic milieu of his mimetic world exerts on the narrator.

42. *Mrs. Dalloway*, pp. 73-74.

43. Without referring specifically to this passage, Leon Edel has commented on the interchangeability of voices in Woolf's novels: "The same vein of poetry runs through all the minds she creates for us" (*The Modern Psychological Novel* [New York, 1955], p. 128).

44. Quoted by Lawrence Bowling ("What is Stream of Consciousness Technique," *PMLA* 65 [1950], 333-345, p. 338) from *An Honest Thief and Other Stories*.

45. *Light in August*, pp. 135, 142. See also pp. 90, 91, 137, 161, 167.

46. Victor Egger, *La Parole intérieure: Essai de psychologie descriptive* (Paris, 1881), p. 1.

47. Egger, p. 120.

48. Joseph Church, *Language and the Discovery of Reality* (New York, 1961), esp. pp. 83 and 99.

49. *The Principles of Psychology*, Vol. I (New York, 1950), esp. pp. 166-271. James discusses Egger on pp. 280-281.

50. For example in the chapter on Joyce in Shiv K. Kumar, *Bergson and the Stream of Consciousness Novel* (New York, 1963), pp. 115-117.

51. Church, p. 147.

52. "*Joyce*. A profile: spiritualized Naturalism. . . . Question: How does one think? His abbreviations are: shortened formulas for orthodox speech formulas. They copy . . . the speech-process. Not the thought-process" (*Tagebücher*, p. 584).

53. *A la Recherche* III, p. 890.

54. *The Age of Suspicion*, trans. Maria Jolas (New York, 1963), pp. 91-92.

55. *Op. cit.*, pp. 78 ff. Her comment on Joyce is compara-

ble to Musil's: "All Joyce obtained from those dark depths was an uninterrupted flow of words" (p. 79).

56. For a typical example, see *Le Rouge et le noir*, p. 283, (Book II, chap. 42). Julien has produced a particularly obnoxious thought; we are told, "Fortunately for him . . . the interior of his soul did not correspond to his cavalier language." Instances of this kind make it hard to agree with Georges Blin, when he says that Stendhal used interior monologue "for the benefit of characters who are specialists in introspection, so that they can be charged with the task . . . of practicing their own psychoanalysis" (*Stendhal et les problèmes du roman* [Paris, 1954], p. 147).

57. "Intimité," p. 134.

58. *A la Recherche* III, p. 187.

59. Cf. the analogous structure and meaning of the final sentence of *To the Lighthouse*: "Yes, she [Lily Briscoe] thought, laying down her brush in extreme fatigue, I have had my vision."

60. Claude Mauriac's novel *Le Diner en ville* (1959) is no doubt the most extreme example. It consists in its entirety of the alternating quotations of the conversational chatter and the private thoughts of eight people seated around a dinner table.

61. *Ulysses*, pp. 30-31.

62. See, for example, Harry Levin, *James Joyce* (New York, 1960), pp. 90-93.

63. Cf. Scholes and Kellogg, *The Nature of Narrative* (New York, 1966), pp. 194-195.

64. *Anna Karenina*, pp. 858-859 (Part VII, chap. 22).

65. Gleb Struve, "*Monologue Intérieur*: The Origins of the Formula and the First Statement of its Possibilities," *PMLA* 69 (1954), 1101-1111, p. 1108.

66. *War and Peace*, p. 285 (Book III, chap. 12).

67. *Ulysses*, p. 382.

68. These contradictions in terms are evident, for example, in Robert Humphrey, *Stream of Consciousness in the Modern Novel* (Berkeley, 1954): after stating initially that stream-of-

consciousness fiction is "a type of fiction in which the basic emphasis is placed on the exploration of the prespeech levels of consciousness" (p. 4), he later identifies "direct interior monologue" as one of the principal techniques of the genre (p. 25), and illustrates it with quotations from *Ulysses*.

69. Steinberg, pp. 20, 249, and passim. See also his statement in "The Stream-of-Consciousness Novelist: An Inquiry into the Relation of Consciousness and Language," *ETC* 17 (December, 1960), 423-439: "the psychological stream of consciousness is not merely a string of words . . . what the stream-of-consciousness writer writes is not a transcription but a simulation of what occurs in the mind" (p. 433).

70. *The Stream of Consciousness and Beyond in* Ulysses, pp. 45 and 51. Steinberg is of course forced to admit that "words" are the most obvious "components of the stream" (p. 44), and he even concedes—in significant understatement—that "People talk to themselves on occasion, and Joyce's characters are no exceptions." But he proceeds to illustrate how Joyce renders "preverbal" components of the stream (sensations, images, and perceptions) by quotations of passages clearly featuring the quoted-monologue technique (pp. 44-61).

71. See Michel Raimond, *La Crise du roman* (Paris, 1966), pp. 270-272, and Steinberg, pp. 22-24, for citations from critics who have understood the technique in this fashion.

72. The only critic who has clearly stated this obvious limitation of the technique is H. A. Kelly: "No other method has been so severely restricted to the intellectual area of consciousness, and to only one portion of this area, the 'verbalizable.' Far from being able to record marginal objects of attention and simultaneous awareness, the method is limited to displaying only one element of thought at a time . . ." ("Consciousness in the Monologues of *Ulysses*," p. 4).

73. J. Laplanche and J.-B. Pontalis, *The Language of Psycho-Analysis*, trans. D. Nicholson-Smith (New York, 1973), p. 169.

74. Scholes and Kellogg, p. 201; several slips of the tongue from *Ulysses* are quoted for illustration.

75. Margaret C. Solomon, "Character as Linguistic Mode: A New Look at Streams-of-Consciousness in 'Ulysses,' " in *Ulysses: Cinquante ans après*, Louis Bonnerot, ed. (Paris, 1974).

76. Emile Benvéniste, *Problems in General Linguistics*, trans. M. E. Meek (Coral Gables, Fla., 1971), p. 74. Cf. Freud's essay "The Unconscious" (quoted by La Planche and Pontalis, p. 448): "The conscious presentation comprises the presentation of the thing plus the presentation of the word belonging to it, while the unconscious presentation is the presentation of the thing alone."

77. For a discussion of "formal mimeticism" see Michal Glowínski, "Der Dialog im Roman," *Poetica* 6 (1974), 1-16, p. 6.

78. As Scholes and Kellogg (pp. 178-188) have shown, the use of a conversational idiom in quoted monologues is an important aspect of the rise of Realist conventions in fiction. They contrast this "psychological" form of monologue with an earlier "rhetorical" form. The latter prevailed in epic and romance, where "words [were] artfully deployed so as to move the reader or the audience by focusing on him and his responses" (p. 185). For a late example of "rhetorical" monologue explicitly based on the conventions of drama, see Sir Walter Scott, *The Fortunes of Nigel* (London, 1901, pp. 388-399), quoted and analyzed by Bickerton, "Modes of Interior Monologue: A Formal Definition" (*Modern Language Quarterly* 28 [1967], 229-239), p. 234. Bickerton, however, erroneously assumes that the rhetorical mode is necessarily associated with *explicitly* quoted monologues, and that colloquial speech patterns appear only when monologues are seamlessly integrated into the narrative context in the Joycean manner. It is plain, however, that eighteenth- and nineteenth-century novels frequently contain explicitly quoted monologues written in a colloquial style.

79. Cf. Benvéniste's essay "The Nature of Pronouns," in *Problems in General Linguistics*, esp. p. 218.

80. *Ivan Ilych*, p. 147.

81. *Ulysses*, pp. 45-46.

82. Mikhail Bakhtin has shown how Dostoevsky's monologues are generally structured in this manner. He quotes an example from *Crime and Punishment*, where Raskolnikov "floods his inner speech with the words of others" (*Problems of Dostoevsky's Poetics*, trans. R. W. Rotsel [Ann Arbor, Mich., 1973], p. 200).

Another remarkably clear example of this "Oedipal" type of internal debate occurs in *Le Rouge et le noir*: Julien, awaiting execution, daydreams about a successful future as a diplomat, when a voice rudely interrupts his fantasy with the words: "Not exactly, Sir, you will be guillotined in three days." He then reflects that "man has two beings inside him," and reveals the true relationship of these two beings by reciting to himself a dialogue from a play in which a father condemns his son to death (Book II, chap. 42, p. 283).

83. Quoted in Kenneth Burke, *A Grammar of Motives and A Rhetoric of Motives* (New York, 1962), p. 562. See also Burke's own discussion of the rhetoric of interior discourse (pp. 561-563).

84. Jan Mukařovskí, *Kapitel aus der Poetik*, trans. Walter Schamschula (Frankfurt a.M., 1967), pp. 132-137.

85. For an English translation of Jakobson's essay, see L. Matejka and K. Pormorska, eds., *Readings in Russian Poetics* (Cambridge, Mass., 1971).

86. See Alan Gardiner's discussion of this semantic criterion for the definition of the sentence: "intelligible purpose is the real differentiating attribute of the sentence," in *The Theory of Speech and Language* (Oxford, 1951), p. 210.

87. See esp. Steinberg, *The Stream of Consciousness* (Part II), Solomon (see n. 75), and Therese Fischer, *Bewusstseinsdarstellung im Werk von James Joyce von Dubliners zu Ulysses* (Frankfurt a.M., 1973), pp. 129-134.

88. *James Joyce*, pp. 92-93.

89. *Ulysses*, p. 377.

90. For an expert stylistic-linguistic analysis of Bloom's monologic language, see John Spencer, "A Note on the

'Steady Monologuy of the Interiors,' " *Review of English Literature* 6:2 (1965), 32-41. Grammatical incompleteness is discussed on pp. 37-39.

91. Lev Semenovich Vygotsky, *Thought and Language*, ed. and trans. E. Hanfmann and G. Vakar (Cambridge, Mass., 1962).
92. Vygotsky, p. 135.
93. *Op. cit.*, pp. 138-139.
94. *Loc. cit.*
95. *Op. cit.*, p. 127.
96. *Ulysses*, pp. 57 and 377.
97. *Ulysses*, pp. 55, 57, 370.
98. Vygotsky, p. 145.
99. *Op. cit.*, p. 147.
100. This is a term used by Humphrey (p. 70).
101. Cf. Steinberg, *The Stream of Consciousness*, pp. 107 and 159.

3 Narrated Monologue—pages 99-140

1. Arno Holz and Johannes Schlaf, *Papa Hamlet* (Stuttgart, 1968), p. 28. Ruby Cohn has drawn attention to this transposition of Hamlet's speech into narrated monologue form in *Modern Shakespeare Offshoots* (Princeton, N.J., 1976), p. 153.
2. This Hamlet speech is not, of course, strictly speaking, a monologue, since he speaks it in the presence of Rosencrantz and Guildenstern. But for my present purposes this fact is not revelant.
3. Cf. Roland Barthes' suggestion that certain passages in third-person texts can be "rewritten" (he uses the Frenchified verb "rewriter") in the first person ("Introduction à l'analyse structurale des récits," *Communications* 8 [1966], 1-27, p. 20). See also Richard Ohmann's application of the "transformation" concept to a Hemingway text containing narrated monologue ("Generative Grammars and the Concept of Literary Style," *Word* 20 [1964], 423-439).
4. *Mrs. Dalloway*, pp. 101-102.

5. *Das Schloss*, pp. 45-46; English based on *The Castle*, trans. Muir, p. 39.

6. *A Portrait of the Artist*, p. 143.

7. This "as if" quality of narrated monologue has been described by Harald Weinrich (*Tempus* [Stuttgart, 1964], p. 235). Paul Hernadi similarly designates the mental life rendered through this technique as "quasi-verbal" ("Dual Perspective: Free Indirect Discourse and Related Techniques," *Comparative Literature* 24 [1972], 32-43, p. 39).

8. For a comprehensive study of all the different "signals" that characterize narrated monologue, see R. J. Lethcoe, "Narrated Speech and Consciousness," Ph.D. Diss. Wisconsin, 1969, pp. 79-169. Ludomír Doležel's survey of "Discriminative Features in Czech Represented Discourse" (*Narrative Modes in Czech Literature* [Toronto, 1973], pp. 20-40) is equally useful.

9. See Eugen Lerch, *Hauptprobleme der französischen Sprache* (Braunschweig, 1930), pp. 132-133. That the *Bovary* trial did in part deal with passages of narrated monologue—misread by the prosecution as authorial statements—has recently been demonstrated by Hans Robert Jauss in *Literaturgeschichte als Provokation* (Frankfurt a.M., 1970), pp. 203-206.

10. Oskar Walzel, "Von 'erlebter' Rede" in *Das Wortkunstwerk* (1926, rpt. Heidelberg, 1968), p. 228. This essay was published before Joyce was known in Germany.

11. Several of the early articles on *erlebte Rede* appeared in the *Germanisch-romanische Monatsschrift* before World War I, notably those of Charles Bally and Eugen Lerch. During the nineteen twenties the following books discussed the subject at length: Etienne Lorck, *Die "erlebte Rede": eine sprachliche Untersuchung* (Heidelberg, 1921); Marguerite Lips, *Le Style indirect libre* (Paris, 1926); Werner Günther, *Probleme der Rededarstellung* (Marburg, 1928). A detailed presentation of the research before 1930 is given in Lethcoe's dissertation, pp. 12-53.

12. Leo Spitzer, *Stilstudien* II (1922, rpt. Munich, 1961), pp. 166-207, and "Zur Entstehung der sogenannten 'erlebten

Rede,' " *Germanisch-romanische Monatsschrift* 16 (1928), 327 ff.;
Oskar Walzel, "Von 'erlebter' Rede" in *Das Wortkunstwerk*;
Albert Thibaudet, *Gustave Flaubert* (Paris, 1935), pp. 246-254.

13. The first German edition of Stanzel's *Narrative Situations in the Novel*, where *erlebte Rede* is discussed as a characteristic feature of the "figural" novel type, appeared in 1955. The first edition of Hamburger's *Logik der Dichtung*, where the technique is viewed as the quintessence of narrative language, appeared in 1957. See also Stanzel's article "Episches Praeteritum, erlebte Rede, historisches Praesens," *Deutsche Vierteljahrschrift* 33 (1959), 1-12, and Norbert Miller, "Erlebte und verschleierte Rede," *Akzente* 5 (1958), 213-226.

14. Genette, whose "Discours du récit" is centered on *A la Recherche*, devotes only one paragraph to *style indirect libre*, which he classifies as a "variant" of indirect discourse, and illustrates with a rather lame example from Proust (*Figures III*, Paris, 1972, p. 192). Todorov leaves it out of consideration in *Littérature et signification*, but discusses it briefly in "Les régistres de la parole," *Journal de Psychologie* (1967), pp. 265-278, esp. pp. 271-272. In view of the importance both these critics give to the relationship between narration and discourse, it is surprising that they have never studied the technique where the borderline between these two language fields becomes effaced.

15. The two books on the stream-of-consciousness novel by Humphrey and Friedman are exceptions of sorts. Humphrey, without referring to the French or German terms, identifies an "indirect interior monologue" which he illustrates with examples from *Ulysses* and *Mrs. Dalloway* (*Stream of Consciousness in the Modern Novel* [Berkeley, 1954], pp. 28-33). His examples make it evident that "indirect interior monologue," far from being a technique special to the stream-of-consciousness novel, however, is in reality identical to the *style indirect libre - erlebte Rede* found in most standard nineteenth- and twentieth-century fiction. Melvin Friedman does make the connection between Humphrey's term and the standard French term. But he confuses the issue by maintain-

ing that *style indirect libre* is an "imperfect" forerunner of "indirect interior monologue" (*Stream of Consciousness: A Study in Literary Method* [New Haven, 1955], p. 21; see also pp. 4, 63, 198, 233). I explain below (n. 24) why I consider Humphrey's term misleading.

16. For Daiches and Watt, see below. Scholes and Kellogg fail to include this technique in their otherwise cogent discussion of methods for rendering consciousness in chap. 5 of *The Nature of Narrative*. Booth's dismissal of *erlebte Rede* is in line with his cavalier treatment of grammatical distinctions in fiction generally; see esp. "Distance and Point of View: An Essay in Classification," *Essays in Criticism* 11 (1961), 60-79, p. 60.

17. *The Passages of Thought: Psychological Representation in the American Novel 1870-1900* (New York, 1969), pp. 64 and 70. See also Ian Watt, "The First Paragraph of *The Ambassadors*: An Explication," *Essays in Criticism* 10 (1960), 250-274. Watt evidently has narrated monologue passages in mind when he says: "because the narrator's consciousness and Strether's are both present, we often don't know whose mental operations and evaluative judgments are involved in particular cases" (p. 261). When Watt describes the transition from the third to the fourth sentence of *The Ambassadors* as a rapid passing "from the objective analysis . . . to what must be a verbatim quotation from Strether's mind" (pp. 261-262), he is actually referring to a quite standard passage from psycho-narration to narrated monologue.

18. William M. Schutte, *Introduction to Twentieth Century Interpretations of* A Portrait of the Artist as a Young Man, p. 12.

19. *Virginia Woolf* (New York, 1963), p. 72. Another critic even criticizes Woolf for her "obtrusive art," because she "adroitly and purposely" conceals the "clear and inviolable line of demarcation" that supposedly separates inner and outer reality in fiction (Stuart Rosenberg, "The Match in the Crocus: Obtrusive Art in Virginia Woolf's *Mrs. Dalloway*," *Modern Fiction Studies* 13 [1967], 211-220, p. 217).

20. See, for example, William O. Hendricks, who singles

out free indirect style as one of the key problems extending linguistics "beyond the sentence in the sense of proceeding from function to form" ("On the Notion 'Beyond the Sentence,' " *Linguistics* 37 [1967], 12-51, pp. 38-40).

In England, free indirect style was a focus of attention for a group of stylistic linguists at the University of Leeds, working under the Romance philologist Stephen Ullmann. Ullmann's own chapter, "Reported Speech and internal monologue in Flaubert," in *Style in the French Novel* (Oxford, 1964) is still one of the best studies of the subject in English. For a recent approach by an American linguist, see Ann Banfield, "Narrative Style and the Grammar of Direct and Indirect Speech," *Foundations of Language* 10 (1973), 1-39.

21. See especially Paul Hernadi, "Dual Perspective: Free Indirect Discourse and Related Techniques," and R. J. Lethcoe's previously mentioned dissertation. See also my "Narrated Monologue: Definition of a Fictional Style" (*Comparative Literature* 18 [1966], 97-112), which represents an early version of the present chapter, and where I first introduced the term "narrated monologue." The new book by the British Germanist Roy Pascal, *The Dual Voice: Free Indirect Speech and its Functions in the Nineteenth-Century European Novel* (Manchester, 1977), reached me only after completion of my manuscript.

22. See, for example, Spitzer and Lips. This spoken aspect has received some attention in English as well: see especially Michael Gregory, "Old Bailey-Speech in *A Tale of Two Cities*," *Review of English Literature* 6, No. 2 (1965), 42-55; and Norman Page, *Speech in the English Novel* (London, 1973), pp. 34-38.

23. For a discussion of terms used in English, see Lethcoe, pp. 4-5. Lethcoe's own approach through descriptive linguistics prompts his preference for the umbrella-term "narrated speech," which he in turn divides into "narrated inner speech" (my "narrated monologue") and "narrated outer speech." This minor terminological difference reflects the different emphasis of Lethcoe's study from my own.

24. Although Humphrey's term "indirect interior mono-

logue" is as limited as mine, its first modifier is based on a misleading analogy with indirect discourse—assuming as it does that this technique for rendering consciousness is "indirect" in the same sense as quoted interior monologue is "direct." Both Humphrey's term and the false analogy stem from Dujardin (*Le Monologue intérieur* [Paris, 1931], pp. 39-40).

25. "Les Régistres de la parole," pp. 271-272.

26. Cf. Hernadi's much broader term "substitutionary narration," which corresponds to *vision avec* (or the figural narrative situation) rather than to what I call narrated monologue. Hernadi's sub-category of "substitutionary thought," however, corresponds exactly to narrated monologue ("Dual Perspective," pp. 35 and 38).

27. See below, pp. 133-134.

28. Phrases like "duplicity," "double perspective," "twofold vision," "dual voice" crop up constantly in analyses of novels using the narrated monologue. Ian Watt, for example, speaks of "the split narrative point of view" and the "dual presence of Strether's consciousness and of that of the narrator" in *The Ambassadors*, when he is actually trying to define their singular fusion in the Jamesian text. ("The First Paragraph of *The Ambassadors*," pp. 260, 266.)

29. This persistently happens in Booth's *Rhetoric of Fiction* (e.g., pp. 164, 279, 282, 300). The same confusion pervades George H. Szanto's book *Narrative Consciousness* (Austin, Texas, 1972).

30. In her linguistic discussion, Ann Banfield cuts through the problem of the narrator-character relationship in narrated monologue texts by suggesting that it makes no sense to talk of a narrator in such texts at all ("Narrative Style," pp. 34-38). I do not find her argument convincing. As she herself admits, narrated monologues are sometimes found in the same texts with audible narrators, and vice versa. In the narrator-less model she proposes for the narrated monologue there would be no way of accounting for the continuity of the voice that refers to the protagonist in the same third-person form in passages of authorial commentary and of narrated monologue.

The model of a narrator who identifies or coheres with the ⌐
figural consciousness still seems the most satisfying one to ac- ⌐
count for the narrated monologue.

31. *The Rise of the Novel* (Berkeley, 1967), pp. 296-297.

32. *Emma*, p. 844 (chap. 16).

33. Cf. Willi Bühler, *Die 'erlebte Rede' im englischen Roman.
Ihre Vorstufen und ihre Ausbildung im Werke Jane Austens* (Leipzig, 1937), and Lisa Glauser, *Die erlebte Rede im Roman des 19.
Jahrhunderts* (Bern, 1948).

34. "A propos du 'Style' de Flaubert," *Nouvelle Revue
Française* 14 (1920), 72-90, p. 78; reprinted in *Chroniques* (Paris,
1927). See also Thibaudet's reply in the same volume of
Nouvelle Revue Française, 426-441, and his chapter on style in
Gustave Flaubert (Paris, 1935), esp. pp. 246-250. See further
Stephen Ullmann, "Reported Speech and Internal Monologue in Flaubert" in *Style in the French Novel* (Oxford, 1964),
pp. 94-120, and Victor Brombert, *The Novels of Flaubert*
(Princeton, N.J., 1966), pp. 76-78 and 167-173.

35. Letter to George Sand, 15-16 December, 1866 (*Correspondence* V [Paris, 1929], p. 257).

36. Quoted in Ullmann, *Style in the French Novel*, p. 119.

37. *Gustave Flaubert*, p. 248.

38. *The Art of the Novel*, p. 66.

39. *Op. cit.*, p. 37.

40. *L'Education sentimentale*, p. 37; English: *Sentimental
Education*, trans. Goldsmith, p. 6.

41. *Op. cit.*, p. 438; trans., p. 378.

42. *Op. cit.*, p. 82; trans., p. 48.

43. See, for example, *Mrs. Dalloway*, pp. 70-71 and 101;
To the Lighthouse, pp. 100 and 226.

44. *To the Lighthouse*, pp. 95-100 and 53-57.

45. *La Chartreuse de Parme*, I, p. 55 (chap. 3); English: *The
Charterhouse of Parma*, trans. Moncrieff, p. 61.

46. See, e.g., Hugo Friedrich, *Drei Klassiker des französischen Romans* (Frankfurt a.M., 1966), p. 128: "The narrator
does not stand next to his figures, but he slips inside them.
. . . He becomes the actor who plays the role of his figures."

47. *Der Zauberberg*, p. 198.

48. In "Erlebte und verschleierte Rede," Norbert Miller points out that this tongue-in-cheek variety has a much longer history than the serious narrated monologue form—a change that corresponds to the general evolution of the novel from the authorial to the figural pole. Modern ironists like Mann and Musil, however, revert to the older form with particular gusto. See Werner Hoffmeister, *Studien zur erlebten Rede bei Thomas Mann und Robert Musil* (The Hague, 1965), pp. 110-127).

49. "L'Enfance d'un chef," p. 220.

50. Robert Humphrey seems to be the only critic to have identified correctly the basic technique of the Gerty-half of "Nausicaa" (*Stream of Consciousness*, pp. 30-31).

51. *Ulysses*, p. 357.

52. *Der Prozess*, pp. 271-272; English based on *The Trial*, trans. Muir/Butler, pp. 254-255.

53. Cf. chap. 1, where I discuss the entirely different technique Broch uses when his protagonists are benighted "sleepwalkers," unconscious of their own mental processes.

54. "Bemerkungen zum *Tod des Vergil*," *Essays* I (Zurich, 1955), p. 265.

55. *Der Tod des Vergil*, p. 9; English: *The Death of Virgil*, trans. Untermeyer, pp. 11-12.

56. *Der Tod des Vergil*, pp. 13-14; *The Death of Virgil*, p. 15. (I have altered the tense of two verb-forms to make the translation correspond to the original; see n. 57 below.)

57. Unfortunately, with a few exceptions, the passages that employ the present tense in the original were translated into the English past tense. This change, as the "Translator's Note" explains, was deliberate (*The Death of Virgil*, p. 488). Though it was made on rather doubtful linguistic grounds, the fact that it was made with Broch's approval is definite proof that he envisioned the present-tense passages as monologic, rather than authorial, language. But the ambiguity created by the present tense in the original gets lost in the English—though it is, in all other respects, a masterful translation.

58. The "Hymns against Beauty" and the "Elegies on Fate" (*The Death of Virgil*, pp. 97 ff. and 200 ff.).

59. *To the Lighthouse*, p. 220.

60. "Now, here we encounter the objective grammatical symptom which in all its inconspicuousness provides decisive proof that the past tense of fictional narration is no statement of past-ness: the fact that deictic temporal adverbs can occur conjointly with the past tense." (*The Logic of Literature*, trans. Marilynn J. Rose [Bloomington, Indiana, 1973], p. 71.)

61. The adjustment of adverbs applies to space as well as to time. To the "now" of the quoted passage Lily will add its spatial counterpart in the immediately following paragraph, when she brings her chair and easel outdoors: "Yes, it must have been precisely *here* that she had stood ten years ago" (pp. 220-221) [my emphasis].

62. My discussion of narrated memories and fantasies is indebted to R. J. Lethcoe, who proposed these terms and illustrated these patterns (pp. 241-257).

63. *To the Lighthouse*, pp. 277-278.

64. Cf. David Daiches' discussion of mnemonic retrospection in stream-of-consciousness fiction (*The Novel and the Modern World* [Chicago, 1960], pp. 15-19). Daiches writes about this general tendency of the modern novel without pinpointing specific techniques.

65. *Mrs. Dalloway*, p. 3.

66. *The Portrait of a Lady* II, p. 186.

67. *Op. cit.*, p. 192.

68. *Loc. cit.*

69. *The Portrait of a Lady* II, p. 205; *The Wings of the Dove*, p. 114; *The Ambassadors*, pp. 336 and 337.

70. For an analysis of the narrative technique in *Tonka*, see Werner Hoffmeister, *Studien zur erlebten Rede bei Thomas Mann und Robert Musil*. Another work structured on the same principle is Claude Simon's *Le Palace* (1962).

71. *The Web and the Rock*, p. 288.

72. *Op. cit.*, pp. 275 and 293.

73. "Ein Hungerkünstler," p. 232.

74. Lethcoe, p. 214.
75. *To the Lighthouse*, p. 228.
76. "Narrated Speech and Consciousness," p. 205. Similar terms have been suggested by other critics: "style indirect libre de perception" (Lips); "erlebter Eindruck" (Willi Bühler); "substitutionary description" (Hernadi).
77. *Narrative Modes in Czech Literature*, pp. 50-53.
78. *Madame Bovary*, pp. 512-513.
79. *L'Education sentimentale*, pp. 40 and 81; English based on *Sentimental Education*, trans. Goldsmith, pp. 9 and 47.
80. *To the Lighthouse*, p. 95.
81. See above, pp. 32-33.
82. It is to allow for these variations that I used the phrase "basic tense of narration" in my initial definition of the narrated monologue, despite the fact that "past tense" would cover 99 percent of the cases.
83. These tense shifts are especially frequent in Schnitzler, Döblin, and Broch.
84. *Le Planétarium*, p. 64. English based on *The Planetarium*, trans. Jolas, p. 76.
85. *The Age of Suspicion*, trans. Maria Jolas (New York, 1963), p. 114.

4   Retrospective Techniques—pages 143-172

1. Quoted in Ian Watt, *The Rise of the Novel* (Berkeley, 1967), p. 119.
2. Jean Rousset, *Narcisse romancier: Essai sur la première personne dans le roman* (Paris, 1973). For another systematic survey of first-person narrative patterns, see Bertil Romberg, *Studies in the Narrative Technique of the First-Person Novel* (Lund, 1962).
3. The distinction between "narrating self" (*erzählendes Ich*) and "experiencing self" (*erlebendes Ich*) was first made by Leo Spitzer in his essay on Proust (*Stilstudien* II [1922, rpt. Munich 1961]), p. 478. It has been adopted by most critics concerned with first-person narration.

4. The difference has been most clearly worked out by Käte Hamburger. See especially her distinction between third-person narrative as a mimesis of reality, and first-person narrative as a "feigned reality statement" (*The Logic of Literature*, pp. 311-318).

5. *David Copperfield*, p. 25 (chap. 2). Many other passages from first-person novels in which a narrator explains how he knows what he knows could be cited. They indicate that the "convention of a perfect memory" is less solidly established than Romberg assumes (see *Studies in the Narrative Technique*, pp. 97-98).

6. "Preface to *The Ambassadors*" in *The Art of the Novel* (New York, 1962), pp. 320-321.

7. Surprisingly, even Beckett, in his famous Proust essay, misunderstands the aesthetics in this fashion; see *Proust. Three Dialogues* (London, 1965), pp. 80-87.

8. This process is the focus of the early pages of the poetics section (*A la Recherche* III, pp. 867-879).

9. *Op. cit.*, p. 896. English based on *Remembrance of Things Past* II, trans. Moncrieff / Blossom, p. 1014.

10. *Op. cit.*, p. 878 f.

11. *Op. cit.*, p. 895.

12. Cf. Gérard Genette, *Figures III* (Paris, 1972), pp. 236-238 and 260-261.

13. See Genette, pp. 149 ff.

14. *A la Recherche* I, p. 156. English based on *Remembrance of Things Past* I, trans. Moncrieff, p. 120.

15. *A la Recherche* I, pp. 174-177. This scene is too long for full quotation. I quote it selectively in the analysis that follows. English based on *Remembrance of Things Past* I, trans. Moncrieff, pp. 134-136.

16. Similes in Proust's self-narrations are often far more expansive, and not always ironic in tone. For one example among many, see the comparison of changing moods to a bird traversing bands of color in a variegated sky (*A la Recherche* I, p. 183).

17. This is a typical example of Proust's employment of in-

terior monologue to point up mendacious rationalizations (see p. 79 above).

18. Cf. Leo Spitzer's discussion of Proust's "psychological apparatus of the parenthesis" and of the pseudo-modest "peut-être" introducing his glosses (*Stilstudien* II [1922, rpt. Munich, 1961], pp. 371, 393-394 and 451-452).

19. It goes without saying that in so vast and varied a work as *A la Recherche* no single technique is used with absolute consistency. As Genette has pointed out, there are occasions when Proust's self-narration becomes "focalized"—with the narrating self adopting the perspective of the experiencing self (*Figures III*, pp. 198 and 216-217). Marcel's past consciousness is then momentarily rendered through a kind of self-narrated monologue.

20. "Ein Bericht für eine Akademie," p. 166.

21. *Three Novels*, p. 31.

22. Percy Lubbock, *The Craft of Fiction* (New York, 1957), pp. 139-140.

23. *The Age of Suspicion* (New York, 1963), trans. George Braziller, pp. 92-93.

24. See *op. cit.*, pp. 65-72 for Sarraute's discussion of the pros and cons of fiction in the first-person, the form she herself used in *Portrait of an Unknown Man*, and in *Martereau*.

25. J. Hillis Miller, "Three Problems of Fictional Form: First-Person Narration in David Copperfield and Huckleberry Finn," in *Experience in the Novel*, ed. Roy Harvey Pearce (New York, 1968), pp. 21-48, p. 32.

26. Recent theorists have begun to give this second type of autobiographical structure its due. See especially Franz Stanzel's discussion of the two contrastive tendencies in first-person narration (*Narrative Situations in the Novel*, trans. J. Pusack [Bloomington, Indiana, 1971], pp. 64-65), and Genette's discussion of "focalization" in Proust (*Figures III*, pp. 214-224). Neither Stanzel nor Genette, however, clearly perceives how this coincidence of viewpoints between the narrating and experiencing self affects the presentation of consciousness.

27. In his Ph.D. dissertation "Anti-Realist Directions in the Novel, 1885-1901" (Indiana University, 1970), David Mickelsen analyzes the narrative technique of Hamsun's novel in detail; see esp. pp. 75-76 for the cohesion between narrating and experiencing self.

28. Quoted in J. W. McFarlane, "The Whisper of the Blood: A Study of Knut Hamsun's Early Novels," *PMLA* 71 (1956), 563-594, p. 574.

29. *Hunger*, trans. Robert Bly, pp. 23-24. With the aid of my colleague Theodore Andersson, I have adjusted the tenses and the punctuation to correspond to the original.

30. "Psychological Literature" (1890), in *Paa Rune* (Oslo, 1960), p. 63. I owe thanks to John Hoberman for translating for me the passages I quote from Hamsun's essays.

31. "From the Unconscious Life of the Mind" (1890), in *Artikler 1889-1929* (Oslo, 1965), p. 42. Hamsun approaches Sarrautean imagery even more closely earlier in this essay when he speaks of inexplicable mental states that are "too fleeting to be captured and held fast; they last a second, a minute, they come and go like moving, blinking lights; but they have left a mark, deposited some kind of sensation, before they vanish. And in sufficiently sensitive persons, out of these almost imperceptible, mimosa-like stirrings thoughts can arise which ultimately lead to decisions and deeds on the day when the mimosa puts forth its leaves."

32. See below, pp. 169-171 for a further discussion of this switching-point between first- and third-person forms of narration.

33. Cf. Albert Guerard's convincing interpretation of Michel as a homosexual who remains unaware of his inclinations (*André Gide* [Cambridge, Mass., 1969], pp. 99-118).

34. *L'Immoraliste*, p. 372; English based on *The Immoralist*, trans. Bussy, p. 11.

35. *Op. cit.*, pp. 418 and 462.

36. *Op. cit.*, p. 399; English based on *The Immoralist*, p. 63.

37. *Op. cit.*, p. 464; English based on *The Immoralist*, p. 190.

38. *Adolphe*, pp. 103-104 (chap. 7).

39. The only mention I have found of this problem is in Leon Surmelian, *Techniques of Writing Fiction: Measure and Madness* (New York, 1968), p. 191. Quite appropriately, this handbook for practicing writers discusses the point in a cautionary way: "The writer should make clear that these [direct monologues] are not the narrator's present thoughts and feelings but those he had when the action of the story took place." The "slight variations . . . from his style in general" that Surmelian recommends for the monologues, however, would be insufficient guards against confusion.

40. Thomas Mann, *Bekenntnisse des Hochstaplers Felix Krull*, pp. 293-295.

41. *Three Novels*, pp. 87-88.

42. See above, pp. 79-80.

43. *Der Steppenwolf*, pp. 73-74.

44. *Free Fall*, p. 168.

45. *A Severed Head*, p. 85.

46. *The Aspern Papers*, p. 119 (chap. 9).

47. My article, "Erlebte Rede im Ich-Roman," (*Germanisch-romanische Monatsschrift* 19 [1969], 305-313) initially drew attention to this technique. See also W.J.M. Bronzwaer, *Tense in the Novel* (Groningen, 1970), esp. pp. 53-62. Bronzwaer demonstrates the existence of an analogue to "free indirect style" in first-person fiction, and illustrates it from Iris Murdoch's novel, *An Italian Girl*. He defines this style, however, far more broadly than I do, including in it all consonant forms of first-person narration.

48. *A la Recherche* III, p. 1044. The final section of *Le Temps retrouvé* (pp. 1032 ff.) contains a number of other narrated monologue passages, symptomatic for the ultimate cohesion of the narrating and the experiencing selves in Proust's novel.

49. *Three Novels*, pp. 167-168.

50. *Der Steppenwolf*, p. 51.

51. For a more detailed analysis of the self-narrated monologue in Hesse's novel, see my article "Narration of

Consciousness in *Der Steppenwolf*," *Germanic Review* 44 (1969), 121-131.

52. See above, pp. 101-102.

53. Quoted from the manuscript of *Das Schloss* (deposited at the Bodleian Library, Oxford).

54. See Roland Barthes, "Introduction à l'analyse structurale des récits" *Communications* 8 (1966), 1-27, p. 20; and Genette, *Figures III*, p. 210. The model sentences from James Bond and Proust that Barthes and Genette use are too innocuous to prove their point. As they admit themselves, the sentence "James Bond saw a man around fifty who appeared youthful for his years" can (and does) neighbor on sentences where Bond is observed from an external vantage-point, and which are therefore pronominally fixed to the third person.

55. I examine this problem in "K. enters *The Castle*: On the Change of Person in Kafka's Manuscript," *Euphorion* 62 (1968), 28-45.

56. *The Art of the Novel*, p. 320.

57. See *The Notebooks for* Crime and Punishment, ed. and trans. Edward Wasiolek (Chicago, 1967), esp. the first-person version reproduced pp. 98-148, and Introduction, pp. 9-10, 20.

58. *The Craft of Fiction*, pp. 144-145. Remarkably Lubbock uses precisely *Crime and Punishment* as his second crown witness (next to *The Ambassadors*) to prove this point, even though he could not have known that the genesis of Dostoevsky's novel shows that the autobiographical method here literally "gave way to the stronger method."

5   From Narration to Monologue — *pages 173-216*

1. Quoted in Richard Ellmann, *James Joyce* (New York, 1959), p. 534. See n. 39 to my Introduction for quotation in French.

2. Cf. above, p. 16.

3. See Edouard Dujardin, *Le monologue intérieur* (Paris, 1931), pp. 65-86.

4. Note that it is only *fictional* antecedents that Dujardin rejects, whereas he stresses the affiliation with the Symbolist movement generally—"*Les Lauriers sont coupés* were the offspring of the movement of 1885" (*op. cit.*, p. 101)—and with the Symbolists' musical conception of poetry and the Wagnerian conception of music in particular (*op. cit.*, pp. 96-97).

5. Most critics discussing the origins of the interior monologue refer to these genres: e.g., Dujardin, Larbaud, Gide, René Lalou, Melvin Friedman, Gleb Struve, Michel Raimond.

6. Michel Butor "L'usage des pronoms personnels dans le roman," in *Répertoire II* (Paris, 1964), p. 65. Cf. Genette's comment on *Les Lauriers sont coupés*: "neither written, nor even spoken—mysteriously captured and transcribed by Dujardin: it is the peculiarity of immediate discourse that it excludes the narrative instance which it constitutes" (*Figures III* [Paris, 1973], p. 240).

7. *Notes from Underground*, trans. Matlaw, pp. 6, 8, 35, 36.

8. *Op. cit.*, p. 5.

9. *Op. cit.*, p. 35.

10. *Op. cit.*, p. 5.

11. *Op. cit.*, p. 35, see also p. 36.

12. This interior dialogization of *Notes from Underground* is discussed in Mikhail Bakhtin, *Problems of Dostoevsky's Poetics*, trans. R. W. Rotsel (Ann Arbor, Mich., 1973), pp. 190-193.

13. *Three Novels*, pp. 304, 305, 301.

14. Cf. Romberg, "The oral, epic situation of a primary narrator easily becomes paradoxical, if presented by the narrator himself" (*Studies in the Narrative Technique of the First-Person Novel* [Lund, 1962], p. 34).

15. Some further examples are Poe's "Imp of the Perverse," Proust's early story "La confession d'une jeune fille," Sartre's "Erostrate," and Kafka's "Burrow" (which will be further discussed later in this chapter).

16. *La Chute*, p. 169; English: *The Fall*, trans. O'Brien, p. 147.

17. Dujardin, *Le Monologue intérieur*, p. 59.

18. In *A Gentle Creature and Other Stories*, trans. David Margarshack (London, 1950), p. 209. In all quotations from the preface to this story, the translation has been amended with the help of Katherine Szczepansky, in order to render the terminology as literally as possible.

19. As Friedman points out, Stendhal had used the identical image of a stenographer when he envisioned the possibility of casting a story in interior monologue form (*Stream of Consciousness: A Study in Literary Method* [New Haven, 1955], pp. 59 and 67).

20. *A Gentle Creature*, p. 210.

21. If we remember that Dostoevsky customarily, and without apologies for using a "fantastic form," quotes his characters' thoughts in third-person novels (e.g., Raskolnikov's in *Crime and Punishment*), we can see from this preface that he sensed the difference that exists between a narrator's quotation of thoughts and his disappearance. The first is, of course, no less "fantastic" than the second, but it is a convention as old as narrative itself.

22. *A Gentle Creature*, p. 211.

23. *Op. cit.*, pp. 210 and 251.

24. See Dujardin, *Le monologue intérieur*, p. 66, and Gleb Struve, "*Monologue Intérieur*: The Origins of the Formula and the First Statement of its Possibilities," *PMLA* 69 (1954), 1101-1111, p. 1111.

25. Letter to Dujardin quoted in *Le monologue intérieur*, p. 66. "Krotkaya" is the original (Russian) title for "A Gentle Creature."

26. *Free Fall*, pp. 10 and 6. See also pp. 7, 8, 9, 25.

27. *Op. cit.*, pp. 6 and 46.

28. See, for example, the delayed narration of three childhood episodes in chaps. 8, 11 and 12.

29. Translated from back cover of Editions de Minuit edition of *La Route des Flandres* (Paris, 1960).

30. Translated from interview with Claude Sarraute reprinted in 10/18 edition of *La Route des Flandres*, p. 273.

31. Cf. Jacques Dubois' comments on the role of memory

in "Avatars du monologue intérieur dans le nouveau roman" (*Revue des Lettres Modernes*, Nos. 94–110 [1964], 17–29, pp. 24–25).

32. These terms have been applied to *A la Recherche* by René Lalou and Gaëtan Picon (See Marcel Muller, *Les Voix narratives dans la "Recherche du temps perdu"* [Geneva, 1965], p. 54).

33. See the analysis of the temporal order of *A la Recherche* in *Figures III*, pp. 85–89.

34. *Chroniques* (Paris, 1927), p. 209, cited by Muller, p. 55.

35. *The Catcher in the Rye*, p. 92 (chap. 13).

36. Emile Benvéniste, *Problems in General Linguistics*, trans. M. E. Meek (Coral Gables, Florida, 1971), p. 209. I will use Benvéniste's terms *discours* and *histoire* in italicized French spelling.

37. *Op. cit.*, p. 208.

38. "We shall define historical narration as the mode of utterance that excludes every 'autobiographical' linguistic form." (*Op. cit.*, p. 206; see also p. 210.)

39. "Le style de l'autobiographie" in *La Relation critique* (Paris, 1970), pp. 83–98. Though Starobinski is concerned with real autobiography, his suggestions are equally applicable to fictional autobiography. Concerning the applicability of Benvéniste's categories to novel theory, see also Genette, "Frontières du récit," *Communications* 8 (1966), 152–163.

40. Starobinski, p. 89.

41. Cf. John Spencer's characterization of interior monologue language as "language written to be read as if overheard" ("A Note on the 'Steady Monologuy of the Interiors,' " *Review of English Literature* [1965], 32–41, p. 41). Although this is an accurate description, it is not a sufficient one, since it applies equally to dialogue in drama.

42. Theorists who analyze fiction from the point of view of communications theory define interior monologue in this way: as a communicative language addressed by an ego to its alter ego (cf. Johannes Anderegg, *Fiktion und Kommunikation* [Göttingen, 1973], pp. 71–73). But the closed circuit of this

communication still has very distinct effects on the language it shapes. See chap. 6, below.

43. Preface to *Les Lauriers sont coupés*, p. 10.

44. *Les Lauriers sont coupés*, p. 63.

45. Quoted in Dujardin, *Le Monologue intérieur*, pp. 15-16.

46. Cited by Genette in *Communications* 8 (1966), p. 163. As Genette points out, this focus of fictional speakers on their act of locution is especially frequent in contemporary writers. Cf. also in the same issue Roland Barthes, "Introduction à l'analyse structurale des récits," p. 21.

47. *Three Novels*, p. 61.

48. *Op. cit.*, p. 66.

49. *Martereau*, p. 24; trans. Jolas, pp. 15-16.

50. *Op. cit.*, p. 25; trans. Jolas, p. 17.

51. *Three Novels*, p. 253.

52. "A Boring Story," trans. Magarshack, p. 58.

53. *Op. cit.*, pp. 58-62.

54. "Der Bau," p. 174; English based on "The Burrow," trans. Muir, p. 46.

55. "Der Bau," p. 179; English based on "The Burrow," p. 51.

56. "Der Bau," p. 194; English based on "The Burrow," p. 64.

57. "Der Bau," p. 206; English based on "The Burrow," p. 75.

58. See esp. Heinrich Henel, "Das Ende von Kafkas *Der Bau*," *Germanisch-romanische Monatsschrift* 22 (1972), 3-23.

59. Otto Jespersen, *Essentials of English Grammar* (London, 1933), p. 239. On the historical narrative present as a metaphoric tense, see Paul Imbs, *L'Emploi des temps verbaux en français moderne* (Paris, 1960), pp. 32 and 201, and Harald Weinrich, *Tempus: Besprochene und erzählte Welt* (Stuttgart, 1964), pp. 125-127.

60. I take the term from Leo Spitzer, who applies it to lyric poetry in "Überzeitliche Perspektive in der neueren französischen Lyrik (Anredelyrik und evokatives Präsens)," in *Stilstudien* II (1922; rpt. Munich, 1961), pp. 50-83.

61. *David Copperfield*, p. 139 (chap. 9).

62. "Ein Landarzt," p. 134. English based on "A Country Doctor," trans. Muir, p. 136. Since this translation fails to reproduce the change to the evocative present on which I focus the following discussion, I have, among other things, adjusted the English tenses to correspond to the original.

63. "Ein Landarzt," p. 138; English based on "A Country Doctor," p. 141.

64. The preceding discussion of "A Country Doctor" duplicates, with some variations, a section from my article "Kafka's Eternal Present: Narrative Tense in 'Ein Landarzt' and Other First-Person Stories" (*PMLA* 83 [1968], 144-150).

65. Vsevolod M. Garshin, "Four Days," p. 15.

66. *Op. cit.*, p. 26. In the original, this final sentence has a passive construction ("and I tell him all that is written here"), which leaves open the question of who actually did the writing. (I owe this information to Katherine Szczepansky.)

67. My ignorance of Russian precluded close stylistic analysis of this text. But my interpretation of its structure is supported by several brief passages where the tense, referring to the same "present" moment as the present tense, changes to the past in midstream (pp. 19, 22, 23-24; these inconsistencies are contained in the original as well as in the translation). A number of summary passages also contradict the monologic aspects of this text (e.g., "several times I almost gave up in despair but at last . . . I succeed" in the passage quoted above. See also the six moments (pp. 14, 16, 19, 20, 25 and 26) when the speaker tells how he loses consciousness.

68. See esp. C. D. King. "Edouard Dujardin, Inner Monologue and the Stream of Consciousness," *French Studies* 7 (1953), 116-128, pp. 123-124; and Gleb Struve, *"Monologue intérieur,"* pp. 1108-1109. These critics have not, however, noticed the problem raised by the last sentence, nor the various inconsistencies in its language I mention in n. 67 above.

69. Darl speaks 19 of the 59 sections; the remaining sections are about equally divided among past tense narrators (Cash and the characters who are not family members), and present-tense monologists (the other family members).

For Darl's privileged role as narrator, see André Bleikasten, *Faulkner's* As I Lay Dying (Bloomington, Indiana, 1973), pp. 46 and 57.

70. *As I Lay Dying*, p. 134.

71. *Op. cit.*, p. 135.

72. *Op. cit.*, p. 141. The analogy between synchronous narration and the language of the radio reporter is made by Christian Paul Casparis (*Tense Without Time: The Present Tense in Narration* [Bern, 1975], pp. 43-44), who suggests the term "current report" for this form of narration.

73. *As I Lay Dying*, pp. 140-141.

74. The interpretation of Darl's sections as narratives in evocative present rather than interior monologues is supported by the manuscript, which—according to R. W. Franklin—shows frequent corrections and hesitations in the tenses ("Narrative Management in *As I Lay Dying*," *Modern Fiction Studies* 13 [1967], 57-65, p. 61). See also Casparis, who interprets Darl's sections as retrospective narratives on the basis of a number of linguistic details (*Tense Without Time*, pp. 86-88).

75. Cf. Genette's similar analysis of the "récit au présent" as an unstable form that can veer either in the direction of objective narration or of inner discourse (*Figures III*, p. 231).

76. Cf. Dubois, "Avatars du monologue intérieur," where the relationship between *La Jalousie* and interior monologue is explored in greater detail. The term "monologue extérieur" one critic has applied to this text is tempting, but misleading (see Bernard Pingaud, "Je, Vous, Il," *Esprit* 26 [1958], 91-99, p. 94).

77. *As I Lay Dying*, pp. 34 and 52.

78. Preface to *Les Lauriers sont coupés*, p. 11.

79. *James Joyce* (New York, 1959), p. 369.

80. These phrases from Richardson's prefaces are quoted by Ian Watt, *The Rise of the Novel* (Berkeley, 1967), pp. 192-193.

81. *Clarissa*, Vol. II, p. 257.

82. *Op. cit.*, Vol. II, p. 371.

83. Quoted in Watt, p. 193.

84. Quoted in Watt, p. 25.
85. "A Gentle Creature," p. 210.
86. *Le dernier Jour d'un condamné*, p. 144.
87. *Op. cit.*, p. 54.
88. *Die Chronik der Sperlingsgasse*, p. 125.
89. *Répertoire* II, p. 64.
90. *La Nausée*, p. 127. English: *The Diary of Antoine Roquentin*, trans. Alexander, p. 134.
91. *Op. cit.*, p. 130; *The Diary*, p. 136.
92. *Loc. cit.*; *The Diary*, p. 137.
93. *Op. cit.*, p. 133; *The Diary*, p. 140.
94. I refer to the title of the article by Jacques Dubois (see note 31).

6   Autonomous Monologue — pages 217-265

1. Letter to Harriet Weaver, 7 October, 1921. *Letters of James Joyce* I, ed. Stuart Gilbert (London, 1966), p. 172.
2. *Letters* I, p. 170.
3. See the reproduction of the schemata in the Appendix of Richard Ellmann, *Ulysses on the Liffey* (New York, 1972).
4. This narrative voice, or "arranger" as David Hayman prefers to call it (*James Joyce's Ulysses*, eds. Clive Hart and David Hayman [Berkeley, 1974], p. 265) is present even in those earlier chapters that are most nearly given over to other voices: in the "asides" of "Cyclops" (see Hayman's comments, *op. cit.*, pp. 265-271), the stage instructions of "Circe," and, of course, in the intermittent narrative passages that interrupt Bloom's or Stephen's thoughts in such chapters as "Proteus" and "Lotus Eaters."
5. Diane Tolomeo reacts against this oversimplification in "The Final Octagon of *Ulysses*" (*James Joyce Quarterly* 10 [1973], 439-454): "This is not a simple linear movement, and yet it is not entirely as circular as it is often made out to be. It cannot steadfastly be maintained that the chapter ends where it began merely because the initial and final words are identical. Quite an amount of yardage has been gained by the time

the eight sentences reach their ending . . ." (p. 449). But even Tolomeo overstresses the circularity of the episode earlier in her article, when she discusses its analogy to the Viconean cycle (pp. 441-442).

6. Page references in the text will be to the "New Edition" (New York: Random House, 1961).

7. Tolomeo, p. 442.

8. See the final chapter of Ellmann, *Ulysses on the Liffey* ("Why Molly Bloom menstruates") for some of these universal implications (esp. pp. 170-171).

9. The autonomous monologue therefore corresponds to what Genette calls "récit isochrone"—a limit case of time-structure, which he takes to be purely hypothetical (*Figures III* [Paris, 1972], pp. 122-123).

10. Erika Höhnisch draws a distinction in interior-monologue texts between "temps du corps" (the experienced present moment) and "temps de l'esprit" (the past, present, and future within the reflecting consciousness). (*Das gefangene Ich: Studien zum inneren Monolog in modernen französischen Romanen* [Heidelberg, 1967], p. 20 and *passim*). The "temps du corps" is chronologically bound, the "temps de l'esprit" totally unbound.

11. Since we gather from the time scheme of "Ithaca" (and from the schemata) that Bloom joins Molly in bed around 2 A.M., "3 quarters the hour wait 2 oclock" (772) thirty-four pages into "Penelope" must be inaccurate counting on Molly's part (unless Joyce is being inconsistent). Two pages before the end it is "a quarter after what an unearthly hour" (781) which is not much help; but we are also told here that "the nuns ringing the angelus" and "the alarm-clock next door at cockshout" still lie in the future.

12. Several critics, pointing out the contrast between Molly and the two male characters in this respect, have noted the correspondence between form and content: the less the surrounding world changes (and the less the body moves), the more dispensable the narrator becomes. See John Spencer, "A Note on the 'Steady Monologuy of the Interiors,' " *Re-*

view of English Literature, 6 (1965), 32-41, p. 40; and William M. Schutte and Erwin R. Steinberg, "The Fictional Technique of *Ulysses*" in Thomas F. Staley and Bernard Benstock, eds., *Approaches to Ulysses* (Pittsburgh, 1970), p. 173.

13. To my knowledge, no close linguistic analysis of "Penelope" has appeared to date. It would be interesting to apply to it the kind of analysis Irena Kaluza applied to the monologues of *The Sound and the Fury* (see n. 65 below).

14. Alan Gardiner, *The Theory of Speech and Language* (Oxford, 1951), p. 98.

15. *Op. cit.*, p. 315.

16. In the article "Les Régistres de la parole" (*Journal de Psychologie* [1967], 265-278) Todorov draws a theoretical distinction between monologue and dialogue on the basis of the contrast between exclamation and interrogation: "Just as one can interpret dialogue as an application and extension of interrogative syntax, so one can interpret monologue, on the statement level, as exclamatory syntax" (p. 278). Although, as Todorov himself points out, examples from classical drama contradict his theory (pp. 276-277), he would find it decisively confirmed in the less rhetorical interior monologues of modern fiction.

17. Emile Benvéniste calls a phrase of the "I suppose" type an "indicator of subjectivity" that characterizes the speaker's attitude toward the statement he is making. (*Problems in General Linguistics*, trans. M. E. Meek [Coral Gables, Florida, 1971], p. 229.)

18. Except when she briefly thinks about tomorrow's menu (764) or the program and wardrobe for her forthcoming concert tour (763).

19. *Stream of Consciousness in the Modern Novel* (Berkeley, 1954), p. 50.

20. David Hayman has previously noted the "proliferation of pronouns" in "Penelope," and their many ambiguities (*Ulysses: The Mechanics of Meaning* [Englewood Cliffs, N.J., 1970], p. 100).

21. Benvéniste, p. 218.

22. *Ulysses on the Liffey*, p. 171.

23. See also: "till they have us swollen out like elephants" (742); "theres always something wrong with us" (769), and *passim*.

24. See also: "thats all they want out of you" (742), "you cant fool a lover" (748), "you want to feel your way with a man" (754), "it makes you feel like nothing on earth" (747).

25. Joseph Campbell's interpretation, as reported by Diane Tolomeo ("The Final Octagon," p. 447).

26. In his dissertation "Anti-Realist Directions in the Novel, 1885-1901" (Indiana, 1970), David Mickelsen gives a comparative analysis of the two works. Schnitzler's knowledge of *Les Lauriers* when he wrote *Leutnant Gustl* is attested by a letter to Georg Brandes dated June 16, 1901 (see Kurt Bergel, ed., *Georg Brandes und Arthur Schnitzler. Ein Briefwechsel* [Berkeley, 1956], p. 88).

27. This dedication is dated November 1921. On October 20, Joyce had sent Larbaud "the virtually completed 'Penelope' " (Ellmann, *James Joyce*, p. 534). By "the form I have adopted" Larbaud thus probably meant specifically the autonomous monologue form common to "Penelope" and "Amants." Larbaud's story is, at any event, the first-born offspring of "Penelope." On the other hand, despite certain similarities of theme and atmosphere with Dujardin's novel, it is improbable that Larbaud had read *Les Lauriers* before 1923.

28. Höhnisch, who draws attention to this style in Dujardin and Larbaud, traces it back to the techniques of impressionistic word-painting developed especially by the Goncourts in their diaries. For a negative evaluation of these enumerative descriptions in *Les Lauriers*, see Michel Raimond, *La Crise du roman: Des Lendemains du Naturalisme aux années vingt* (Paris, 1966), p. 276.

29. *Les Lauriers sont coupés*, p. 39.

30. *Op. cit.*, p. 63.

31. The term is used by Jacques Dubois, *Romanciers français de l'instantané au 19ème siècle* (Bruxelles, 1963), p. 135. As we

have seen in Part I, descriptions of the passing scene also occur frequently in quoted monologues within a third-person narrative (Bloom's in *Ulysses*), but there they are supplemented by the narrator's report.

32. *Les Lauriers*, p. 84.

33. *Fräulein Else*, pp. 371-373.

34. *Les Lauriers*, pp. 39-45. One must agree with H. A. Kelly who regards these moments of *Les Lauriers* as flaws in the basic technique of the text: "he [Dujardin] made the mistake of having the character whose mind was on display become his own narrator from time to time, with a result that is highly unrealistic" ("Consciousness in the Monologues of Ulysses," *Modern Language Quarterly* 24 [1963], 3-12, p. 5). Cf. also Mickelsen, p. 187.

35. *Fräulein Else*, p. 378.

36. Unless, of course, punctuation is left latent, which is a different way of stressing syntactic peculiarity. Beauvoir punctuates Murielle's run-on sentences sparsely, in obvious imitation of "Penelope."

37. *Les Lauriers*, p. 114.

38. Michel Raimond points out that immobility and regular movement through space (on foot or in trains) are the two favorite postures of monologists (*La Crise du roman*, pp. 291-292).

39. Cf. Raimond's distinction between monologues that center on the self (which he associates with a "psychoanalytic perspective"), and those that center on the surrounding world (which he associates with a "phenomenological perspective") (*La Crise du roman*, pp. 273-274).

40. See p. 83 above.

41. Cf. Genette's association of dialogue and monologue, both of which he sees as equally pure mimetic forms, in the Platonic sense of the term (*Figures III*, pp. 192-193).

42. Cf. Mickelsen's discussion of this "awkwardness" in the rendering of dialogue in the two works (*Anti-Realist Directions*, p. 188).

43. *Fräulein Else*, pp. 343-346.

44. "Monologue," p. 117.

45. The narrated time spans roughly eight hours in *Leutnant Gustl* (10 P.M. to 6 A.M.), four hours in *Fräulein Else* (6 P.M. to 10 P.M.). The time-markers are less precise in "Goethe" (from his waking moment to sometime in mid-morning) and "Monologue" (from midnight to pre-dawn); "Amants" has the longest narrated time (morning to early evening, about 12 hours) but covers this time-span only intermittently.

46. A rough word-count shows that *Les Lauriers* and *Fräulein Else* are about the same length as "Penelope" (45 densely printed pages in the Modern Library edition). *Leutnant Gustl*, "Amants," and "Goethe" (discounting the intermittent dialogue scenes) are considerably shorter.

47. "Monologue," p. 114.

48. *Leutnant Gustl*, p. 356.

49. *Lotte in Weimar*, p. 684.

50. The break between chaps. III and IV, for example, corresponds to no temporal pause. At the end of III, Daniel stands before the door of his house; at the beginning of IV the concierge calls to him as he enters.

51. *Lotte in Weimar*, pp. 617, 619, 623.

52. Dujardin's own word, *Le Monologue intérieur*, p. 57.

53. Melvin Friedman, *Stream of Consciousness: A Study in Literary Method* (New Haven, Conn., 1955), p. 149.

54. I use the concept of "tenor" here in the sense of "degree of formality," following the definition given in John Spencer and Michael Gregory, "An Approach to the Study of Style," in *Linguistics and Style*, John Spencer, ed. (London, 1964), pp. 86-87.

55. *Le Monologue intérieur*, p. 59.

56. *Lotte in Weimar*, p. 620.

57. *Op. cit.*, pp. 619-621.

58. *Fräulein Else*, p. 365.

59. In *Les Lauriers* thoughts of the past are almost entirely limited to chap. V, which significantly starts with the words "Since I have nothing to do—". Here Daniel remembers previous rendezvous with Lea as he rereads his correspondence with her.

60. See above, pp. 183-184.

61. Note, however, that one is free to attribute a *post mortem* origin to Quentin's monologue, as Sartre does in his well-known interpretation: "when Quentin's memory begins to unravel its recollections . . . *he is already dead*" ("On *The Sound and the Fury*," in *Faulkner: A Collection of Critical Essays*, ed. Robert Penn Warren [Englewood Cliffs, N.J., 1966], p. 92; Sartre's emphasis).

62. There is no evidence in the novel for placing the moment of verbalization during the night with Corinne, as some commentators have done: see, for example, Léon S. Roudiez, *French Fiction Today* (New Brunswick, N.J., 1972), pp. 166-168. I agree with Dominique Lanceraux, who declares the "enunciatory position" of the text to be "undecidable" ("Modalité de la narration dans *La Route des Flandres*," *Poétique* 4 [1973], 235-249, p. 238).

63. The terms "actual scenes" and "remembered scenes" were used by Faulkner himself in a letter to his editor describing the Benjy Section, as quoted by James B. Meriwether in "The Textual History of *The Sound and the Fury*" (*The Merrill Studies in* The Sound and the Fury [Columbus, Ohio, 1970], pp. 1-32, p. 10). I prefer these terms to the more usual, but more misleading, designation of the episodes as "present" and "past."

64. *La Route des Flandres* (Paris, 1960), pp. 256-294.

65. For a rigorous linguistic-stylistic analysis of the three monologues from *The Sound and the Fury*, see Irena Kaluza, *The Functioning of the Sentence Structure in the Stream of Consciousness Technique of William Faulkner's "The Sound and the Fury": A Study in Linguistic Stylistics* (Krakow, 1967). Dominique Lanceraux offers a structural analysis of *La Route des Flandres* in "Modalité de la narration."

66. *The Sound and the Fury*, pp. 2-3.

67. Meriwether, "The Textual History," pp. 9-10.

68. *The Sound and the Fury*, pp. 165-166.

69. *Op. cit.*, p. 216.

70. *Op. cit.*, pp. 185-203.

71. See above, p. 165.

72. *The Sound and the Fury*, pp. 243-256.

73. *Op. cit.*, p. 250.

74. *Op. cit.*, p. 290.

75. Simon's formulation in *Histoire*.

76. A closer approximation to interior monologue can be achieved in cinema, where the monologue can be spoken by the actor's voice, but not emitted by his mouth—creating the illusion that it is "in his head," internal.

77. *Le Monologue intérieur*, pp. 36-37.

78. When modern critics discuss the "dramatic" element in dramatic monologue, they usually attribute to it a purely internalized meaning: the self presented in the process of inner debate, split into antagonists. See, for example, Robert Langbaum, *The Poetry of Experience: The Dramatic Monologue in Modern Literary Tradition* (London, 1957), and Francis Scarfe, *The Art of Paul Valéry: A Study in Dramatic Monologue* (London, 1954).

79. This kind of poem could, with equal justification, be called "a narrative monologue in verse": a term I do not seriously propose since it is no less one-sided and confusing than the one we have. The German *Rollengedicht* has the great advantage of being generically more neutral. Its English equivalent, role poem, has in fact been used in Marilynn J. Rose's translation of Käte Hamburger, *The Logic of Literature* (Bloomington, Indiana, 1973). It is in this work also that we find the analogy between dramatic monologue and first-person narrative most clearly drawn: "it [the role-poem] presents itself as the lyric counterpart to the major epic form of the first-person narrative . . ." (p. 310). This relationship between dramatic monologue and first-person narrative has been disregarded by critics writing in English. Langbaum does not allude to it, and Scarfe's remarks touching on the relationship to interior monologue are cursory and imprecise.

80. Cited in Scarfe, p. 182; my translation, Valéry's emphasis and ellipsis.

81. Paul Valéry, *Œuvres* I (Paris, 1957, Pleiade edition), pp. 103-104.

82. *Ulysses*, p. 742.

83. See the chapter entitled "Rhythmus und freie Verse bei Dujardin und Larbaud" in Höhnisch, *Das gefangene Ich*, pp. 138-152.

84. *The Anatomy of Criticism* (New York, 1967), p. 249.

85. See C. D. King, "Edouard Dujardin and the Genesis of the Inner Monologue," *French Studies* 9 (1955), 101-115, pp. 103-107.

86. Charles Baudelaire, *Œuvres complètes* (Paris, 1961, Pléiade edition), p. 229; English: *Paris Spleen*, trans. Louise Varèse (New York, 1947), pp. ix-x.

87. *Œuvres complètes*, p. 232; *Paris Spleen*, p. 3.

88. In this regard I disagree with George T. Wright's views in *The Poet in the Poem: The Personae of Eliot, Yeats, and Pound* (Berkeley, 1962). Wright regards all first persons who speak in a poem as "personae," regardless of whether they seem to speak in the poet's own name, or whether they speak through fictional - historical masks. Käte Hamburger views this problem more lucidly: she demonstrates that in lyric poems, as in prose texts in the first person, no distinction can be drawn between speaker and author, unless this distinction is marked in the text itself. (*The Logic of Literature*, pp. 309-310.)

89. *Beschreibung eines Kampfes* (New York, 1946), p. 140.

90. *A Writer's Diary*, ed. Leonard Woolf (New York, 1954), pp. 103, 107, 134 and 156.

91. *The Waves*, pp. 28, 54-55, 63.

92. "The Lyric Present: Simple Present Verbs in English Poems," *PMLA* 89 (1974), 563-579. The replacement of the progressive form by simple present in *The Waves* has been noted by J. W. Graham, who interprets it somewhat differently ("Point of View in *The Waves*: Some Services of the Style," *University of Toronto Quarterly* 39 [1970], 193-211).

93. See esp. Robert O. Richardson, "Point of View in Virginia Woolf's *The Waves*," *Texas Studies in Literature and Language* 14 (1972-73), 691-709; see also Graham, pp. 207-211, and Magdalene Brandt, *Realismus und Realität im modernen Roman* (Bad Homburg, 1968), pp. 106-122.

94. *A Writer's Diary*, p. 140.

Editions Cited

Editions Cited

Austen, Jane. *Emma* in *The Complete Novels*. New York: Random House (Modern Library) [no date].

Balzac, Honoré de. *Le Père Goriot, La Comédie Humaine* II. Paris: Gallimard (Bibliothèque de la Pléiade), 1951.

Beauvoir, Simone de. "Monologue" in *La Femme rompue*. Paris: Gallimard, 1967.

Beckett, Samuel. *Three Novels*. New York: Grove Press, 1965.

Broch, Hermann. *Die Schlafwandler*. Zürich: Rhein-Verlag, 1952.

———. *Der Tod des Vergil*. Zürch: Rhein-Verlag, 1952.

———. *The Death of Virgil*, trans. Jean Starr Untermeyer. New York: Grosset and Dunlap, 1965.

Camus, Albert. *La Chute*. Paris: Gallimard, 1956.

———. *The Fall*, trans. Justin O'Brien. New York: Knopf, 1957.

———. "Le Renégat" in *L'Exil et le royaume*. Paris: Gallimard, 1957.

Capote, Truman. *In Cold Blood*. New York: New American Library (Signet Book), 1965.

Chekhov, Anton. "A Boring Story," trans. David Magarshack, in *Lady with Lapdog and Other Stories*. Baltimore, Md.: Penguin Books, 1964.

Constant, Benjamin. *Adolphe*. Paris: Editions Garnier Frères, 1963.

Dickens, Charles. *David Copperfield*. New York: New American Library (Signet Classic), 1962.

———. *Little Dorrit*. London/New York: Oxford University Press [no date].

Döblin, Alfred. *Berlin Alexanderplatz: Die Geschichte vom Franz Biberkopf*. Olten und Freiburg im Breisgau: Walter Verlag, 1961/1967.

Dostoevsky, Fyodor. *Crime and Punishment*, trans. Constance Garnett. New York: Modern Library (Random House), 1950.

Dostoevsky, Fyodor. "A Gentle Creature," trans. David Magarsshack, in *A Gentle Creature and Other Stories*. London: John Lehmann, 1950.

———. *Notes From Underground* and *The Grand Inquisitor*, trans. Ralph E. Matlaw. New York: E. P. Dutton, 1960.

Dujardin, Edouard. *Les Lauriers sont coupés*. Paris: Bibliothèque 10/18, 1968.

Faulkner, William. *As I Lay Dying*. New York: Vintage Books (Random House) [no date].

———. *Light in August*. Harmondsworth: Penguin Books, 1960.

———. *The Sound and the Fury*. New York: Random House (Vintage Books), 1954.

Fielding, Henry. *Tom Jones*. New York: Random House (Modern Library Paperback), 1950.

Flaubert, Gustave. *L'Éducation sentimentale, Oeuvres* II. Paris: Gallimard (Bibliothèque de la Pléiade), 1951.

———. *Sentimental Education*, trans. Anthony Goldsmith. New York/London: Everyman's Library, 1941 [1966].

———. *Madame Bovary, Oeuvres* I. Paris: Gallimard (Bibliothèque de la Pléiade), 1951.

Garshin, Vsevolod M. "Four Days," trans. Rowland Smith, in *The Signal and Other Stories*. New York: Knopf, 1917.

Gide, André. *Les Faux-Monnayeurs* in *Romans*. Paris: Gallimard (Bibliothèque de la Pléiade), 1958.

———. *L'Immoraliste* in *Romans*. Paris: Gallimard (Bibliothèque de la Pléiade), 1958.

———. *The Immoralist*, trans. Dorothy Bussy. New York: Knopf, 1951.

Golding, William. *Free Fall*. New York/Burlingame: Harcourt, Brace & World (Harbinger Books), 1960.

Hamsun, Knut. *Hunger*, trans. Robert Bly. New York: The Noonday Press, 1967.

Hesse, Hermann. *Der Steppenwolf*. Frankfurt a.M.: Suhrkamp, 1961.

Hoffmann, E.T.A. *Meister Floh* in *Späte Werke*. Munich: Winkler-Verlag, 1965.

Holz, Arno and Schlaf, Johannes. *Papa Hamlet, Ein Tod*. Stuttgart: Reclam, 1968.

Hugo, Victor. *Le dernier Jour d'un condamné*. Paris: J. Hetzelt & Cie/Maison Quantin [no date].

———. *Les Misérables*, 2 vols. Paris: Garnier Frères (Classiques Garnier), 1957.

——— *Les Misérables*, trans. Charles E. Wilbour. New York: Modern Library [Random House], [no date].

James, Henry. *The Ambassadors*. New York: New American Library (Signet Classic), 1960.

———. *The Aspern Papers, The Spoils of Poynton*. New York: Dell Publishing, 1959.

———. "The Beast in the Jungle" in *Complete Tales*, Vol. 11, ed. Leon Edel. London: Rupert Hart-Davis, 1964.

———. *The Portrait of a Lady*. New York: Modern Library (Random House), 1951.

———. *What Maisie Knew*. New York: Doubleday Anchor Books, 1954.

———. *The Wings of the Dove*. New York: New American Library (Signet Classic), 1964.

Joyce, James. *A Portrait of the Artist as a Young Man*. New York: Viking Press (Compass Books), 1964.

———. *Ulysses*. New York: Modern Library (Random House), 1961.

Kafka, Franz. "Der Bau" in *Beschreibung eines Kampfes*. New York: Schocken Books, 1946.

———. "The Burrow," trans. Willa and Edwin Muir, in *The Great Wall of China*. New York: Schocken Books, 1970.

———. "Ein Bericht für eine Akademie" in *Erzählungen und kleine Prosa*. New York: Schocken Books, 1946.

———. "Ein Hungerkünstler" in *Erzählungen und kleine Prosa*. New York: Schocken Books, 1946.

———. "Ein Landarzt" in *Erzählungen und kleine Prosa*. New York: Schocken Books, 1946.

———. "A Country Doctor," trans. Willa and Edwin Muir, in *The Penal Colony: Stories and Short Pieces*. New York: Schocken Books, 1961.

Kafka, Franz. *Der Prozess*. New York: Schocken Books, 1946/1963.

――――. *The Trial*, trans. Willa and Edwin Muir. Revised with additional chapters and notes by E. M. Butler. London: Secker and Warburg, 1956.

――――. *Das Schloss*. New York: Schocken Books, 1946/1962.

――――. *The Castle*, trans. Willa and Edwin Muir. New York: Modern Library, 1969.

Larbaud, Valéry. "Amants, heureux amants" in *Amants, heureux amants*. Paris: Gallimard, 1972.

Lawrence, D. H. *Women in Love*. New York: Viking Press (Viking Compass Edition), 1960.

Mann, Thomas. *Bekenntnisse des Hochstaplers Felix Krull, Gesammelte Werke* Vol. VII. Frankfurt am Main: S. Fischer Verlag, 1960.

――――. *Buddenbrooks, Gesammelte Werke* Vol. I. Frankfurt am Main: S. Fischer Verlag, 1960.

――――. *Lotte in Weimar, Gesammelte Werke* Vol. II. Frankfurt am Main: S. Fischer Verlag, 1960.

――――. *Der Tod in Venedig, Gesammelte Werke* Vol. VIII. Frankfurt am Main: S. Fischer Verlag, 1960.

――――. *Der Zauberberg, Gesammelte Werke* Vol. III. Frankfurt am Main: S. Fischer Verlag, 1960.

Murdoch, Iris. *A Severed Head*. New York: Viking Press, 1963.

Musil, Robert. *Die Verwirrungen des Zöglings Törless* in *Prosa, Dramen, Späte Briefe*. Hamburg: Rowohlt, 1957.

――――. "Die Vollendung der Liebe" in *Prosa, Dramen, Späte Briefe*. Hamburg: Rowohlt, 1957.

――――. "The Perfecting of a Love," trans. Eithne Wilkins and Ernst Kaiser, in *Five Women*. New York: Dell Publishing Co. (Delta Books), 1966.

Proust, Marcel. *A la Recherche du temps perdu*, 3 vols. Paris: Gallimard (Bibliothèque de la Pléiade), 1954.

――――. *Remembrance of Things Past*. 2 vols: Vol. I, trans. C. K. Scott Moncrieff, Vol. II, trans. Moncrieff and Frederick A. Blossom. New York: Random House, 1932.

Raabe, Wilhelm. *Die Chronik der Sperlinggasse, Gesammelte Werke in drei Bänden*, Vol. I. Gütersloh: Sigbert Mohn Verlag [no date].

Richardson, Samuel. *The History of Clarissa Harlowe*, in eight volumes. London, Miller and Carpenter, 1811.

Salinger, J. D. *The Catcher in the Rye*. Boston: Little, Brown and Co. (Bantam Books), 1951.

Sarraute, Nathalie. *Martereau*. Paris: Gallimard, 1953.

————. *Martereau*, trans. Maria Jolas. New York: George Braziller, 1959.

————. *Le Planétarium*. Paris: Gallimard (Livre de poche), 1959.

————. *The Planetarium*, trans. Maria Jolas. New York: George Braziller, 1960.

Sartre, Jean-Paul. "L'enfance d'un chef" in *Le Mur*. Paris: Gallimard, 1939.

———— "Intimité" in *Le Mur*. Paris: Gallimard, 1939.

————. *La Nausée*. Paris: Gallimard, 1938.

————. *The Diary of Antoine Roquentin*, trans. Lloyd Alexander. London: John Lehmann, 1949.

Schnitzler, Arthur. *Fräulein Else, Die Erzählenden Schriften*, Vol. II. Frankfurt am Main: S. Fischer Verlag, 1961.

————. *Leutnant Gustl, Die Erzählenden Schriften*, Vol. I. Frankfurt am Main: S. Fischer Verlag, 1961.

Simon, Claude. *Histoire*, trans. Richard Howard. New York: G. Braziller, 1968.

————. *La Route des Flandres*. Paris: Editions de Minuit, 1960.

Stendhal (Beyle, Henri). *La Chartreuse de Parme*, 2 vols. Paris: Librairie Armand Colin (Bibliothèque de Cluny), 1957.

————. *The Charterhouse of Parma*, trans. C. K. Scott Moncrieff. New York: Modern Library, 1937.

————. *Le Rouge et le noir: Chronique du XIXe siècle*. Paris: Bibliothèque de Cluny, 1937.

Sterne, Laurence. *The Life and Opinions of Tristram Shandy*. New York: The Modern Library, 1950.

Thackeray, William Makepeace. *Vanity Fair*. New York: New American Library (Signet Classic), 1962.

Tolstoy, Leo. *Anna Karenina*, trans. Constance Garnett. New York: Modern Library (Random House) [no date].

———. *The Death of Ivan Ilych* in *The Death of Ivan Ilych and Other Stories*, trans. Aylmer Maude. New York: New American Library (Signet Classic), 1960.

———. *War and Peace*, trans. Louise and Aylmer Maude. New York: Simon and Schuster, 1942.

Wieland, Christoff Martin. *Agathon, Werke* Vol. I. Munich: Carl Hanser/Verlag, 1964.

Wolfe, Thomas. *The Web and the Rock*. Garden City, N.Y.: Sun Dial Press, 1940.

Woolf, Virginia. *Mrs. Dalloway*. New York: Harcourt, Brace & World (Harvest Book) [no date].

———. *To the Lighthouse*. New York: Harcourt, Brace & World (Harvest Book) [no date].

———. *The Waves*. London: The Hogarth Press, 1963.

Index

*Library of Congress Cataloging
in Publication Data*

Cohn, Dorrit Claire.
   Transparent minds.

   Includes index.
   1.   Psychological fiction.   I.   Title.
PN3448.P8C6   809.3'83   78-51161
ISBN 0-691-06369-9
ISBN 0-691-10156-6 (pbk.)

Printed in the United States
95796LV00003B/70-81/A

9 780691 101569